United States–Cuban Relations

United States–Cuban Relations

A Critical History

ESTEBAN MORALES DOMINGUEZ
AND GARY PREVOST

LEXINGTON BOOKS

A division of
ROWMAN & LITTLEFIELD PUBLISHERS, INC.
Lanham • Boulder • New York • Toronto • Plymouth, UK

LEXINGTON BOOKS

A division of Rowman & Littlefield Publishers, Inc.
A wholly owned subsidary of The Rowman & Littlefield Publishing Group, Inc.
4501 Forbes Boulevard, Suite 200
Lanham, MD 20706

Estover Road
Plymouth PL6 7PY
United Kingdom

British Library Cataloguing in Publication Information Available

Library of Congress Cataloging-in-Publication Data
Morales Dominguez, Esteban.
  United States-Cuban relations : a critical history / Esteban Morales Dominguez
and Gary Prevost.
      p. cm.
  ISBN-13: 978-0-7391-2443-7 (cloth : alk. paper)
  ISBN-10: 0-7391-2443-9 (cloth : alk. paper)
  ISBN-13: 978-0-7391-2444-4 (pbk. : alk. paper)
  ISBN-10: 0-7391-2444-7 (pbk. : alk. paper)
  1. United States--Foreign relations--Cuba. 2. Cuba--Foreign relations--United
States. I. Prevost, Gary. II. Title.
  E183.8.C9M67 2008
  327.7307291--dc22   2008003542

Printed in the United States of America

Contents

Introduction

The long standing view of the U.S. government, much of the U.S. mass media and some academic treatments of the relations between the United States and Cuba begin from the perspective that U.S. domination of the island is a natural phenomenon of history determined by the geopolitical positions of the two countries. These writers view the era of the Cuban revolution from 1959 forward as an aberration, or a brief period of history that will ultimately end with the full reintegration of Cuba into the U.S. sphere of influence and control. These writers believe that the period of U.S. neocolonial control of the island from 1899-1959 was the norm and that any deviation from that pattern was primarily the result of poor U.S. planning in the final days of the Batista regime and the clever intervention of the Soviet Union to shore up the fledgling revolutionary government. This view has been challenged by the survival of the revolutionary government fifteen years after the collapse of the Soviet Union, but the same analysts now argue that the return of U.S. control of Cuba is simply awaiting the death of the revolution's aging leader, Fidel Castro. The authors agree that Fidel is an important player. He is one of those figures of the contemporary world who evokes strong emotions: either fierce loyalty and admiration or intense hatred. To many Cubans living in the United States, and to the government of the United States, he is evil incarnate, a bearded dictator who has led Cuba down a disastrous path for the last forty-five years. In contrast to the authors and many others around the world, Castro is seen as a revered leader, a person who has overseen the fundamentally positive transformation of Cuban society and has confidently defied the U.S. government and nine U.S. presidents for more than four decades in defense of Cuba's national interests. However, important as Fidel Castro has been to the Cuban revolution and to U.S.-Cuban relations, the authors reject the view that he is the revolution and that he alone will dictate the future direction of U.S.-Cuban relations. In analyzing contemporary Cuba the authors argue that in the last ten years an important transition to a post-Fidel era has already begun in Cuban political life. A new generation of political leaders who came to political maturity long after 1959 have taken control of the daily

1

political life of the country. Figures like Ricardo Alarcon, head of the National Assembly, Carlos Lage, Vice President of the Council of State and Secretary of the Executive Committee of the Council of Ministers, and Felipe Perez Roque, Foreign Minister, represent primary continuity of the revolutionary process and the continuing rule by the Communist Party, not unlike transitions that have occurred in China and Vietnam. This group of leaders gained legitimacy by being at the center of carrying out Cuba's successful economic and political strategies in the 1990s that allowed it to survive the catastrophic circumstances created by the collapse of the Soviet bloc. The recent illness of Castro that has at least temporarily removed him from day to day decision-making is a validation of the transition that is underway in Cuba. During Castro's illness the Cuban political and economic system moved forward in a normal manner under the leadership of Raul Castro and the younger leaders discussed above. The authors acknowledge that the eventual departure of Fidel from the scene will be a difficult moment for the revolutionary movement but reject the notion that fundamental change in Cuban society is inevitable when that day comes. In fact, the longer that Fidel plays some role in the system, the likelihood of gradual transition is even greater. It is the scenario of the gradual transition to a Cuban government without the leadership of Fidel Castro, but equally committed to a project of national independence and socialism, that represents the feared scenario for the U.S. government and all of those analysts who view the last fifty years as an aberration.

The overall approach, mirroring the political science background of both authors, will not focus on historical detail that has been provided by many other authors, but rather a broad analysis of trends and patterns that have marked the long relationship between the two countries. The general thesis of the book is that U.S. policy toward Cuba is driven in significant measure by developments on the ground in Cuba. From the U.S. intervention at the time of the Cuban Independence War down to the most recent revisions of U.S. policy in the wake of the Powell Commission, the authors demonstrate how U.S. policy adjusts to developments and perceived reality on the island. Of course, the unending constant of U.S. policy is the desire to economically, militarily, and politically dominate the island. Because that domination has been lacking after 1959, its reestablishment has been the primary basis of U.S. policy. To the contrary, Cuba's position toward the United States since 1959 has been geared almost solely toward the maintenance of its independence from the United States. For thirty years that meant Cuba accepted a dependent relationship with the USSR as the lesser of two evils. For the past decade it has meant the rebuilding of trade and political relations with the capitalist world while keeping its distance from the United States. The authors acknowledge the position of the U.S.-Cuban community but do not believe that U.S. policy toward Cuba is primarily determined by it. An analysis of the Elian Gonzalez episode makes that case. The final chapters in the book focus on the contemporary period with particular emphasis on the changing dynamic toward Cuba from U.S. civil society. The authors describe how the U.S. business community, fearful of being isolated from Cuba's reinsertion in the world market place, united with long standing opponents of the U.S. embargo to win the right to sell food and medicines to Cuba over the last five years.

The authors believe that the attitude of contemporary U.S. rulers toward Cuba is rooted in perspectives toward the island that go back to the U.S. founders. From Thomas Jefferson to James Monroe, the U.S. leaders of the first twenty-five years of the nineteenth century looked at Cuba as a territory that needed to come under U.S. control for a combination of political, military, and economic reasons. The United States witnessed the Latin American wars of independence against Spain and saw the situation as an opportunity to extend its influence southward. Buoyed by the successful purchase of Florida from Spain in 1819, the U.S. leaders considered that ultimate possession of Cuba was inevitable. This perspective was enshrined in the Ripe Fruit Doctrine enunciated by James Monroe in 1823, which would provide the framework under which several U.S. presidents from James Polk forward made strong overtures toward Spain for the purchase of the island. U.S. designs on the island were largely thwarted during the nineteenth century by Spain's unwillingness to sell and by U.S. weakness in the face of British and French power. However, during that century, the United States became Cuba's leading trading partner and slowly built up its industrial base to become a world power.

The authors argue that the events surrounding the Cuban-American-Spanish War of 1898 are crucial to a full understanding of the relationship that exists between the two countries. By 1898 Spanish control of the island was clearly coming to an end as the Cuban independence forces under Jose Marti relaunched their offensive in 1895 and fought the Spaniards to a stalemate. Seizing that opportunity, the resurgent United States entered the Cuban-Spanish War and tipped the balance to the independence forces. However, the cost to the Cuban side was that the U.S. intervention denied them the achievement of their full national independence. Instead, under U.S. presence, Cuba was established as a neocolony of its northern neighbor, nominally independent but dominated politically, militarily, and economically. This domination was enshrined in the U.S. drafted Platt Amendment that was inserted into the 1901 Cuban constitution and served as the basis of regular interference in Cuban internal affairs over the next thirty years until its abrogation by the U.S. Good Neighbor Policy in 1933. The events of 1898 were crucial because for both sides they remain salient today. From the Cuban side, the U.S. humiliation of Cuba that occurred when their victory over Spain was taken from them leads to a perspective of fundamental distrust of U.S. intentions and the primary goal of Cuba to maintain its national sovereignty at all costs. From the U.S. perspective, the victory over Spain in 1898 established a right of domination over the island paid for in U.S. lives.

During the Era of Gunboat Diplomacy (1898-1933) that followed the 1898 war, Cuba was emblematic of U.S. policy throughout the Central American and Caribbean region. The United States worked by a variety of means to ensure governments in power that catered to the needs of U.S. business interests. From companies engaged in food production to those in banking and communications, the region was a prime target for U.S. foreign direct investment in the first quarter of the twentieth century. Cuba alone would receive more than $2 billion in U.S. investment that resulted in North American control of Cuba's sugar, banking, and mining industries. Central to the U.S. economic strategy was having local governments in power that gave preference to U.S. business interests over European ones and generally allowed the businesses to proceed with little regulation and few taxes. In most countries the United States found local elites who were willing to govern under those rules. The Tomas Estrada Palma government that assumed power in Cuba under U.S. tutelage in 1902 was typical of this pattern. These local elites were rewarded by substantial perks to guarantee their allegiance. However, as happened in Cuba, sections of the local elites and the working masses as a whole were left out of any significant benefit from the neocolonial arrangements. As a result, significant resistance to U.S. domination developed throughout the region forcing the United States to turn often to armed actions to impose its will, causing the time period to become known as the Era of Gunboat Diplomacy. In all, the United States would make fifty-four separate armed incursions into the region over a thirty-five year period and twice U.S. troops landed on Cuban soil to rescue Cuban governments facing resistance to U.S.-based policies. Other countries in this region, especially Nicaragua and Haiti, faced even more frequent U.S. military occupations. U.S. domination was not limited to the military incursions, however, and the incursions led in many situations to almost direct U.S. governance of countries in the region. In the case of Cuba, General Enoch H. Crowder served as the defacto ruler of the island in the 1920s from his position as the U.S. Ambassador.

However, the Era of Gunboat Diplomacy and its naked form of imperial intervention eventually created unacceptable costs for the United States. The most striking costs came in Nicaragua in the late 1920s when the guerrilla army of Agosto Cesar Sandino fought the U.S. Marines to a stalemate in a six-year long war that ended in 1933. Events in Cuba came to a head in the same year when the Cuban people, under the leadership of primarily university students known as the Generation of 1930, brought down the U.S.-backed dictator, Gerardo Machado. The events in Cuba tested the newly-enunciated Good Neighbor Policy of the Roosevelt administration which committed the United States to a policy of not using armed intervention as a regular tool of diplomacy. The United States did not intervene against the revolutionary movement directly, but rather worked behind the scenes to bring to power a government acceptable to the United States. Using the ambitious army sergeant Fulgencio Batista, mobilizer of the army against Machado, the United States succeeded in blocking the radical reform government of Grau San Martin from holding on to power. Wedded to defending U.S. interests and enhancing his own position, Batista would dominate Cuban politics for most of the next twenty-five years. He was a model leader for the United States, a strongman who through a variety of policies, including the highly progressive 1940 Constitution, gained enough credibility with the populace that direct U.S. military intervention was not necessary to defend

U.S. interests. Support for Batista would save U.S. interests well until his cata-strophic fall from power in the face of the revolutionary upsurge of 1957-58.

Revolution

The revolution and its fundamental challenge to the U.S. domination of the isl-and began in July, 1953 following a Batista-led coup that cancelled the sche-duled 1952 elections. Fidel Castro and other opponents of Batista's coup orga-nized an attack against the Moncada army barracks in Santiago on July 26 that was intended to spark a nationwide uprising. The attack failed badly, but Castro survived and after an amnesty from Batista in 1955 went to Mexico and re-launched their revolution in Oriente Province in December 1956. Though initial-ly nearly defeated, the revolutionaries survived and quickly built up a significant movement that was well supported by comparable guerrilla groups and other anti-Batista forces in the cities. Castro's forces, now called the July 26th Move-ment after their day of defeat in Santiago, gained considerable public sympathy both in Cuba and in the United States. The U.S. government grew wary of Batis-ta's ability to hold power and began to isolate him, assuming that the July 26th Movement was simply another Cuban group that could be successfully maneu-vered as the Generation of 1930 rebels had been twenty-five years before. This judgment proved to be a serious miscalculation by the U.S. authorities. Castro and his fellow leaders were very well aware of the events of both 1898 and 1933 and were determined that history would not repeat itself with North American actions stealing Cuban independence. Once in power, the rebels moved quickly to consolidate revolutionary power and carry out programs of land reform and rent control to win the allegiance of Cuba's poor citizens. A turning point in U.S.-Cuban relations came in April 1959 when Castro made a non-state visit to Washington but did meet with Vice President Richard Nixon. Quite consciously, the Cubans did not request any aid during the visit, sending the signal that the revolution could not be bought. The U.S. government responded in the summer of 1959 with hostile actions toward the Cuban government that would set the tone for the U.S. policies that have continued down to the present. From those days forward it became the policy of the U.S. government to seek the downfall of the revolutionary government by any means necessary. Over the next forty-five years the U.S. government under presidents both Democratic and Republi-can would pursue policies that had one fundamental intent—return control of the island to the United States.

Faced with this hostility and with near total dependence on imported ener-gy, the Cuban government turned to the Soviet Union for assistance, and for its own Cold War reasons the Soviets responded positively. This relationship with the Soviet Union proved to be both long-standing and complex and brought the world to the brink of nuclear war in 1962. This book will deal with the events that the Cubans call the October Crisis in considerable detail because in the last fifteen years, a wealth of declassified material has been made available by all sides in the confrontation that sheds much more light on what happened in those fateful days of October 1962. Common wisdom on the events, generally known to the wider world as the Missile Crisis, is that the Soviet Union, seeking a strategic advantage in the nuclear standoff with the United States, brought the world to the brink of Armageddon by attempting to secretly place missiles on Cuban soil. The common wisdom also saw the Cubans as adventurous revolutionaries pushing the Soviets even further into confrontation with the United States once the plans were discovered. In our view, the reality is far more complex. The roots of the October Crisis and the decision by the Soviets to place missiles on the island was based on the range of policies carried out by the United States from 1959 forward to overthrow the Cuban government. The initial denial of Cuba's sugar quota grew into a full-fledged economic embargo by the end of 1960 that was designed to wreck a Cuban economy that had been almost completely tied to the United States for over a century. The failed invasion of Cuban exiles organized by the CIA at the Bay of Pigs in 1961 was just one of hundreds of operations under the title of Operation Mongoose that were designed to kill leaders of the revolution and put exiled leaders back into power. The United States also organized international pressure by gaining the suspension of Cuba's membership in the Organization of American States.

The culmination of the October Crisis was contradictory for Cuba. On one hand, Khrushchev exacted a pledge that the United States would not invade Cuba as a tradeoff for the removal of the missiles. However, Cuba was entirely excluded from the negotiations and was therefore denied the possibility of moving to a more normal relationship with the United States. More importantly, the Cubans have never trusted the non-invasion pledge because U.S. policies toward Cuba remained fundamentally hostile with both the economic embargo and Operation Mongoose in place after 1962. Recent documentation has shown how much Cuba's relations with the USSR were strained by the October Crisis. In a secret speech to the Communist party in 1968, Castro revealed a deep distrust of the Soviet Union rooted primarily in their handling of events at the end of October 1962.

Throughout the 1960s Cuba pursued a policy of revolutionary internationalism in its foreign policy. It actively supported revolutionary movements throughout Latin America, embodied in Che Guevara's own death supporting Bolivian rebels in 1967. Cuba's involvement was not limited to Latin America. Before his Bolivian activities, Guevara worked with revolutionaries in the Congo. In the framework of the Tricontinental conferences, Cuba hosted gatherings that brought together revolutionaries from across the globe. Such policies irritated the Soviet Union and Communist parties throughout most of Latin America because they were oriented toward reformist, not revolutionary politics. Of course, these policies only served to deepen Washington's hostility toward the Cuban revolution making any sort of détente between the countries impossible throughout the 1960s.

Cuba's international position shifted somewhat after 1968 as the Cuban leaders moved closer to the Soviet Union. Following failure of the ten million ton sugar campaign in 1970, Cuba accepted a position within the Council of Mutual Economic Assistance (CMEA) in 1972. This action effectively tied Cuba's economy to socialist nations led by the USSR. For the sugar, nickel, fish, and citrus products that Cuba produced it received oil, food, and manufactured goods from Eastern Europe at a favorable rate of exchange. This arrangement brought considerable benefit to Cuba for twenty years. Shielded from the vagaries of the international capitalist markets—especially the dramatic increases in the cost of oil in 1973 and 1981—the Cubans were able to develop a planned economy and make significant investments in health, education, and food security. By the 1980s, Cuba was a model Third World country in terms of socioeconomic development. In foreign policy, the Cubans, while still maintaining support for select revolutionary movements such as the FSLN in Nicaragua and the FMLN in El Salvador, began to reestablish diplomatic relations with selected Latin American countries and concentrated most of its diplomatic efforts with progressive countries in the Third World, especially Africa. Its most dramatic action in the 1970s was to provide troops, with Soviet backing, to revolutionary governments in Ethiopia and Angola. These governments faced military attacks from forces backed by the United States and in the case of Angola by South Africa. These actions in Africa and the Non-Aligned Movement that elected Cuba and Fidel Castro to its presidency in 1979, earned Cuba tremendous prestige on that continent. Cuba's successes in Africa and elsewhere actually brought to an end a brief thaw in U.S.-Cuban relations that had occurred between 1977-1979. The Carter administration, acting in part from the desire by segments of the U.S. business community to do commerce with the island, made overtures toward Cuba that might have led to a more normal relationship between the two countries. Low-level diplomatic relations were established. The long shuttered U.S. embassy building on the Malecon in Havana was reopened. The United States lifted its restrictions on travel by U.S. citizens to the island and negotiations were begun on a number of issues including migration of Cubans to the United States. However, by 1979, this opening began to close as hard-line elements in the Carter administration objected strongly to Cuba's aforementioned activities in Africa. Given its solid trading position with the Eastern bloc and rising prestige in the Third World, Cuba was not interested to make significant concessions to the United States to change their basic relationship. Throughout the 1980s Cuba continued its activities in Africa and with 87% of its foreign trade with the CMEA saw little need to orient significantly toward its neighbor to the North. The Reagan administration, for its part, viewed Cuba as a tool of the evil USSR and increased its pressure on the island. With the exception of Cuban Americans visiting their relatives and a few other narrow categories of travel, U.S. citizens were again barred from visiting Cuba from 1982 onward.

Post-Cold War Cuba

Cuba's privileged position in the CMEA came to a sudden and dramatic end between 1989 and 1991. First, in the fall of 1989 the Eastern European revolutions effectively ended the CMEA as the newly capitalist countries walked out of the socialist common market and tore up their trade agreements with Cuba. This dealt a blow to the Cuban economy but nothing compared to the collapse of the Soviet Union in the fall of 1991. Overnight Cuba lost 75 percent of its international trade and its GDP shrunk by more than 50 percent over the course of three years. Outside the context of war it was arguably the hardest blow that any country's economy suffered in the twentieth century. Of course, these events impacted Cuba's foreign relations, including those with the United States.

The authors argue that in the wake of the collapse of the Soviet Union in the early 1990s a set of variables have defined U.S.-Cuban relations down to the present time. We identify those variables as:

- the internal Cuban situation
- power relations in the U.S. Congress related to U.S. Cuba policy
- internationalization of the economic blockade against Cuba by the Untied States
- international resistance to the internationalization of the blockade
- the attitude of the U.S. executive branch toward policy changes regarding Cuba
- the attitude of various sectors of U.S. society, including heterogeneous economic interests, toward Cuba.

This latter variable basically describes the anti-embargo lobby since the embargo and blockade is the main obstacle to normalizing economic and trade relations with Havana. First of all, it is necessary to look at the role of the internal Cuban situation as a factor in the bilateral relations. Once the most pressing difficulties of the Cuban economy during the period 1989-94 started to subside with minor GNP growth in 1995, the economic impact of the Soviet collapse could be broken down into a small set of intimately related elements: the dynamics of economic recuperation, the development of economic reforms, and the social and political impact of the new economic policies.

The stratification implicit in the initial macrovariables is valid, for there is a close relationship among the necessity to maintain economic recuperation, the measures needed for economic reform, the impact of these measures, and the evolving social and political (ideological) situation in Cuba. The government sought to avoid any more shock therapy like the population had experienced in the initial years of deprivation caused by the collapse of the Soviet economy. The government drastically reduced its own size, taking such steps as reducing the number of civilian functionaries and armed forces and decreasing purchases of gasoline and consumer items used by workplaces.

The government strategy was successful to the extent that, in spite of the critical situation, the revolution survived, and the political leadership managed to safeguard its political project while maintaining its capacity to lead. Nevertheless, the government was not able to avoid certain social inequalities and social problems such as prostitution and corruption at various levels. In addition, a negative correlation among labor capacity, employment, and income affected the ability to manage the economy. This led to intense efforts to maintain the workforce, particularly the most qualified workers, in the positions most needed by the country: industry, agriculture, basic services, education, and public health. Although tourism, foreign investment, and the legalization of transactions in foreign currency dynamically impacted on the economic crisis, at the same time these activities competed with the rest of the economy, especially those parts that did not operate within the new schemes. Thus, the Cuban government thought it was imperative to take the necessary measures to undo the negative conditions present in the internal economy.

The economic challenge seriously threatened the distribution, stability, and renovation of the country's qualified labor force. It also encouraged families to search for added income, and it promoted emigration. Dual forms of income and growing inequalities decreased the incentive to work and even promoted criminal behavior. Such situations brought into play social, political, and ideological contradictions that undermined the socialist project. These were the kinds of situations that the Cuban policy of the United States sought to encourage for its potential to incite an overthrow of the Cuban political leadership and the socialist system.

Congress, Other Political Actors, and U.S. Cuba Policy

The United States Congress has been the center of debate for U.S. Cuba policy since Helms-Burton became law in 1996, precisely because under this law only Congress can make any significant policy change. The power of Congress to affect U.S. policy toward Cuba derives less from its constitutional power than from the prerogatives that President Clinton granted to the legislative branch when, in the midst of the 1996 electoral campaign, he signed the Helms-Burton law. In addition to Congress, there are other actors within the U.S. government and within the political system in general that aim to secure their participation in the debate. Additionally, the influence of nongovernmental organization should not be underestimated. On the governmental front, the Drug Enforcement Administration, the United States Information Agency, and the Defense Department are among the best known actors representing perspectives that separate them from the aggressive stand of extreme conservatives.

On the nongovernmental front are found extreme conservative and right-of-center organizations within the Cuban community who favor continuation of the embargo. Foremost among these is the conservative Cuban American National Foundation (CANF). Many other nongovernmental organizations maintain an interest in Cuban affairs and most a change in current U.S.-Cuba policy:

- Academic and cultural organizations interested in U.S. policy toward Cuba

- Organizations such as the Chamber of Commerce and other business groups (especially farm interests)
- The media, including newspapers like the New York Times and the Washington Post, which publish points of view sometimes critical of U.S. Cuba policy
- Religious organizations of various denominations;
- Solidarity groups and organizations such as Pastors for Peace
- Left-leaning organizations, including Cuban American groups
- An important part of the African American, Hispanic, and labor community.

Whatever the consequences, there is a wide array of political actors within U.S. society concerned with Cuban policy, spanning the whole internal political spectrum. Their number has grown as the conflict has dragged on in the face of ineffective policies and there has been a qualitative change regarding Cuban policy. Today, it is not possible to count those interested in Cuban policy, while ten years ago such a count was easy to accomplish. Also, solidarity with Cuba and opposition to the blockade are no longer ignored as in the past. In the United States Congress, positions against the blockade are not limited to the small group of liberal legislators who for years have called attention to the contradictions of Washington's Cuba policy.

Today, the antiblockade stance is a relevant alternative. Within Congress, the number of legislators supportive of at least a partial lifting of the blockade has grown. This development was prompted by the bilateral conflict itself and has brought along an increasing number of political actors involved in Cuban policy. The debate sprang from the very survival of the Cuban Revolution—without a socialist Cuba such political dynamics would not have evolved. The context for analysis is the domestic Cuban situation and the so-called national interests of the United States vis-à-vis the island. The two positions may be summarized as follows:

One sector believes there should be a change in policy because the island continues to progress in its social project and U.S. policy is clearly ineffective. Thus, a new mode of relations with Havana must be found. Most of all, this position is upheld by the business and farming community, which understands keenly that it is missing profitable trade opportunities.

A second sector maintains that, while Cuba has begun to overcome its economic crisis, it still faces difficult challenges and current U.S. policy is effective and must be strengthened. This sector included the Clinton administration but is more stridently represented by President George W. Bush's administration, the Cuban American political right (as exemplified by the CANF and the changing political tactics it has followed since the death of its founder, Jorge Más Canosa), and counterrevolutionary and terrorist groups. In coalition with the Cuban American political right are five members of Congress: Lincoln Díaz-Balart (R-FL), Ileana Ros-Lehtinen (R-FL), Mario Díaz-Balart (R-FL), Bob Menéndez (D-NJ), and Mel Martinez (R-FL).

Legislative efforts to roll back the economic embargo have not made much headway because of the dominance exercised by conservative groups operating in the inner circles where U.S.-Cuba policy is made. The ever-increasing number of individuals and groups who advocate a real policy change have been deterred by the prevailing political context. The political reality is that a long road has yet to be traveled before Washington's Cuba policy is transformed into the kind of change that the Cuban side of the conflict would welcome.

The Blockade's Transnationalization

The Torricelli law, as well as the Helms-Burton law enacted four years later, expressed the will in American politics to continue using the embargo/blockade as the cornerstone of U.S. policy toward Cuba.[1] These laws provoked conflicts in the international arena with traditional U.S. allies. Still, the United States and its allies have made every effort to avoid turning Cuba into an "apple of discord" among them. Arguably, when the United States stands as the only world hegemonic power, it is inclined to impose its will on its own allies. In this sense, Cuba became a test case by which the United States has probed how far it can go in forcing its policies on the international community. By defining the blockade as a transnational political action, the United States has turned it from a bilateral to a multilateral action.

With passage of the Helms-Burton law, the contradiction between the United States policy toward Cuba and the sovereign rights of nations became clearly visible. This triangular conflict became manifest during the process of Cuba's international economic reintegration in the 1990s. Many nations sought to establish economic links with the island, but the United States created many obstacles. Since the United States has had a long-standing desire to make Cuba an extension of its sphere of influence, it chose to legislate transnationally to accomplish its objectives with Cuba. Hence, this political factor has been formed by three basic components: U.S. blockade policy, Cuba's national and economic sovereignty, and the sovereign rights of nations that would like to start or continue trading with Cuba.

These three categories are expressed in the conflict of interests that resides at the international level, including the many fronts of resistance to U.S. policy. The confrontation is then acted out at three parallel levels, between the U.S. blockade and other states, U.S. business circles, and solidarity groups with Cuba.

The United States government could not reach any accommodation with the solidarity groups but tried to pressure them to stop providing aid to Cuba or tried to infiltrate them in an attempt to subvert Cuban civil society. In addition, there have been many instances involving U.S. allies that have required an avoidance of direct confrontation. Negotiations have been necessary whenever sensitive issues arose as the European Union and Canadian interests confronted U.S. economic pressure. But from the perspective of the economic reintegration of Cuba, the confrontation at the international level takes a triangular shape on the following stages:

- Cuba—Latin America—United States
- Cuba—Caribbean—United States
- Cuba—Europe—United States
- Cuba—Asia—United States

Within Europe it is important to highlight Russia and the former Socialist countries of Eastern Europe. Russia was a primary U.S. concern due to its continuing relationship with Cuba, to the point that it received special attention in the Helms-Burton law. The Eastern European nations were also of particular interest to Washington, which made significant efforts to prevent their establishing economic rapprochement with Cuba, such pressure was effective because these former Soviet satellites were eager to carry favor with the United States. As far as the Asian triangle is concerned, China, Vietnam, and North Korea require special consideration for their position vis-à-vis Cuba since they did not heed U.S. pressure aimed at isolating them from Havana.

Several stages of confrontation and negotiations ensued in the late 1990s and have repeated themselves under President Bush. At first, the Helms-Burton bill given Clinton's initial reservations was viewed by some commentators as not likely to be implemented, but in reality, Clinton used the new law as an instrument to pressure American allies and other international actors. The President's special envoy, Stuart Eizenstat, played an essential role in explaining Helms-Burton to skeptical allies in an attempt to make U.S.-Cuba policy acceptable at the international level. It must be pointed out that U.S. allies generally do not grant Cuba any significant priority in their foreign policy. As a result, European nations have sought to avoid direct confrontation over Cuba provided that their citizens and businesses are not prevented from doing business with the island if they choose to do so.

It is within this framework, riddled with contradictions between the United States and its allies, that Cuba finds an opportunity to move forward with its international economic integration. Still, while these pressures to impose a particular policy approach against Cuba have not been fruitful on the economic front, the United States and its allies still maintain strategies that do not differ markedly on the political front. The allies share with the United States the strategic objective of returning Cuba to capitalism. The difference lies in the strategy, whether to demand it overtly, negotiate it discreetly, or seek it merely as a desirable goal. Hence, the contradictions lie mainly in the methods, not the desired ends.

The methods used to further the goal of returning Cuba to capitalism differ in the various arenas: the United States, Latin America and the Caribbean, the European Union, and Asia.[2] The U.S.-Cuba policy has been conceived as an amalgam of blockade pressures, the absence of economic relations (notwithstanding the paid-in-cash American food trade initiated in late 2001, and continued since), and setting political obstacles to the acceptance of Cuban socialism and characterizing it as incompatible with peaceful hemispheric and international coexistence. U.S. pressure to move Cuba toward "liberal democracy" really seeks to forge the internal conditions that would destroy Cuba's political system.

This includes creating the domestic circumstances that could precipitate and justify U.S. military intervention. The conditions were pragmatically stated by President Clinton (and repeated by President Bush): Havana must carry out free elections, certified by an international team of observers, as a demonstration of its willingness to promote a transition to democracy and capitalism. Cuba's current political leadership is to be excluded from such transition, as defined in Helms-Burton and the "common position" that was agreed upon with the European Union in 1996.

The fundamental difference between the European Union's position and that of the United States is that the former maintains economic relations with Cuba and has not accepted the dictates of Title III of the Helms-Burton law because of its extraterritorial reach and its insensitivity toward other nations' sovereignty. The dispute even led to the selection of a panel of judges to review charges brought by the European Union against the United States at the World Trade Organization (WTO). This EU-US dispute has been mitigated because in reality the United States has regularly suspended implementation of the most controversial aspects of Helms-Burton, Titles III and IV. Such non-activation still works for U.S. policy because the very presence of the provisions, that could be implemented in the future, serve to deter at least some new private investors in Cuba from outside of the United States.[3]

In the Latin American and Caribbean area, Cuba's progress in its economic relations with the region, the gradual reestablishment of diplomatic relations, and the cooperation the island has promoted with Central America all stand out, especially in its provision of medical aid and its willingness to train specialists from and for the region. Also, Cuba has become a participant in such organizations as the Association of Caribbean States (ACS), ALADI (Latin American Integration Association), SELA (Latin American Economic System), CARIFORUM (Caribbean Forum), and others. This has taken place in spite of Washington's attempt to exclude Cuba from hemispheric, economic dynamics. The linkage against the obstacles caused by the blockade could open so-called windows of vulnerability. A most interesting case is Canada, a Western country that has maintained a permanent political dialogue with Cuba while also expanding economic relations with it.[4]

Such Cuban foreign policy initiatives as its membership in ALADI, its observer status in the negotiating group for Lomé, its numerous United Nations resolutions against the U.S. blockade, its role hosting the Iberian-American Summit in November 1999, its medical aid to Central America, its presentations at the Group of 77 meetings, and the speeches by Cuba's foreign minister at the United Nations on numerous occasions all provide factual indication that the island is not isolated in the manner hoped for by the U.S. government.

This recovery process is not only economic but also political and includes Cuba's new image in the hemisphere. The positive emerging image has diluted any lingering animosity from previous times. Thus, such issues as Havana's participation in the Organization of American States (OAS) and its transition to liberal democracy have lost their urgency under the political reality of a new century (demonstrated by the newly elected leftist and center left presidents in Latin America). Cuba is repeatedly maintaining its personality as a nation in the hemisphere and on the world stage. In turn, the United States has been continuously condemned by the General Assembly of the United Nations for its blockade against Cuba.[5] Although Washington keeps its pressure over the hemisphere and internationally to enforce discriminatory practices against Cuba, the policy has lost support and suffered numerous defeats. In Asia, China, Vietnam, and Korea ignore U.S. pressure against Cuba. Japan responds to American pressure by maintaining a degree of independence in its relations with Cuba and has looked for ways of widening its economic links with the island.[6]

Havana has been steadily recovering its international links. Today the country has more than 360 joint ventures with foreign capital, 170 of which were created after the signing of the Helms-Burton law. Marketing and investment agreements have been signed with forty countries. It has been elected or appointed to twenty governing bodies of the United Nations, and currently has 118 diplomatic, consular, or interests offices abroad—ninety-eight of them are embassies, the highest number in the history of Cuba.[7] Furthermore, Cuba has commercial relations with seventeen hundred companies from 150 nations, hosts seventy-nine embassies representing countries from all continents, and has accredited 138 foreign correspondents from 104 media organizations and thirty-one countries, compared with 93 correspondents from 62 media organizations a decade ago. Faced with this reality, is it proper to speak of Cuba's isolation, or is it more accurate to speak of the growing international opposition to U.S. policy, particularly the blockade against Cuba?

Clinton's and Bush's Approach to Cuba

The Clinton Years

William Clinton began his first term as president in 1993 with no real commitment to support the United States' long-held aggressive policy against Cuba. In contrast to George W. Bush in 2000, Clinton did not have a strong Miami connection "deciding" his Cuba policy. However, during the 1992 presidential campaign, Clinton supported the Torricelli bill in his search for South Florida Cuban American votes. He even forced the former President Bush to sign the Torricelli bill into law to avoid having Cuban Americans switch to Clinton. In the end, Bush won Florida but lost the reelection, while Clinton lost the Cuban American vote but won the White House. Still, an electoral seed was planted for a future political campaign strategy vying for Cuban American votes—George W. Bush's troubled victory depended largely (to some analysts, entirely) on Florida's electoral mishaps, including the Cuban American vote and political activism.[8]

The Clinton administration kept its Cuba policy on hold until the August 1994 balseros (rafters) crisis. Until then, two contradictory incidents were salient. On the one hand, wanting to keep some distance from the head of the conservative CANF, the White House did not invite Jorge Más Canosa to the May 20 (a Cuban national holiday) celebration. On the other hand, the appointment of a political moderate, Mario Baeza, as Assistant Secretary of State for Latin America was cancelled after a lobbying campaign by Más Canosa's CANF. Clinton decided in favor of extant Cuba policy and used the Cuban Democracy Act (Torricelli bill) as his political mantra.

For reasons escaping objectivity, the Cuban-American right suspected that Clinton was going to make changes in U.S. Cuban policy at the beginning of his administration. The signing of the immigration accord in September 1994 aimed at ending the rafters' crisis, and the Dennis Hayes-Ricardo Alarcon exchange during the signing of the second immigration accord in May 1995, both reinforced the conservative belief that Havana and Washington were negotiating in secrecy.

Throughout the 1996 election year Clinton confronted the contradictory dilemma of having signed Helms-Burton into law in spite of his initial intention of deciding the Cuba policy more rationally. Before signing the Helms-Burton bill, Clinton knew that it could cause serious problems for his reelection if Congress decided to approve it without his support. His search for a formula that would make Helms-Burton politically profitable paid off when two planes flown by Brothers to the Rescue (BTTR), an anti-Castro Miami organization, were shot down on February 24, 1996, by the Cuban air force. Richard Nuccio (Clinton's Cuban policy advisor) would state later that he had warned about the possibility of such an incident and the dangers it would bring.[9]

The most intimate and real causes of the incident could be found in the numerous provocative threats to Cuban national security by Brothers to the Rescue and the repeated warnings and complaints Cuban had filed with American authorities. Washington turned a blind eye to these warnings and complaints. It seems certain that Havana's attack on the Brothers to the Rescue planes allowed Clinton to overcome some of the political difficulties encountered during his first term. However, under Helms-Burton the White House could only decide its Cuban policy within the narrow limits established by this law. Hence, Clinton continued supporting the blockade and used Helms-Burton adroitly, seeking a consensus for the political subversion of the Cuban Revolution even as he maintained fundamental doubts about the bill and its limitations on the power of the presidency. Clinton's final Cuba policy was mostly a mix of antagonistic rhetoric and actions hardened by the blockade (although he decided to ease it partly by the end of his administration), and of pressures on U.S. allies to make them accept Torricelli's Track II and some of the Helms-Burton measures.[10] The Clinton paradox is evident: the president who appeared as least committed to extreme-right-wing aggressiveness contributed to some of the most contentious means to put an end to the Cuban Revolution.

Cuba Policy under George W. Bush

In 2000 a Council of Foreign Relations task force, chaired by Julia Sweig, Bernard Aronson, and Walter Mead, issued a report, "US-Cuban Relations in the 21st Century," that provided positive guidelines for the United States' Cuba policy. Since the first months of President George W. Bush's administration, an array of hostile initiatives toward Cuba has been approved. However, Title III of the Helms-Burton Act continued to be suspended in 2001, 2002, and 2003, as was done by the Clinton administration. The financing of the internal opposition to the Cuban government in the amount of $100 million was one of the early Bush initiatives. Paradoxically, with such an action Washington was confirming Havana's long-standing charge that regime opponents were being paid by the U.S. government.

Despite the Senate's opposition but with the CANF's blessing—and taking advantage of a congressional recess in December 2001—President Bush appointed Otto Reich, a conservative Cuban American, as Assistant Secretary of State for Latin America, an appointment that lasted until the end of 2002, when Reich was moved to the National Security Council. Another hard-line Cuban American, Col. Emilio González, was assigned to the Western Hemisphere post at the National Security Council.

The situation that ensued after the attack on the Twin Towers and the Pentagon on September 11, 2001, turned tense due to Cuba's opposition to the way the war against terrorism was being pursued. In his address to the United States Congress, President Bush had dichotomized the world into countries "supporting the United States or supporting terrorism," which posed a hegemonic challenge to the international community. Cuba reacted, making public its opposition to the war in Afghanistan. Havana had offered earlier its sincere condolences and deepest sympathy for the horrific attack against the American people and had expressed its willingness to share intelligence and to permit its airports and airspace to be used as needed to fight terrorism. Finding it of little value, Washington dismissed Havana's good-faith offer.

Pleasing the hard-line Cuban Americans that made up the audience, Bush used a Miami political rally celebrating a Cuban holiday on May 20, 2002, to announce his Cuba policy. Repeating issues raised earlier, he demanded that Havana allow internationally supervised democratic elections, freedom of expression, and freedom for all political prisoners, before an end to such punitive measures as trade and travel restrictions could be considered. By then, the White House had welcomed the 2001 UN Human Rights Commission's condemnation of Cuba by a majority of one vote; the close decision was made possible by the relentless campaign of the United States seeking support for the anti-Cuba resolution, including arm twisting of reluctant delegations whenever necessary.

The diplomatic situation was appraised by the head of the Cuban Interests Section in Washington, Dagoberto Rodríguez: "What we hear from the American public is that there is a great desire to have normal and civilized relations....[But] what we hear from government officials is that there are no great possibilities that it could ever happen." And yet, "we are always ready to sit down to discuss in a civilized fashion any bilateral issue, but never our internal affairs," added Rodríguez.[11]

Nonetheless, some events contrary to Bush's Cuba policy were already taking place during the administration's first years. Notably, acting against Washington's long-held restrictions, Americans continued visiting the island some of them illegally. By the end of 2001, approximately one hundred eighty thousand U.S. tourists had traveled to Cuba, demonstrating a growing interest in their neighboring island. In spite of the severe penalties increasingly imposed on travelers without the required Washington-issued license, the flow of visitors continued in 2003. However, after the administration stopped issuing licenses for the people-to-people educational program and later most of the university educational programs, the number of American visitors began to decrease. Representing a cross-section of American society, visitors seemed bound by their common concern for finding proper ways to relate to Cuba. Americans from many walks of life—political leaders, students, teachers, personalities, industrialists, businessmen, farmers, and many others—were included among the visitors. Several hundred students participating in the University of Pittsburgh's Semester at Sea program, members of Congress, city mayors, Illinois governor George Ryan (for the second time), former president Jimmy Carter (who was later honored with the Nobel Peace Prize), the 2000 presidential candidate Ralph Nader, and others were welcomed personally by President Castro.

The general secretary of INTERPOL, Ronald Noble, during a visit to the island in early 2002, supported Cuban efforts in international law enforcement, stating "Cuba has sustained an outstanding campaign combating drug trafficking as well as the illicit transit of people and the use of counterfeited credit cards." Noble also endorsed Cuba's condemnation of terrorism and of the terrorist attack suffered by the United States on September 11, 2001, characterizing it as "sincere and honest." He added that both "Cuba and the INTERPOL agree that a 'refuge/paradise' [in any country] for criminals and especially for terrorists could not be tolerated."[12] While attending a regional conference studying ways to stop drug trafficking, Congressman William Delahunt (D-MA) proposed a cooperative approach by Washington and Havana to combat the problem. Ricardo Alarcon, head of the Cuban National Assembly, responded, saying, "I see no reason that could prevent the United States and Cuba from having an anti-drug agreement."[13]

In the year 2000, President Clinton approved the sale of food and medicines to Cuba under restrictive conditions; no private or public credit or financing were allowed—all sales had to be paid in cash. But until Hurricane Michelle caused major havoc to the island in the fall of 2001, Clinton's partial softening of the long-held embargo had no real impact. With winds of 250 kilometers per hour, affecting 53 percent of the population and 45 percent of the national territory, Michelle caused material losses estimated in the millions of dollars, which severely harmed the nation's gross domestic product (GDP) for that year. In the face of such disaster, Washington offered humanitarian aid to relieve the hardship. After respectfully declining the Bush administration's offer, Havana reversed its earlier refusal to proceed with needed purchases under such onerous conditions and announced its willingness to pay cash for U.S. food products. The administration refused at first but then accepted Cuba's offer—an initial dispute concerning how to transport the cargo ended when it was agreed to use third countries' merchant ships. Soon thereafter, the first shipments of food from U.S. ports in over four decades were sailing for Havana.

Characterizing it as a "Castro political maneuver," southern Florida Cuban Americans voiced their disapproval of the ensuing, mutually profitable commercial exchange. Showing her frustration, Rep. Ros-Lehtinen stated that "it is up to American farmers if they want to run the risk of not being paid by Castro for their products." Contrary to such gloomy predictions, however, the shipments arrived on time throughout 2002 and since and have been properly paid for in cash by Cuba.

The political fallout generated by American farmers' sales to Cuba gained a life of its own. Under pressure, Congress became sympathetic to ending restrictions in order to facilitate further trade (although allowing Cuban products to enter the United States was not part of the legislation under consideration). The Republican-dominated House approved in 2002 the commercial financing of sales to the island, as well as putting an end to travel restrictions and lifting the limits imposed on money remittances by Cuban Americans to their relatives.

Rather than political abstractions and partisanship, the social and economic needs of American farmers and businessmen were the force behind the growing movement seeking to end the politics of sanctions and embargo against Cuba. However, militant conservative forces in Congress and in the Republican Party, acting with the administration's support, were adamant in their opposition to even a partial softening of Bush's Cuban policy.

In addition, the new U.S. envoy in Havana, James Cason, stepped up his highly public contacts with Cubans opposed to the revolutionary government. These actions by Cason were followed by the arrests of some seventy-five "dissidents" in the first months of 2003. In 2004-2005 the momentum for potentially better U.S.-Cuban relations was broken. The harder line elements of the Bush administration gained the upper hand with the issuance of the Powell Commission report in May 2004. Acting upon its recommendations, the U.S. government put further restrictions on U.S. citizen travel to the island and on the payment of remittances to Cuban citizens. The United States unilaterally suspended the regular migration talks between the two sides and in 2005, the Bush administration issued new regulations that were aimed at reducing the growing U.S.-Cuban agricultural trade. The hard line elements in the United States were buoyed by Cuban economic and infrastructure difficulties resulting from the Fall 2004 hurricanes. As 2008 approaches there are renewed calls in the U.S. Congress for an end to the embargo on Cuba but the White House and its allies remain as committed as ever to the nearly fifty-year status quo.

Notes

1. A "dog" and a "throwback to the 1960s" was the language used by congressional aides to characterize the Torricelli law (Cuban Democracy Act, CDA) when it was initially introduced in the House. Still, "then-Congressman Robert Torricelli (D-N.J.), chairman of the House Subcommittee on Western Hemisphere Affairs, and the Cuban American National Foundation [CAIN-F] leader at the time, Más Canosa—the real force behind the bill—were committed to having it become law. [Congressman, later Senator] Torricelli, [Senator Jesse Helms, R-N.C.] . . . and other elected officials benefited from the support by the . . . [CANF] and its leaders (soft money) for politicians and political parties who would play an anti-Castro role." The Torricelli bill was finally signed into law by President George Bush just before the 1992 presidential elections.

"The Helms-Burton Act [signed into law by President Clinton in 1996] is organized in four separate titles or sections. Title I solidifies a . . . network of sanctions against Cuba [i.e., seeking an international embargo, opposing Cuba's business with international lending organizations, sanctioning former socialist countries aiding Cuba, supporting independent organizations and individuals on the island, and codifying the embargo] . . . Title II covers U.S. aid to a free and democratic Cuba . . . Title III protects American citizens who lost property [nationalized by the Cuban government]. [Included in this category are Cuban Americans who are American citizen today but were not at the time. However, the legislation authorizes the U.S. president to cancel its application for security reasons for a six-month period, which Presidents Clinton and Bush have done with no exception.]. Title IV empowers the secretary of state and the attorney general to suspend visas of officials from corporations trafficking in American property and those officials' spouses and children." Max Azicri, *Cuba Today and Tomorrow: Reinventing Socialism* (Gainesville: University Press of Florida, 2000), 181-3, 208-9.

2. See Esteban Morales Dominguez, Carlos Batista, and Kanaki Yamaoka, *The United States and Cuba's International Economy Reinsertion,* Joint Research Program Series no. 126 (Tokyo: Institute of Developing Economies, 1999).

3. See for example, "José Maria Aznar's, Spain President," statement in *Granma,* September 11, 1999.

4. Morales Domínguez, Batista, and Yamaoka, *Reinsertion,*139-44.

5. "For the 10th year in a row [twelfth year in 2003], the General Assembly voted overwhelmingly . . . for an end to the United States trade embargo against Cuba. The vote was 167 to 3, identical to [the year before]. Those opposing the resolution, in addition to the United States, were Israel and the Marshall Islands, which also supported Washington in 2000. Latvia, Micronesia and Nicaragua abstained, as they did last year. Despite United Nations support for American positions since the Sept. 11 attacks against the United States, sympathy for Cuba's financial plight and condemnation of the blockade remained unchanged."

"U.N. again chastises U.S. on Cuba trade," *New York Times,* November 28, 2001.

6. Morales Dominguez, Batista, and Yamaoka, *Reinsertion,* 152-77.

7. "Informe del Ministro de Relaciones Exteriores," *Granma,* September 15, 1999.

8. For a discussion of the different political forces that brought President Bush to the White House, see Michael Lind, *Made in Texas: George W. Bush and the Southern Takeover of American Politics* (New York: Basic Books, 2003).

9. *El Nuevo Herald* (on line), February 21, 1999.

10. The Torricelli law (Cuban Democracy Act, CDA) and its two-track policy have been implemented by the administration of President George Bush, President Bill Clinton, and President George W. Bush (who in 2003 suspended its person-to-person exchange provision to curb further the inflow of U.S. dollars to Cuba). Under this legislation, "while the embargo [has been] tightened (track one, the stick), at the other end (track two, the carrot) a window [has been] opened facilitating exchange of information and travel by certain individuals. To Havana and some political analysts, under the guise of increased person-to-person relations, Washington's real objective with track-two [has been] to undermine the revolution from within." Azicri, *Cuba Today and Tomorrow,* 189.

11. *El Nuevo Herald* (on line), January 24, 2002.

12. *Granma,* January 17, 2002.

13. *El Nuevo Herald* (on line), November 11, 2001.

Chapter One

Historical Background of United States-Cuban Relations (1800-1959)

To understand the nature of contemporary relations between the governments of the United States and Cuba it is necessary to delve deeply into the history of the two countries. We will argue that the framework of U.S.-Cuban relations, largely unchanged since the triumph of the Cuban revolutionaries, can best be understood in the context of imperial designs held by U.S. rulers since the era close to the founding of the United States. This historical perspective is crucial to understanding why there has been little change in U.S. policy toward Cuba since the fall of the Soviet Union. Throughout the nineteenth century U.S. rulers, as part of an imperial outlook embodied in the concept of Manifest Destiny, viewed Cuba as an island that would eventually fall into the hands of the United States. As Spain's status as a world power declined over the course of the century, the United States would make repeated overtures to Spain for the purchase of the island. For a variety of reasons that acquisition never happened, but the opportunity for U.S. domination of the island came at the end of the century when U.S. military forces intervened during the war for Cuban independence on the side of the forces fighting the Spanish. As the superior military force, the United States dictated the terms of the Spanish surrender and in the process, established Cuba as a neocolony, thoroughly dominated politically, militarily and economically from 1902 onward. The triumph of the Cuban revolutionaries in 1959 and their subsequent integration into the socialist bloc abruptly ended that era of U.S. domination and remains by far the single most important defeat of U.S. imperial designs in the Western Hemisphere. This defeat is exacerbated from the U.S. perspective by the fact that the same revolutionary leaders, led by Fidel Castro, remain in power today and continue to pursue an anti-imperialist foreign policy that regularly challenges that United States. In what has been dubbed by many observers as the post-Cold War world, the United States has normalized relations with former adversary countries still led by Communist parties, namely Vietnam and China. However, unlike Cuba, these countries are not in the Western Hemisphere, the perceived natural sphere of influence of U.S.

influence and both Asian countries, while nominally socialist, have pursued strategies of economic development that openly welcome large scale foreign direct investment and allow the development of significant indigenous capitalist classes. In contrast, Cuba, while welcoming foreign investment on its own terms, remains committed to a socialist path. This chapter will show the depths of the historical confrontation that has prevented into the twenty-first century the development of a normal relationship between the two countries. In fact, the authors will show that there have never been normal relations between the two countries.

There were many dimensions to the relations between the United States and Cuba in the nineteenth century, but always crucial to U.S. designs on the island, they were economic in nature. As the U.S. historian Leland Hamilton Jenks expressed in his work *Our Cuban Colony*,[1] economic relations between Cuba and the United States can be traced to contraband and piracy times, when the island of Cuba was still a part of the old Spanish colonial system. However, from the inception of the United States as an independent state, Cuba's northern neighbor showed a special interest in the possession of the island. Early U.S. policymakers recognized that Cuba had the necessary conditions to complement the U.S. economy given Cuba's proximity and strategic geographic position halfway between the two Americas along international trading routes. U.S. merchants saw Cuba as a potential market and also a base from which to reach out to the rest of the Caribbean and Central America.

Military considerations were also a part of these ambitions of the United States. During Thomas Jefferson's first presidential term (1801-1805), the idea that U.S. interests in Cuba went beyond the growing commercial interests gained impetus among North American power circles.[2] Cuba's geographic position at the entrance of the Gulf of Mexico and its closeness to Florida could provide an advance post for the defense of U.S. territory in an era of continuous incursions by European powers trying to extend their colonial domains in the region.

Jefferson stated:

> I consider that the Florida Cape and Cuba form the mouth of the Mississippi as well as other rivers that empty their waters in the Gulf of Mexico and, therefore, its purchasing for our Union is of the uppermost importance because of what it represents to our internal tranquility and to our prosperity and enlargement.[3]

He continued:

> On my part I sincerely confess that I have always considered Cuba as the most important addition to our system of states. The control that, together with Florida, it would give over the Gulf of Mexico and over the countries of the isthmus surrounding it, as over those whose waters empty there, would come to fulfill our political wellbeing[4]

In effect, Cuba's exceptionally advantageous geographic position made the island, more than any other territory, the object of U.S. ambition for commercial expansion and industrial development. Such considerations led the United States to consider acquisition of the island as a matter of national policy.

In November 1805, President Jefferson notified the British ambassador in Washington that, in the event of war between Great Britain and Spain, the United States would seize the Spanish held colonies of Cuba and Florida in order to defend the southern border of the United States. Jefferson persisted in this threat of invasion throughout his term of office ending in 1809.[5] U.S. threats to annex Cuba were tempered by the fact that the more powerful British and French also had interests in Latin America. The weakness of the United States in the face of Great Britain was underscored by the U.S. defeat in The War of 1812 and the subsequent pledge by the United States not to invade the island. However, these setbacks to U.S. power did not diminish long term U.S. interests in acquiring the island, but rather led to the formulation in 1823 of the famous "Ripe Fruit Theory."

This theory, stated in the instructions sent by the Secretary of State John Quincy Adams to Hugh Nelson, U.S. ambassador in Spain, expressed the irrevocable desire to take possession of Cuba, as well as the acknowledgment of the circumstances that advised patience in waiting for the right moment for Cuba to fall.[6]

It could be taken for a fact that Spanish domination over the American continents, Northern and Southern, has irrevocably ended. But the islands of Cuba and Puerto Rico remain nominally, and to such a point really, under its dependence that it still has the power to transfer to others its control over them, and with that, its possession. These islands for their local position are natural appendages of the North American continent, and one of them, the isle of Cuba, almost in view from our shores, has become for a number of reasons of the uppermost importance for the political and commercial interests of our Union. The dominant position it has in the Gulf of Mexico and in the Antilles Sea, the character of its population, its location halfway between our east coast and the isle of Santo Domingo, its vast and protected Havana harbor, facing a long line of our coasts deprived of the same advantage, the nature of its productions and its own needs, that support an immensely beneficial commerce for both parts, all combine to give it such importance in the sum of our national interests that any other foreign territory can compare, and that our relations with it are almost identical to the ones that tie the different states in our Union.

Indeed, such are the interests between that isle and this country, the geographical, commercial and political links, formed by nature and gradually fomented and strengthened with the passage of time, that when we turn our eyes to the probable course of events in the next fifty years is almost impossible to resist oneself to the certitude that the annexation of Cuba to our Federal Republic will be indispensable to the continuation to the Union and its integrity. . . .

It is self evident that for that event, the annexation of the isle to the United States, we are not yet prepared, and that at first sight numerous and formidable objections presented themselves against the extension of our domains beyond the sea . . . But there are laws of political gravitation as well as physical gravitation; and if an apple, severed by the tempest from its native tree can not

choose but fall to the ground, Cuba, forcibly disjoined from its unnatural connection with Spain and incapable of self-support, can gravitate only toward the
North American Union, which, by the same law of nature can not cast her off
from its bosom.[7]

There is no doubt that the concept of seeking absolute control over Cuba
became an inextricable part of the American political culture. However, the
declaration of policies was not enough. It became necessary to develop a suita-
ble policy and set of instruments to accomplish the early-defined objectives
regarding Cuba. In light of U.S. military weakness at the time and the lack of
willingness of Spain to sell Cuba to the United States as it had done with Florida, the U.S. leaders tried to place U.S. designs in a broader framework.

In a move to raise barriers to the British appetite in Latin America, and especially with respect to Cuba, President Monroe enunciated his policy toward
the territories to the south of the United States in his message to Congress in
December 1823. In that statement, known since as the Monroe Doctrine, it was
clear that any effort on the part of a European nation to take over any of the
Latin American lands would be understood as, "the manifestation of a hostile
disposition toward the United States."[8]

The Ripe Fruit Theory, the Monroe Doctrine and the proclamation of the
Manifest Destiny, which stipulated aggressive expansionism as a foreign policy
principle, were sign posts of U.S. policy toward Latin America. Cuba played a
singular role as the launching platform for taking control over the young neighboring republics to the south. In this respect, the island would become the scenario for the clash of British and North American interests regarding Latin America.[9]

Before the Panama Congress in 1826, Henry Clay, Secretary of State for
President Adams, expressed the U.S. position.

Not any power, not even Spain, has in any sense a higher interest in Cuba's
destiny than the United States . . . and as for (the Anglo-American), we do not
want any change in the Isle's possession or the political condition and we
would not see with indifference that Spain's power would pass to another European power. We would not want either that it be transferred or additioned to
any of the new states of America.[10]

At the same Congress, the United States officially and forcefully opposed a
plan proposed by Simón Bolivar, the South American Liberator, to facilitate the
independence of Cuba and Puerto Rico. After Adams and Monroe, every U.S.
President reiterated the policy that Cuba would remain a Spanish colony only
until the United States was strong enough to take control. Under this policy
Cuba would never realize its independence. As a premonition of the island's fate
in the twentieth century and its increasing dependence on the United States, the
U.S. trade policy toward Cuba became the tool to prepare the ground for ultimate U.S. control. By 1848 Cuba imported products from the United States
valued at $6,938,538.[11] That same year Cuba exported products to the United

States for $8,825,826, which represented a third of the island's total exports.[12] There is no doubt that Cuba had started to strongly depend on exportation with importation with the United States while it remained a Spanish colony. By the 1850s, the United States had firmly established a model of commercial relations with Cuba that continued to function until the island obtained its independence from Spain. As this trend in commercial relations between Cuba and the United States continued, the Spanish trade was replaced in the Cuban market in spite of Spanish resistance to U.S. trade with the island. By the mid-1860s, Cuba was becoming an economic colony of the United States without losing its role as a political colony of Spain.

The first formal offer to purchase Cuba from Spain was made during the James Knox Polk administration (1845-1849). President Polk undertook the negotiations with the support of Cuban annexionists in the U.S. Congress. The June 1848 negotiations in Madrid were unsuccessful as the Spanish refusal was strong. The answer, given by the Marquis de Pidal, Spain's Minister of Foreign Affairs, is famous: "The unanimous opinion of the country is that it would prefer seeing the isle under the ocean before giving it away to another power."[13]

In the years preceding the Civil War, U.S. efforts to purchase the island continued. President Franklin Pierce's ambassador to Spain, Pierre Soule, was particularly aggressive in pursuit of the sale. President Buchanan secured in 1860 Congressional approval for a $30 million fund as a down payment for the purchase.[14] The Civil War served to adjust U.S. designs on Cuba to a degree. The defeat of the slave states ended the hopes of the Southern slaveowners that the annexation of Cuba would bolster their cause. However, in other aspects the triumph of the Northern industrialists and their model of capitalist development further whetted the appetite of the United States for the control of Cuba.

The last quarter of the nineteenth century saw the rapid growth of U.S. industry and with it the development of the United States as a power with the potential for global reach. It is during this time period that the United States developed the military power, especially naval forces that made the option for empire declared more than fifty years earlier in the Monroe Doctrine a realistic possibility. The United States emerged by the 1880s as a country with transoceanic interests. The interest in Cuba became recast in a new context linked to wider strategic motivations including an eventual interoceanic canal through Panama.[15]

The decade of the 1880s was an epoch openly characterized by the penetration of U.S. capital investments in Cuba. This involvement encountered a very favorable soil already fertilized by the strong influence of trade with the United States, trade which had for a number of years served as an effective vehicle to gradually tie Cuba's productivity lines to U.S. needs. During President Grover Cleveland's first administration (1885-1889), a fusing process had begun, closely linking U.S. industrial capital with banking investments. The search for markets, investment sources, and above all else, increased profit margins, moved the United States to direct its expansionist intentions to the less developed countries, especially Cuba.

While this process was taking place in American society, another process of great importance for Cuban history was also developing in the United States. On April 10, 1892, José Marti, poet, orator, and above all, a Cuban patriot, founded the Cuban Revolutionary Party, which;

> is constituted in order to obtain, with the combined efforts of all men of good-will, the independence of Cuba, and to foment and assist in the independence of Puerto Rico . . . and to gather all existing elements of revolution . . . that could be attracted . . . in order to create a Cuban nation, republican in spirit and method warfare, a nation capable of securing the lasting happiness of her children and of accomplishing, in the historical life of the continent, the hard duties imposed by its geographic position.[16]

From that moment on, Marti dedicated himself to the organization of what he called the Necessary War, which started on February 24, 1895. Over the next three years, even though Marti himself perished in the struggle, the Cuban independence forces gathered momentum and by 1898 represented a serious threat to the continuation of Spanish colonial rule in Cuba.

Meanwhile, U.S. monopolies strengthened their power even more by beginning to play an increasingly active role in that country's politics. One of their first victories was the election of Republican President William McKinley in 1896. The Republican Party received $16 million from various companies including Rockefeller Oil, Havemeyer Sugar and Morgan Steel.[17] McKinley's foreign and domestic policies were responsive to the interests of these special donor groups. The terms of McKinley's electoral platform bound him with the independence of Cuba. However, even though the Republican Party's program included this acknowledgment, the new president did not refer to it in public speeches. In February, 1897, incoming Secretary of State John Sherman outlined the political projection of the administration on Cuba and the President accepted his assertion that the government's policy should be guided more by commercial interests than by sympathy toward a people fighting for independence.

While McKinley became committed to a policy favoring the annexation of Cuba, there were other businesses already investing and trading with Cuba who did not favor annexation. The latter position found support with a majority of U.S. citizens and factions of Congress. Collectively, these sectors demanded the recognition of Cuban insurgence and the independence of Cuba.[18] In May, 1897, the Secretary of State received a petition signed by 3,000 prominent entrepreneurs in banking, industry, commerce and shipbuilding, all of whom were commercially linked with Cuba. These businessmen petitioned the administration to save their enterprises but to do so within the framework of Cuban independence.

Later in 1897, McKinley designated William T. Calhoun to head a judicial investigation about the Cuban situation. The report from the Danville, Illinois judge acknowledged just cause in the Cuban war of independence and criticized Spain. Furthermore, Calhoun reported that the insurgents would not be defeated and that both sides were exhausted. The report concluded that the military outcome would be on the basis of resistance and emphasized that independence would sink Cuba into an internal class and race war. This prognosis was inimical to the commercial future and general U.S. interest in Cuba. From that point of view, it was more dangerous for the United States to witness the victory of the Cuban independence forces than Spain's continued colonial rule. In response to the report, all U.S. action from there forward was designed to prevent a Cuban victory.

The United States pressured Spain to negotiate a truce with the Cuban rebels and to grant significant reforms short of independence. However, this position resonated with neither side in the Cuban struggle. The Spanish government was not in a mood for concessions and the Cuban insurgent army would settle for nothing short of independence. Thus, McKinley's option languished in the face of the reality of a revolutionary war. At this point McKinley revived the idea of purchasing Cuba from Spain, but this option was effectively blocked by Senatorial opposition. Concerned by Congress's inability to pursue the purchase of Cuba, a group of bankers and businessmen from New York were willing to exert their political influence in exchange for future commercial advantages and monetary remuneration. Heading this group were: Samuel M. Janney, a member of the banking firm Chrysty and Janney, and John McCook, a lawyer and financier from the firm Alexander and Green. McCook was also the administrator of the Wardine Steamship Company that made trips between the United States and Cuba and, as a personal friend of McKinley, had been considered for the posts of Attorney General and Secretary of the Interior.

On August 5, Tomás Estrada Palma, who, after Marti's death, became the head of the Cuban Revolutionary Party in 1897, entered into an agreement with this group in New York. The goal was to negotiate a tripartite accord among the United States, Spain and Cuba. The plan was reminiscent of old formulas to purchase Cuba from Spain. Janney was to receive 140 million pesos in bonds from the Cubans at four percent interest.[19] In November, 1897, the accord was still unsigned because President McKinley, who was in favor of annexation, considered that the implied legal contractual ties in the wording of the accord would give Cuba the international judicial standing that would hamper U.S. annexionist purposes.

It was in this context that Spain issued a Royal Decree in November, 1897 establishing an allegedly autonomous regime for Cuba and Puerto Rico. For Cuba, the decree created a bicameral Parliament, an Administration Council and a Chamber of Representatives. The latter would be formed by popular election, but the former would have eighteen elected members and seventeen members designated by the King. The true government of Cuba would be in the hands of a General Governor appointed by the King. Although this regime was in place during all of 1898, its existence was a farce. When Spain granted Cuba an autonomous regime aimed at stopping the independence movement and avoiding direct action by the United States, it was too late. The circumstances left only one option to U.S. interests: direct intervention.

Direct intervention was advocated by a group of military officers and politicians linked to the most aggressive sector of U.S. capital. The group's strategy was based upon the expansionist needs of the United States, focusing south of the continental boundary and seeking control of the Caribbean Sea. Its goal was to guarantee the building of an interoceanic canal in Panama that would allow marine traffic between the U.S. shores in the Atlantic and the Pacific Oceans for military and economic purposes. U.S. control of Cuba and Puerto Rico would permit the domination of the Caribbean and possible U.S. expansion to the rest of the continent, while Spain's possessions in the Philippines would open the way in Asia for the United States.

The pretext for U.S. intervention in the Hispanic-Cuban War was the explosion of the U.S. naval cruiser *Maine* on February 15, 1898, causing the death of 276 U.S. sailors. The ship had been sent to Cuba in the last days of January of that year as a warning to the Spanish government.[20] The explosion of the *Maine* brought about an eruption of collective anger in the United States. A Spanish commission determined that the explosion had occurred in the interior of the ship, while an American commission attributed the cause to an external agent.

On April 11, 1898, President McKinley asked for Congressional authorization to take the necessary measures to put an end to hostilities between the Spanish government and the Cuban people.[21] Congress answered the presidential request with the Joint Resolution of April 19. This resolution began with the statement that ". . . Cuban liberators have already won their independence and the right to its recognition that the isle of Cuba is, and rightfully should be free and independent."[22] It further authorized the President to employ all sea and land forces in order to achieve the pacification of Cuba, including the establishment of a competent and stable government, and the expulsion of Spain from Cuba. The war of the United States against Spain extended from April 21 to July 16, 1898, the date of the capitulation of Spanish forces in a military barracks near Santiago de Cuba.

The entrance of the United States into the Cuban Independence War was a military and political action that allowed the U.S. government to seize the remains of the Spanish Empire in America. The participation of the U.S. Navy, first in Santiago de Cuba and later in Manila, served the purpose of cutting short Spanish resistance. With the signing of the Paris Treaty in December of 1898, the negotiations between the representatives from the United States and Spain concluded with full Spanish surrender. The Cubans were not allowed to participate in the surrender of Spanish forces, in spite of the important role that Cuban forces under Calixto Garcia played in the defeat of the Spanish. The Cubans were also not included in the peace talks with Spain, thus allowing the United States to dictate the terms of the transfer of power. These steps ratified an essential element of U.S. tactics toward the Cuban insurgents: the non-recognition of the representation and authority of the three fundamental organs that incarnated the independent aspirations of the Cuban people: the delegation of the Cuban Revolutionary Party abroad, the Government Council of the Republic in Arms and the Liberation Army. Such non-recognition was crucial because the political forces contained in these organizations would have strongly resisted the U.S.

plans to turn the island into a neo-colony.

The inauguration of a U.S.-controlled Cuban government on January 1, 1899, immediately ratified the agreement between Spain and the United States. This action legally ended the U.S. military occupation of the island that had been in place since the Spanish surrender in July. In reality, the U.S. military occupation would last for another three years while U.S. authorities laid the groundwork for the creation of Cuba as a permanent neocolony.

Although there was a republican form of government established for Cuba, the reality was that the implementation of these republican intentions were doomed as a result of the hidden U.S. agenda. An interventionist U.S. military government was established. The mission of these military forces was to achieve three goals: 1) to serve as an occupation force, to guarantee internal order in the country; 2) to gather economic, social and political data with an emphasis on noting capital investment possibilities in each military jurisdiction; and 3) to establish norms of life more compatible with U.S. culture through military regimentation. These orders established the judicial foundations for ruling Cuba, not just during the period in which the interventionist government functioned and authority was in place, but carried over to the entire Republican period (1902-1959), as historical events have attested.

The Cuban tariff system was modified through military orders making it more amenable to U.S. imports. Procedures for land transfers were simplified to facilitate U.S. investments. Railroad and port concessions were granted to U.S. companies. These edicts as well as many others were issued, thus molding the Cuban identity in U.S.-driven political, social and economic terms. Military orders decreed by the interventionist government became the foundation of future Cuban legislation and were repeatedly confirmed through complementary mechanisms, such as the Platt Amendment, imposed on the Constitutional Assembly of 1901 and the first Cuban Republican Government in 1902.

Once the conflict between the United States and Spain was eliminated, Cuba was freed of interference by a third country in its relationships with major trading markets for its products. With U.S. intervention, the foreign appropriation of Cuban material and human resources was no longer realized through fiscal exploitation and commercial imbalances, as had been the case with Spain during the eighteenth and nineteenth centuries. The new method of appropriation established the direct exploitation of labor forces and natural resources by direct foreign investments as subsequent increases in Cuban trade and industrial production became reliant upon U.S. capitalism.

With the Cuban Revolutionary Party, founded by José Marti, effectively dissolved, the U.S. interventionist government used the contradictions between the Representative Assembly and the Liberator Army, personified in the figure of General Máximo Gomez, to eradicate the institutions of radical independence. Within these circumstances, the national sovereignty ideal was left without organizational form. However, the building of an independent republic was the prevailing wish of the majority of the Cuban people. That ideal continued to manifest itself even in the context of U.S. intervention. This sentiment for independence helps to explain why the idea of annexation to the United States, supported by many in U.S. ruling circles, could not become a viable option; most Cubans resisted any variant short of independence. As a result, this chapter of U.S.-Cuban relations ended with the formal establishment in 1902 of the Cuban Republic, with formal political power transferred to the government of Tomas Estrada Palma, who, after Marti's death, became head of the Cuban Revolutionary Party in 1897. Palma represented those elements within Cuban society that were prepared to accept limited Cuban sovereignty in the face of overwhelming U.S. political, military, and economic power.

U.S. Policies in the Twentieth Century

During the first half of the 20th century, the United States dominated Cuba's economic and political life via Cuban governments loyal to U.S. designs and reciprocal treaties that favored the Northern neighbor, thus guaranteeing a preponderant role in Cuba's foreign trade, the same way that the capital flow from the United States to Cuba guaranteed high profit margins. Congress made the provision that an amendment to an appropriations bill introduced by Senator Orville H. Platt be incorporated in the Cuban constitution of 1901. The amendment limited Cuban sovereignty in fiscal and treaty-making matters and allowed the United States to intervene at any time to maintain a "government adequate for the protection of life, property, and individual liberty." The Platt Amendment also provided for a North American naval base at Guantanamo, a site still occupied by the United States against the objections of the Cuban government. Cuban products now went almost exclusively to North American markets, and the island became, in essence, a political protectorate of the United States. The Cuban political system was constructed and modeled on U.S. lines. A presidential system was imposed, complete with checks and balances following the U.S. Constitution. A capital building, copied from the one in Washington, D.C., completed the picture. Twice, in 1905 and in 1917, the United States intervened militarily under the Platt provision.

U.S. Cuban economic ties were also strengthened. The Treaty of Reciprocity was signed in 1903, making Cuba's economic growth subservient to U.S. interests.[23] The Treaty of Reciprocity guaranteed the continuation of the commercial relations developed throughout the nineteenth century. Now the newly invested capital, strongly linked to U.S. banking, would do the rest. A British-American agreement set up an International Sugar Committee to control the sale of Cuban sugar, dividing the export market exclusively between the two countries and giving them the power to establish the price. U.S. investment in Cuba, in addition to sugar refineries and lands, included mining, communications, and the railways. The U.S. Federal Reserve Bank established its only foreign branch in Havana. By 1926 U.S. direct investment on the island totaled nearly $1.4 billion.

The political system of the new republic proceeded under the watchful eye of the United States. The first president of the Republic, Estrada Palma, served his first term from 1902-1906. His reelection in 1906 was an example of the electoral frauds that were to become commonplace in Cuba. The furor over his fraudulent electoral victory led Estrada Palma to request U.S. intervention. Faced with potential civil war, he stepped aside and for the next three years the island was ruled by Judge Charles Magoon of Nebraska. His tenure was unpopular with the Cuban people and the president he chose to succeed him, José Miguel Gomez, was exceptionally corrupt during his four year rule from 1909-1913. During his presidency, there was a significant black rebellion that began on May 20, 1912, with demonstrations and strikes protesting a law banning the formation of "movements composed of persons of the same race or color." The law was aimed at the Independent Party of Color (PIC) which had been founded in 1908 by Evaristo Estenoz to challenge the domination of the newly founded Republic by Cubans of European origin. Gomez's army suppressed the revolt, killing more than three-thousand people, including Estenoz and the entire leadership of the PIC. The Americans sent naval forces and marines but they were not needed to carry out the massacre. Politically, the Cubans of African descent were largely driven underground after these events, not resurfacing until the revolutionary events in the 1950s. These events underscored the reality that while a neocolonial system had been imposed on Cuba by the United States, the majority of the Cuban people did not endorse this domination and could be held at bay only by superior military force.

When the successor to Gomez, General Mario Garcia Menocal, assumed power for his second term in 1917 in the midst of vote rigging charges, there was a brief uprising by the opposition Liberal Party against the Conservative president. President Woodrow Wilson supported Menocal and stated that the United States would not recognize any Cuban government brought in by armed means. Marines from the American force established at Guantanamo left their base in support of Menocal advancing as far as Camaguey and remaining there until January 1922.

Between 1921 and 1925 the island was virtually ruled by an American commission headed by General Enoch Crowder, who had been brought in because of an economic crisis caused by a dramatic fall in sugar prices. The commission left in 1926, but by then, General Gerardo Machado had assumed power, having been elected president in 1924 for a four-year term. In 1927, Machado changed the constitution, extending the presidential term to six years and had himself reelected, which, in essence, destroyed the party system in Cuba. During the Machado presidency, student and university activism grew. Julio Mella, a law student and Secretary-General of the Student Federation, organized a national student congress. He later founded the Popular University José Martí, patterned on the Popular University Gonzalez Prada, established by Haya de la Torre and José Carlos Mariategui in Peru, to expand education to the working class. Strongly anti-imperialist and highly critical of the role of the United States, Mella worked with the Mexican Enrique Flores Magón to organize the

Cuban Communist Party in 1925. Through Mella's efforts, students began to attack the increasingly dictatorial government of Machado, who responded by jailing Mella. After his release, Mella left for exile in Mexico. Opposition to the Machado dictatorship continued in the University of Havana, where students organized the University Student Directorate, focusing anti-Machado sentiment in Havana. The directorate leadership was ousted from the university, ending the first phase of struggle against Machado.

However, the economic collapse of 1929 caused a precipitous drop in the world price of sugar, followed by political unrest and severe repression. The assassination of Mella in Mexico and the increased repression by Machado led to a second directorate in 1930, which began organizing open demonstrations against the government. The new leadership included future president Carlos Prío Socarras, Raúl Roa (later foreign minister under Fidel Castro), and Eduardo Chibas, future founder of the Cuban People's Party (Orthodox). A clash with police killed one of the student leaders and brought the closing of the university by Machado. Now known as the Generation of 1930, the students turned to urban violence. Directorate leaders were arrested, as were most of the faculty, including physiology professor Ramón Grau San Martin. Other groups developed in opposition to the increasingly unpopular Machado. U.S. Ambassador Summer Welles tried to mediate the conflict between Machado and his opposition but failed, and a general strike, uprisings among the unionized sugar workers, and an army revolt forced Machado into exile in August 1933. He was replaced by Carlos Manuel de Céspedes, son of the hero of 1868 who restored the 1901 constitution. The new government immediately received U.S. backing aimed at isolating the most radical forces.

Directorate leaders continued to agitate against the government, accusing Céspedes of being too close to Machado and the United States. Students demanded a new constitution, plus social and economic reforms. Government plans to freeze army promotions and reduce pay led to a takeover of the army by noncommissioned officers headed by Sergeant Fulgencio Batista. Batista, who had worked as a stenographer at the military trials of the students under the Machado regime, invited directorate leaders to a meeting. Together they agreed to a coup, and on the composition of a new government, ousting Céspedes in September 1933. Although Batista did not accept a post in the new government, the action placed Batista in a position where he dominated politics through the control of the army for the next twenty-five years.

The new government was headed by Professor Grau San Martin whose short-lived administration initiated important social and nationalist legislation. For example, Antonio Guiteras, Minister of Government, nationalized the Cuban electrical system. Simultaneously, a series of workers' protests, land confiscations by peasants, and a takeover of sugar mills by sugar workers resulted in strong opposition to the new government from Cuba's wealthy elites and U.S. Ambassador Welles. The context of the uprising against Machado was a new administration in Washington. Franklin D. Roosevelt had assumed power in March 1933 and promised a new approach to Latin America, called the "Good

Neighbor Policy." Initially conceived by his predecessor Herbert Hoover, the policy shift acknowledged that there were growing costs to the policies of "Gunboat Diplomacy" that had been pursued in Central America and the Caribbean for more than thirty years. Following the bogging down of U.S. troops in Nicaragua's wars of the late 1920s there was some apprehension about using U.S. soldiers to intervene in Cuba's problems. In May, 1933, Roosevelt sent his friend, Sumner Welles, to Havana as ambassador to mediate the crisis but he failed to find a solution acceptable to the United States. As a result, the United States withheld the recognition without which Grau's government was doomed. He hung on until January 15, 1934 but eventually conceded to reality—the combined power of Batista and the U.S. government. The embittered "Generation of 1930" blamed the United States for blocking their legitimate revolution. The Platt Amendment to the Cuban constitution had become an anachronism. It was no longer needed by the United States and it was resented by the Cubans except by those who might have sought U.S. intervention. Roosevelt had it abrogated on May 29, 1934, but in reality, the United States was dominating Cuba just as much in 1934 as it had in 1902, albeit without direct military or political intervention.

The 1930s proceeded forward with Batista as the clear power behind the scenes and operating with the full blessing of the Roosevelt administration. A key aspect of the administration's policy in Latin America was the promotion of democracy. Such a stance became especially relevant with the rise of fascism in Europe. The Roosevelt administration believed that moderate social reform could actually forestall the advent of radical, revolutionary movements. It was in this context that Batista entered into a seemingly contradictory alliance. On September 13, 1938, he made a deal with the Cuban Communists, legalizing the party and permitting the publication of its newspapers. In January, 1939, the Cuban Workers Confederation was formed with Communist leader Lázaro Peña as the general secretary.

Such an alliance was not as surprising as it might seem. The Cuban Communists, like other Communist parties, had moved in a reformist direction under Soviet guidance beginning in 1934. Viewing fascism as the main enemy, the Soviets urged all Communist parties to enter into "popular fronts" with all anti-fascist parties. Batista's pact with the Communists was a forerunner of the wartime alliance between the United States and the Soviet Union, and there is no evidence that the United States disapproved of Batista's alliance with the Communists. The alliance worked well for Batista who was planning his own run for the presidency in 1940 and wanted to build a broad electoral coalition. Batista easily won the 1940 election and took two communists, Blas Roca and Carlos Rafael Rodriguez, into his cabinet. Both men would later be prominent officials in the revolutionary government. Batista's election also resulted in the enactment of a strong progressive constitution that replaced the 1901 version. It promised many things and went beyond the U.S. Constitution in the arena of social rights by adding compulsory free education, social insurance, minimum wage and other workers' benefits to the usual list of political and civil rights.

The constitution may have been more progressive than that of the United States, but it was fully in keeping with the social democratic outlook of the Roosevelt administration and was emblematic of the promotion of democracy called for in the Good Neighbor Policy.

Batista hoped to continue his legacy in the 1944 elections through his hand-picked candidate Dr. Carlos Saladrigas. Saladrigas was also the favored candidate of the U.S. Ambassador, Spruille Braden. Grau San Martin, running on the ticket of the Cuban Revolutionary Party (Authénticos), prevailed in the election; however, Batista's coalition retained control of the Congress. Grau San Martin and his Authentic successor, Carlos Prio Socarras, maintained good relations with the United States and generally ruled in a highly corrupt manner in spite of progressive promises. As much as Batista, these corrupt presidents would lay the groundwork for the Cuban Revolution. Their corruption was well known to the United States. U.S. Ambassador Philip Bonsal, in his book *Cuba, Castro, and the United States*, wrote: "I know of no country among those committed to the Western ethic where the diversion of pubic treasure for private profit reached the proportions that it attained in the Cuban Republic."[24]

A reform movement, the Cuban Peoples Party (Orthodoxos), emerged in 1947 under the leadership of Eduardo Chibas, a veteran of the 1933 revolution. Chibas came from a wealthy family but his party was reformist and populist in orientation. One person drawn to the party was Fidel Castro. From a landowning family on the Eastern end of the island, Fidel had entered the University of Havana to study law in 1945. Active in student politics and in abortive revolutionary struggles in Colombia and the Dominican Republic, Castro filed as a congressional candidate on the Orthodox ticket for the 1952 elections.

Batista had gone into exile following the 1944 elections but returned to the country in 1948 and won a seat in Congress from Las Villas Province. He later formed a political party called The Party of Unitary Action (PAU). Another presidential election was scheduled for June 1952. In a December, 1951 poll, the Orthodox candidate Roberto Agramonte, a professor at the University of Havana, was leading with the Authentic candidate, Carlos Hevia, in second. Batista of the PAU was a distant third.

Batista could not win at the polls but desired to return to the Presidency. A number of military officers also wanted to see him in power. On March 10, 1952, Batista and his army supporters seized Camp Columbia in Havana, the largest garrison in Cuba. President Prio Socarras did not resist the coup and went into exile. Neither the Cuban Communists nor the Workers Federation resisted, fully expecting to renew their alliance with Batista. Most importantly, Batista figured that U.S. government and corporate interests would support a strong, pro-U.S. government. He declared himself president and cancelled the scheduled presidential elections. Once in power, Batista moved to establish his anti-Communist credentials. By 1952, the Cold War was well-entrenched and the Roosevelt framework that had tolerated his alliance with the Communists was long gone. As a result, once in power, Batista outlawed the Communist Party, restricted the activity of the labor movement, and broke diplomatic relations with the USSR. From the perspective of Washington, his anti-Communist credentials were now impeccable. Batista had demonstrated again that he was the ultimate opportunist, interested only in his own personal wealth and political power. Washington responded with military assistance grants of $1.5 million annually from 1954 to 1956 and doubled this figure during the 1957-1958 period. A U.S. military mission assisted in training Batista's army. Cuba was opened up to increased U.S. investment, and Havana became an ever more popular gambling and nightclub center just a few miles off the Florida coast. American fascination with Cuba had begun in the 1920s during U.S. prohibition times when U.S. citizens went to Cuba to drink and gamble in facilities operated by North American mobsters. In the 1950s, organized crime and the Batista government cooperated in personal enrichment.

Revolution

On the surface it seemed that the coup had been accepted by the populace, but that was deceiving. The opposition to the new Batista government was centered in the urban areas. Following the example of the Generation of 1930, students organized urban guerrilla warfare, using the universities as sanctuaries from the national authorities. In Havana, students formed the Revolutionary Directorate under the leadership of José Antonio Echeverría. On the other end of the island in the city of Santiago de Cuba, Frank País, son of a Protestant minister, organized students at the University of Oriente.

Fidel Castro gathered a number of students and workers around him and sought to begin a national uprising by capturing the army barracks at Moncada, Santiago, and the Céspedes barracks in Bayamo. They attacked on July 26, 1953. In the ensuing battles, most of the attackers were killed and Castro was captured. At his trial, Castro defended himself and described Cuba's social-economic situation in the 1950's in his speech "History Will Absolve Me."[25]

Eighty-five percent of the small farmers in Cuba pay rent and live under the constant threat of being evicted from the land they till. More than half of our most productive land is in the hands of foreigners. In Oriente, the largest province in Cuba, the land of the United Fruit Company and the West Indian Company link the northern and southern coasts. There are two hundred thousand peasant families who do not have a single acre of land to till to provide food for their starving children. On the other hand, nearly three hundred thousand caballerias (one caballeria equals thirty-three acres) of cultivable land, owned by powerful interests remains uncultivated.

Except for a few food, lumber and textile industries, Cuba continues to be primarily a producer of raw materials. We export sugar to import candy. We export hides to import shoes. We export iron to import plows. . . . Everyone agrees with the urgent need to industrialize the nation, that we need steel industries, paper and chemical industries, that we must improve our cattle and grain production, the technique and the processing in our food industry in order to defend ourselves against the ruinous competition of the Europeans in cheese products, condensed milk, liquors and edible oils, and the United States in canned goods; that we need cargo ships; that tourism should be an enormous source of revenue. But the capitalists insist that the workers remain under the yoke. The state sits back with its arms crossed and industrialization can wait forever.[26]

This speech established Fidel as the primary opponent of the Batista regime and also spelled out the key conditions that would spawn the revolution to follow.

Castro was sentenced to prison on the Isle of Pines (now renamed the Isle of Youth), but was released after twenty-two months as a part of a general amnesty by Batista under popular pressure. An agreement between Castro and Frank Pais created the 26th of July Movement (M-26-7), named for the date of the Moncada barracks attack. After Castro had made a number of appearances in continued opposition to Batista, he was advised to leave the country and began to enlist and train a guerrilla army in Mexico. There he met and began work with an Argentine doctor, Ernesto "Che" Guevara, who had been in Guatemala with the government of Jacobo Arbenz until the CIA-backed overthrow of that government in 1954. After successful fund-raising among anti-Batista Cubans, Castro bought a yacht, the *Granma,* from a retired American couple. In November, 1956, he loaded the *Granma* with eighty-two men and sailed for Cuba, landing in Oriente Province. In a coordinated effort, Frank Pals tried to divert the attention of Batista's forces to the city of Santiago, but the invaders were met by army units and were almost completely defeated. The survivors, including Castro, his brother Raúl, and Che Guevara, took refuge in the Sierra Maestra Mountains.

For the next two years the war against Batista proceeded on two fronts, the 26th of July Movement guerrilla campaign in the Sierra Maestra of Eastern Cuba and an urban resistance campaign consisting of several different political groupings. During 1957, the guerrillas worked to consolidate their position in the mountains by recruiting local peasants to join them and to provide logistical support. During this period, the 26th of July Movement articulated its political program and publicized it with the aid of a small radio transmitter and the favorable coverage given their movement by a *New York Times* reporter, Herbert Matthews.

Meanwhile, many Cubans were bombing government installations, executing police, and undermining confidence in the Batista government. In March, 1957, the Revolutionary Directorate under the leadership of José Antonio Echeverría tried to kill Batista in an armed attack on the presidential palace. The attempt failed and resulted in the death of Echeverría and most of the directorate leadership. Other nonstudent armed revolutionary groups included the Civic Resistance (affiliated with the 26th of July Movement); the Montecristo movement of progressive army officers led by Colonel Ramón Barquín, which attempted a failed coup against Batista; and the Puros, who briefly held the Cienfuegos naval station in September 1957. Batista responded to the rebellion with widespread repression. Close to 20,000 Cubans would die in the struggle between 1953 and 1959, mostly civilians.

The ultimate military success of the 26th of July Movement was surprising both in the quickness of its triumph and the small numbers of its starting point. Of the eighty-two men who boarded the *Granma* in Mexico only twelve made it to the mountains. After a year of accumulating a few hundred cadre, the guerrillas launched their first attacks in early 1958, just a year before their ultimate triumph. Batista's defeat began in May, 1958, when his army carried out an ill-fated, all-out offensive against the rebels in the Sierra Maestra. The turning point was a ten-day battle in Jigue when the rebels surrounded a government unit of greater firepower and defeated them. Following that defeat, the morale of Batista's primarily conscript army was very low. Seizing the moment, the 26th of July Movement went on the offensive. In the decisive battle at Santa Clara in December, 1958, the rebel forces under the leadership of Che Guevara and Camilo Cienfuegos totally routed Batista's forces and the army collapsed. Batista had no reliable defenses around him in Havana and on December 31, 1958, he fled the country. Victory came to the rebels even sooner than it had expected.

Beyond the broad outlines of the military campaign just detailed, the triumph of the revolutionaries was a complex phenomenon. It was not a mass-based revolutionary war by a peasant army like those that occurred in China or Vietnam. Peasants were recruited to the 26th of July Movement and gave it important support, but the guerrilla army, only 800 as late as September 1958, was primarily a force of students, professionals, and workers from Cuba's middle sectors. The Cuban insurrection was not an urban proletarian revolution. Organized labor, whose ranks were heavily influenced by the Communist Party (PSP), opposed the 26th of July Movement until almost the very end, when the communists gave their belated support.

The revolutionaries also carried out a broad alliance strategy that culminated at a July, 1958 meeting in Caracas, Venezuela, where the Revolutionary Democratic Civic Front was organized, encompassing almost all of the anti-Batista forces. The front, combined with the military weakening of Batista, eroded U.S. government support for the regime. In March, 1958, under pressure from the Senate, the U.S. State Department placed an arms embargo on Cuba. The July 26th Movement leaders, deeply aware of the anti-communist sentiments in Washington kept their distance from the Cuban Communists often stressing their democratic credentials and desire to restore the constitution of 1940. Such a strategy was designed to forestall a direct U.S. military intervention that could have denied victory to the rebel forces.[27]

In his excellent personal account of U.S.-Cuban relations, Wayne Smith, who served in the U.S. embassy in Havana at the time of the revolution, recounts that to most of the U.S. Foreign Service professionals it was clear that Batista was quickly losing control of the country throughout 1958. As a result, the strategy of the U.S. government became one of seeking a means to keep the Cuban capitalist system in place without Batista at its head. U.S. policy was built around having Batista cede power to non-revolutionary political forces that could somehow gain popular support from the Cuban people while marginalizing the role that forces from the 26th of July Movement would have in the new government. Such a scenario was in all likelihood a U.S. dream, but it did not matter because according to Wayne Smith's account, the role played by U.S. Ambassador Earl E.T. Smith guaranteed that the U.S. hope of transition to a non-Batista government could not be filled. Ambassador Smith repeatedly ignored directives from Washington to distance itself from Batista and eventually threw all of his support behind what proved to be fraudulent November, 1958 elections that would have passed power in early 1959 to a hand-picked Batista successor Rívero Agüero. When the election ploy had clearly failed, Washington sent a private mission, headed by an acquaintance of Batista, businessman William Pawley, to seek Batista's departure from the country. Batista was offered exile in the United States if he agreed to step down, but the dictator refused believing that Ambassador Smith's more positive views of his regime would still carry the day.[28] Batista's stubborn refusal to hand over power ultimately undermined U.S. plans for a transition that would have kept Cuba in its neocolonial status. Buoyed by a series of military successes against Batista's forces the rebels moved decisively in December 1958 to remove the old regime from power. Batista's largely conscripted army crumbled quickly and following a decisive defeat at the hands of rebel forces in Santa Clara at the end of December the dictator fled the island on New Year's Eve ending his quarter century of rule. Within hours after Batista's departure the leaders of the July 26th Movement consolidated power and began to move Cuba down a path of revolutionary change that would inevitably bring it into direct confrontation with the United States.

Notes

1. Leland Hamilton Jenks, *Our Cuban Colony: American Imperialism* (New York: Vanguard Press, 1928), 28.

2. Jefferson Papers "The Library of Congress," Monroe-Jefferson, Washington D.C., June 30, 1823, in Herminio Portel Vilá ed. Historia de Cuba en sus relaciones con los Estados Unidos y España, (History of Cuba and its Relations with United States and Spain), (Vol I, Havana: Jesus Montero, 1938), 229-30.

3. For further information, see: "Letter of Thomas Jefferson to John Stuart: Conservative Politician from Virginia", January 25, 1786, in José Fuentes Mares, Poin Sell, *Historia de una intriga (History of an Intrigue),* (Mexico City: Ediciones Oceanos, S.A., 1985), 34.

4. Phillip S. Foner, *A History of Cuba and its Relations with the United States* (New York: International Publishers, 1962), 133.

5. Emilio Roig de Leuchsenring, *Los Estados Unidos contra Cuba libre (The United States against Free Cuba)* (Santiago de Cuba: Editorial Oriente, 1982, Vol.1), 3, 94.

6. For further information, see: Emilio Roig de Leuchsenring, *Cuba no debe*

su independencia a Estados Unidos (Cuban independence does not rely on the United States), (Buenos Aires: Editorial Hemisferio, 1965), 74-84.

7. Instructions sent by the Secretary of State John Quincy Adams to Hugh Nelson, U.S. Minister in Spain. Quoted by Emilio Roig de Leuchsenring, *Cuba no debe su independencia a Estados Unidos,* (Cuban independence does not rely on the United States), (Buenos Aires: Editorial Hemisferio, 1965), 74-84.

8. Graciela Chaillox, *Las Relaciones cubano-norteamericanas,* 161.

9. Ramiro Guerra, *La expansion territorial,* 131-56.

10. Ramiro Guerra, 131-56.

11. Eduardo del Llano, *La exportación de capital de Estados Unidos hacia Cuba (United Status capital export to Cuba),*(Havana: Editora Politica, 1979), 28.

12. Eduardo del Llano, 28.

13. José O. Cayuela Fernández (Coordinator), *Un siglo de Espana: Centenario 1898-1998 (A Century in Spain History 1898-1998),* (Cuenca: Ediciones de Ia Universidad Castilla-La Mancha, 1998), 410.

14. Referring to the meeting among U.S. ambassadors before Great Britain, France and Spain held in Ostend, Belgiun, on October 1854. The Manifesto of Ostend strongly suggested that the U.S. should take Cuba by force if Spain refused to sell it. For further information, see: *Un siglo de Espana,* 412.

15. Fernando Portuondo del Prado, *Asalto a Cuba por la oligarquta financiera yanqui* (Assault to Cuba by Yankee financial oligarchy), (Havana: Casa de las Américas, 1965), 22-23.

16. Fernando Portuondo del Prado, *Historia de Cuba (History of Cuba),* (Havana: Editorial Nacional de Cuba, Vol. I, 1965), 506-7.

17. Instituto de Historia, *Historia de Cuba: Las luchas por Ia independencia nacional y las transformaciones Estructurales 1868-1898 (History of Cuba: The Struggles for National independence and Structural Transformations).* (Vol.11. Havana: Editora Politica), 519.

18. Instituto de Historia, 519-20.

19. For further information about the conditions, see: Instituto de Historia, *Historia de Cuba: Las Iuchas por la independencia nacional,* p.521.

20. Instituto de Historia, 570.

21. Instituto de Historia, 570.

22. For further information, see: *Un siglo de España,* 420.

23. For more details about the Treaty of Commercial Reciprocity of 1903, refer to: Oscar Zanetti Lecuona, *Los cautivos de Ia reciprocidad (the Captives of Reciprocity),* (ENPES, Ministerio de Educación Superior. Havana, 1989), 69-75.

24. Philip Bonsal, *Cuba, Castro, and the United States* (Pittsburgh, Pittsburgh University Press, 1971).

25. After the attack at the Moncada Garrison, Fidel Castro was captured and in the trial he defended himself and the speech he gave is known as "History Will Absolve Me."

26. Fidel Castro Ruz, *History Will Absolve Me,* The Moncada Trial defense speech, Santiago de Cuba, October 16, 1953, (Jonathan Cape, London: Cape Editions, 1974).

27. See Julia Sweig, *Inside the Cuban Revolution: Fidel Castro and the Urban Underground* (Cambridge, MA: Harvard University Press, 2002).

28. For a detailed treatment of U.S. diplomatic maneuverings in 1958 see Wayne Smith, *The Closest of Enemies* (New York: Norton and Co., 1987), 13-41.

Chapter Two

U.S. Policy Toward Cuba Following
The Triumph Of The Revolution

On January 8, 1959, Fidel Castro and the 26th of July Movement entered Havana. He noted that the U.S. military had prohibited the Liberator Army under General Calixto García from entering Santiago de Cuba in 1898 and commented that history would not be repeated. Castro took no position in the new government but set about consolidating Cuba's military forces under his command. He sent one of his trusted lieutenants, Camilo Cienfuegos, to relieve Ramón Barquín, who had taken command of Batista's remaining troops. The forces of the Directorate initially refused to disarm and had to be persuaded to accept Castro's authority.

At the time the revolutionary forces took power, the national political and economic reality could be defined as follows:

There was total dependence upon elite financial interests, both domestic and foreign, which controlled basic exporting industry, 1,200,000 hectares of the most productive land, the generation of electricity, most of the milk industry, the total fuel supply and the financial system;

Cuba had an economic structure based on agriculture. The basic Cuban industry was the production of the sugar cane, and the remaining industrial structure represented an insignificant portion of Cuba's Gross Domestic Product (GDP);[1]

The extensive agricultural economy was based on large landed estates (latifundium) owned by foreign companies and by a wealthy Cuban minority who controlled twenty percent of the land, while the majority of farmers lived in extreme poverty, without security, and in miserable living conditions.

There was permanent and massive unemployment and underemployment levels of twenty-five percent of the labor force, higher than other Latin-American countries. During non-harvesting periods, more than 600,000 people were laid off. In addition, over 300,000 people were permanently unemployed. Other economic features included a totally open economy in which every produced peso was equivalent to twenty-five to twenty-eight cents of imports and to an equal percentage of exports and sugar mono-exportation system accounting for eighty percent of the total amount of exports.

There was a geographical concentration of exports and imports since approximately sixty percent of all exports were dependent on the U.S. market, as well as seventy-five percent to eighty percent of all imports.[2]

The new government came to power intent on reversing the previously described conditions. Starting in January 1959, a new era in Cuban history began in which a reform program, called the "Moncada Program" proposed by the revolutionary movement, was to be fulfilled. In his 1955 "History Will Absolve Me" speech, Fidel Castro had previewed the first five laws that were to be passed after the triumph of the revolution:

1. The First Revolutionary Law will restore sovereignty to the people and will proclaim the 1940 Constitution as the State Supreme Law, giving the people the right to modify it. The revolutionary movement, as a manifestation of this law and the only source of authentic power, will assume the role of its implementation and enforce exemplary punishment of those who do not obey it, as well as all the authority inherent to it.
2. The Second Revolutionary Law will grant unrestrained and nontransferable property of the land to all planters, subplanters, lessees, and all those owning parcels of land as big as five caballerias. The state will compensate the former owners on the basis of an annuity within ten years.
3. The Third Revolutionary Law will grant all workers and employees the right to take 30% of all facilities of industrial, commercial and mining enterprises, including sugar mills, with the exception of purely agricultural enterprises, for which other laws will be implemented.
4. The Fourth Revolutionary Law will give all planters the right to receive a share of 55% of the sugar cane they produce based on a minimum production quota of 40,000 arrobas (one arroba equals twenty-five pounds).
5. The Fifth Revolutionary Law will enact the confiscation of all personal property misappropriated by previous government officials and from their heirs. Special Courts of Justice will be created which will have access to all sources of investigation for that purpose. These courts can also intervene anonymous companies registered in the country or operating in a country that could hide misapplied funds, and request from foreign governments the extradition of people and the embargo of property. Half the property thus intervened will go to retirement funds for workers, and the other half to hospitals, asylums, and poorhouses.[3]

Four years later, with political power in the hands of the revolutionary forces led by the July 26th Movement, the government moved to implement the above stated promises. Additional measures were directed at redistributing revenues and recovering property embezzled by officials of the previous regime.

One of the first measures carried out by the Revolutionary Government was to punish criminals from Batista's tyranny. That step, taken in some measure in response to popular hatred, led to an anti-revolutionary reaction from the international press. On January 9, 1959, the *New York Times* commented on the earliest actions of the new Cuban government: "If there is a blemish in its record so far, it is the expeditious execution of its former opponents, and the proposed trials for 'war crimes' of hundreds more."[4] On one occasion, a leader of the Revolution, being interviewed about the rising anti-Cuban revolutionary campaign in the press, said: "The Americans are now concerned about the processes and executions we are performing. But Batista killed people without even holding a trial and they never cared about it. Only now are they reacting."[5]

At the same time the U.S. government and U.S. businesses with interests in Cuba began to express the idea of a possible trade embargo of Cuba. Scarcely thirty days after the triumph of the revolution, the possibility of a reduction in the Cuban sugar quota was first suggested. With regard to this idea, the *Journal of Commerce,* a publication of the U.S. Chamber of Commerce noted: "Probably other Latin-American producers would like to have a higher sugar quota in the market."[6] Fidel Castro responded to this veiled threat in his address to massive crowds in Guantánamo and Manzanillo on February 4, 1959: "If they are going to take economic measures, let them. We will find solutions. I don't want them to tell me that they are going to reduce the sugar quota. The Cuban people, united, will find a solution of any situation by means of any sacrifice." [7]

With respect to the Moncada Program, it should be noted that in January and February, 1959, as the U.S. press articulated the measures to be taken against Cuba, the Revolutionary Government proceeded with the immediate confiscation of property ill-acquired by Batista officials and dismantled the former army. Public administration was cleared of elements that had cooperated with the Batista regime. Additionally, common practices of the former regime, such as the misappropriation of public funds, the conferring of privileges, and the common practice known as "botellas" (paying salaries to people who didn't actually work), were eradicated. The political parties that had served the old regime were dissolved; corrupt union management officials were removed and workers' rights restored. In addition, workers who had been fired from their jobs, without just cause, were reinstated.

On March 3, 1959, the Cuban Telephone Company, a U.S. subsidiary which had been involved in private business dealings with Batista, was placed under Cuban government control. On March 6, a law was passed reducing the onerous monthly housing rental rates by fifty percent. This measure was enthusiastically received by the urban working classes while it created uproar among the landowning classes. The nationalization of the Cuban Telephone Company and the Housing Law stirred up further verbal attacks from the United States. Also, on March 6, 1959, during a public speech in Holguin, Fidel Castro made reference to Agrarian Reform, which would cause great concern in Washington.

It was in the early months of 1959, when Cuba showed its capacity to per-

form as an independent nation internally and externally, that the conflict between Cuban sovereignty and U.S. hegemony took its definitive form. Consequently, the permanent components of this conflict were drawn. These components included military-strategic, economic, political-ideological, diplomatic,
and legal. At the same time, the anti-Cuban Revolution campaign continued in
U.S. publications, including photographs and articles aimed at alarming the U.S.
public about the events taking place in Cuba.

   With all of its maneuverings to prevent Fidel Castro and the July 26th
Movement from taking power, clearly a failure, the United States faced the
reality that it would have to deal with the new government. Ambassador Smith
was quickly replaced by career foreign service officer, Philip Bonsal. Bonsal
was chosen because he spoke Spanish and had been the U.S. ambassador to
Bolivia following the 1952 revolution, and had also developed a rapport with the
then new government. In hindsight, it was viewed that he had helped to moderate the Bolivian revolution and the hope was that he could do the same in
Cuba. The United States was initially hopeful that the revolution would not
proceed down a radical course and was made cautiously optimistic by the composition of the first revolutionary government. That government had Manuel
Urrutia as president and included politically centrist figures such as Foreign
Minister Roberto Agramonte of the Orthodox Party, Regino Botti as minister of
economy and Rufo Lopez Fresquét as minister of the treasury. The presence of
such pro-capitalist figures in key governmental posts led the U.S. authorities to
believe that the radical forces could be contained and the traditional position of
U.S. dominance over Cuba maintained. U.S. anti-Communist fears were also
mitigated at the beginning by the fact that for the first months of 1959 the Soviet
Union was very much in the background. The Soviets offered diplomatic recognition to the new government but initially there was no response from Cuba.
Initially, the Cuban leadership was uncertain as to how to proceed with relations
with the Soviet Union. They did not know how the Soviets would respond to an
overture for support, nor how far their relations with the United States would
deteriorate. The first direct link with the Soviets would not come until October
1959 when a KGB official, Alexandr Alekseev, arrived in Havana. The first
Soviet visit came only after officials of the Cuban Communists visited Moscow
to vouch for the revolutionary credentials of the new government and their own
developing role within it. Prior to the PSP visits to Moscow the Soviets had been
skeptical of the new government that they perceived to be anti-communist.[8] The
United States also focused on the fact that the local Communists, the Popular
Socialist Party, had been marginal to the revolutionary triumph and largely dis-
trusted by the 26th of July leaders. Castro and other officials had categorically
denied any links with the Communist Party or the USSR, but the reality was that
their collective vision of Cuba's future was one of radical change that would
likely place them in a large confrontation with the United States.

   In the midst of the rapidly changing situation in Cuba, Fidel made his first
visit to the United States in April.[9] Apart from a visit to the United Nations in
1960, his next visit would not come until 1995 when he visited New York City

to attend the 50th anniversary celebrations at the United Nations. Fidel's trip was not an official state visit, but rather, he was invited to address the annual conference of the American Society of Newspaper Editors (ASNE). In the more than forty-five years since this trip, there has been almost endless speculation over whether the United States missed an opportunity to win over or influence Castro during his visit. What if the United States had offered assistance? What if President Eisenhower rather than Vice President Nixon received Fidel with open arms? In our view such speculation misunderstands the history of U.S.-Cuban relations and the dynamic that was developing on the island.

President Eisenhower showed no inclination for a conciliatory policy with the new government. In his memoirs he wrote about his irritation with the ASNE for inviting Castro to Washington. In addition, Vice President Richard Nixon had a long conversation with Castro which left both men with a low opinion of the other. Castro was infuriated by Nixon's criticisms of developments on the island, including the execution of Batista loyalists. The vice president produced files to show how many communists there were in the Cuban administration, a fact obviously already approved and well-known to Fidel. However, it can be argued that the interview did have dramatic, though not unpredictable, results. Nixon convinced himself that Fidel was directly under the influence of Communist ideology and as a result must be overthrown. Nixon acted on this belief suggesting that a force of Cuban exiles be armed and sent in to overthrow the revolutionary government. This was the first move that would lead to the Bay of Pigs confrontation in April, 1961.

Fidel's impression of Nixon and others whom he met, including a three hour private conversation with the CIA's chief expert on Latin American communism, was that U.S. leaders were obsessed with the Communist question and did not really care about the well being of Cuba and its inhabitants. During a press conference at the end of his visit, Fidel denounced "the systematic attempt of the United States to sabotage our cause," and "the intense campaign that this country has been launching for more than three months to discredit the revolution."[10]

Fidel also made a conscious decision to not discuss any aid requests during his U.S. visit. This stance was interesting because about ten days before the trip a note was sent to Washington, presumably with Castro's approval, suggesting a list of economic subjects for negotiations. However, on the plane to Washington, Fidel instructed his delegation not to discuss the aid requests. Fidel was not principally opposed at that time to the question of U.S. aid, but he had clearly decided that it would have to come primarily on Cuban terms. U.S. leaders were clearly taken aback when the requests for aid were not discussed, signaling to Washington that they were dealing with a new Cuban leader who would not easily be dissuaded from the revolutionary course on which he was proceeding.

Up until that point U.S. officials had expected to control Cuba through the normal give-and-take of foreign aid. However, in spite of the U.S. press and government anti-revolution campaigns, Cuba continued to carry out the Moncada Program. On April 21, 1959, all beaches were declared public, thus putting an end to the exclusivity and discrimination established by the Cuban elites with respect to many of these recreational areas. One of the most important measures adopted by the Revolutionary Government was the First Law of Agrarian Reform, passed on May 17, 1959. This law decisively affected the country's class polarization by taking away the economic base from the large domestic and foreign landowners. Cuba's agriculture and economy in general were dramatically backward and thus required an agrarian reform which ultimately eliminated native and foreign large landowners, liberalized indigent farmers and freed agricultural workers from exploitation. This historic law provided for a secure solution to the farmer's situation, who, until the Revolution, had lived in permanent fear of being evicted.

Speculations arose among sugar businesses and the U.S. administration about the possible effects of Agrarian Reform. They even said they would do everything possible against its implementation. An article appeared in the *New York Times* asserting that: ". . . apparently the agrarian reform in Cuba will have an adverse effect on American investments in the island."[11] In June, the U.S. government sent a diplomatic note to Cuba raising concern about the compensation features of the new agrarian law. This memo was one of the first by the U.S. government making clear that it would not accept reforms in Cuba that threatened U.S. economic interests. By making such threats, the United States was raising the specter of Guatemala, where in 1954 the United States had sponsored a military coup against a government that had proceeded with a land reform program against the interests of the U.S.-based United Fruit Company. On June 15, 1959, Senator George A. Smathers proposed legislation in the U.S. Congress to reduce the Cuban sugar quota in the U.S. market. Agrarian reform forced a direct confrontation between the Cuban Revolution and U.S. economic interests because many Americans owned large sugar cane plantations. As a result, the U.S. government hardened its position towards Cuba, questioning the legitimacy of the measure and demanding explanations.

The U.S. government's discontent was related to what they felt constituted a violation of the 1940 Constitution, Clause 38, regarding expropriation. In which case, prior to the act of expropriation, the expropriated person or entity must be paid the amount legally agreed upon in cash. Nevertheless, the Revolutionary Government cited the text of the Agrarian Reform Law, which stated that the expropriations would be paid in official bonds within 20 years, with an annual interest rate of 4.5 percent, the only form of payment available in those circumstances. In a 1960 speech before the United Nations, Fidel Castro explained Cuba's position:

How are we supposed to pay? You must first ask: with what are we going to pay, not how, but with what? Can you conceive a poor country like ours, underdeveloped, with 600,000 people unemployed, with high levels of illiteracy, plagued by diseases, with exhausted resources, that for the last ten years has been contributing one-hundred million dollars to the economy of a powerful country; paying for the lands affected by Agrarian Reform or at least, to pay for them under the conditions the U.S. wanted?[12]

From May 1959 on, the anti-Cuban Revolution campaign in the American press was heightened. In part, it was spurred on by further executions of many officials connected to the Batista regime. By the end of August 1959, the American Foreign Power Company, a subsidiary of Electric Bond and Share and principal stock holder of the Cuban Electricity Company, announced it was canceling a $15 million financing bond already agreed upon. This measure was in response to the Revolutionary Government's thirty percent reduction of electrical rates.

At that point, the confrontation between Cuba and the United States heightened. U.S. government legal advisers recommended a reduction in the price the United States paid for Cuban sugar, and suggested the possibility of suspending telephone connections between the United States and the island. Cuban fruits were prohibited from entering the port of West Palm Beach and the selling of arms or spare parts for military equipment to the new Cuban government was prohibited. Additionally, the training of Cuban armed forces personnel was suspended.

From the perspective of the U.S. government, shifts made in the leadership of the Cuban government in the fall of 1959 signaled the movement of the Cuban government in a more radical direction. In October, Huber Matos, military commander of Camaguey province, was arrested after he denounced "Communist infiltration of the Revolution." By the end of the year, all of the pro-capitalist government leaders were gone. Manuel Urrutia had been forced out in July and was replaced with Osvaldo Dorticós, a man with close ties to the Communists. Che Guevara replaced Felipe Pazos as President of the National Bank. Roberto Agromonte was replaced as foreign minister by the more radical Raul Roa. By the beginning of 1960, all key government posts were held by revolutionaries from the July 26th Movement or their new allies from the PSP. Also, in a prelude to government-to-government relations that would flower in the following year, in November, a Soviet trade delegation received a red carpet treatment and soon after, Fidel supported the inclusion of key Communists in the leadership of the Cuban Confederation of Labor.

On March 4, 1960, La Coubre, a Belgian ship carrying weapons purchased by Cuba in France, exploded. The Cuban Government blamed counterrevolutionary forces with connections to the U.S. CIA. There is no direct proof of CIA involvement in the La Coubre explosion, and it may have been an accident, but the United States was already moving quickly toward a position of armed actions against Cuba. On March 17, 1960, the United States formally approved a program of covert operations aimed at toppling the Cuban government. It was this order that within thirteen months would lead to the exile invasion at the Bay of Pigs. In the El Coubre explosion, one hundred people were killed and more than two hundred were wounded. In the memorial to the victims, Fidel first used the slogan of patria o muerte, (homeland or death) representing a deepening of the revolutionary process. Following the La Coubre event, the United States prohibited the travel of commercial vessels to and from Cuba. From the Cuban perspective, this act of violence against Cuba, allegedly carried out by Cuban exiles in the pay of the CIA, would be only the first in a long line of such violent acts against Cuba that have been carried until the present.[13]

On February 13, 1960, a transcendent event for Cuban history took place as the Soviet Prime Minister Anastas Mikoyan visited Cuba. As a result of that visit, diplomatic relations between the countries were restored and advantageous contracts for both parties were signed, among them, the purchasing of Soviet petroleum by Cuba. Subsequently, new diplomatic relations and collaborative agreements were established with the USSR and with the rest of the Socialist community, especially with the German Democratic Republic, the Republic of Hungary, the People's Republic of China, the Republic of Vietnam, and Mongolia. As a result, these countries began to develop strong economic ties with Cuba.

In June, 1960, Texaco, Shell, and Esso, the companies that owned the Cuban oil refineries, openly violated the 1938 Cuban Mining and Fuel Law by refusing to refine Soviet petroleum in order to paralyze the country's economy. Following that refusal, the Revolutionary Government nationalized those companies on June 28. On July 6, the United States retaliated against these measures. President Eisenhower ordered a 700,000 ton reduction of the Cuban sugar quota in the U.S. market for the last quarter of 1960.[14] This measure represented more than a $600 million loss of revenue, but the USSR immediately decided to buy the suppressed quota.

This climate of tension between the countries was additionally aggravated by the Cuban government's decision to pass Law 851 on July 6, 1960, which provided for the nationalization of all properties or enterprises owned by natural or legal U.S. nationals or enterprises in which those persons had any interest or participation, by means of forced expropriation. The law also included a provision for the payment of confiscated property.[15] Law 851 took effect in August, 1960, and in September of the same year, the U.S. Department of State issued a traveler's advisory, cautioning U.S. citizens to travel to Cuba only in extreme emergencies. At the same time, U.S. financial credits to Cuban banks for commercial operations were suspended to hinder Cuba's international trade. On September 17, 1960, the Cuban government responded by nationalizing U.S. banks as a means to end the campaign of economic destabilization.[16] On October 13, the U.S. government put regulations into effect banning exports to Cuba, with the exception of food, medicine, and medical equipment, thus depriving Cuba's industry and transportation of the indispensable spare parts to keep its factories working. The escalating war of sanctions was accompanied by harsh rhetoric on both sides. Various U.S. newspapers and members of Congress labeled Fidel as a "Communist madman." In turn, the Cuban press portrayed Eisenhower as a senile old man. In a pattern that has now become routine, large and angry demonstrations against U.S. policy often surrounded the U.S. embassy building on Havana's seafront. As a counter-measure against what was an embargo of the Cuban economy, the Revolutionary Government issued Resolution No. 3 on October 24, 1960, which nationalized the remaining U.S. property in Cuba.[17] On December 16, the U.S. government responded by zeroing the Cuban sugar quota for the first quarter of 1961.[18] In 1961, international solidarity from socialist countries grew larger with their commitment to buy 4,860,000 tons of Cuban sugar annually, while radical anti-Cuba measures within the United States continued to increase.

In addition to the punitive economic measures imposed on Cuba, the U.S. government announced a formal breaking off of diplomatic relations with the Cuban government on January 3, 1961. On March 2, 1961, recently elected President John F. Kennedy announced that he would consider the implementation of the 1918 "Trading with the Enemy Act," which would mean a total embargo of imports and exports from or to Cuba. Concomitantly, he eliminated the Cuban sugar quota for all of 1961 by virtue of Presidential Proclamation No. 3401. In June, the United States suspended the importation of Cuban molasses for one year.

On April 15, it became clearer that Washington was determined to destroy the Cuban Revolution. On that day, U.S. aircraft bombed three airports (Santiago de Cuba, Ciudad Libertad, and San Antonio de los Baños) signaling support to an imminent invasion. Cuban mercenaries, armed, trained, and transported by U.S. warships landed at the Bay of Pigs on April 17, but were defeated in seventy-two hours by the Rebel Army and the revolutionary militia. The events of Playa Giron will be addressed in detail in Chapter Three.

With the defeat of the Bay of Pigs invasion, it became clear to the United States that economic measures would be a potentially effective means to halt the Revolution, considering that in 1958 the U.S. market represented seventy-three percent of Cuba's total commerce. Thus, in September, the U.S. Congress prohibited all assistance to the Cuban Government and gave the President the authorization, by means of an amendment to Section 620 (a) of the Foreign Assistance Act of 1961, to impose and maintain an embargo on all commerce between both countries. On December 1, 1961, President Kennedy announced Presidential Proclamation No. 3440,[19] which suspended the Cuban sugar quota for the first semester of 1962.

In addition to economic and military measures, Washington coerced the Organization of American States (OAS) to expel the Cuban government from the organization on the supposed basis of incompatibility with the inter-American system. That decision was made during the 8th OAS Summit held in Punta del Este, Uruguay, on January 31, 1962, which demonstrated the dominance that the United States had over the Latin American nations at that time. Following Cuba's expulsion from the OAS, President Kennedy issued Presidential Proclamation No. 3447, acting in accordance with Section 620 (a) of the Foreign Assistance Act of 1961, effective February 7, 1962, in which he decreed the economic embargo of Cuba. The above-mentioned law established that:

1. Under this Chapter no assistance will be offered to the current Cuban gov-
    ernment, unless the President determines that such assistance is a matter of
    national interest for the United States . . . the President has the right of im-
    posing and keeping a total embargo over the commerce between both coun-
    tries.
2. Under this Chapter no assistance will be offered to any Cuban government,
    nor does Cuba have the right to receive any quota that authorizes Cuban
    sugar importation into the United States, or to receive any benefit under any
    law . . . unless the President determines that such government has taken
    steps . . . toward restoring American property, or unless an equal compensa-
    tion to those citizens or entities is provided.
3. Under this Chapter, no funds will be authorized to assist any country that
    has failed to take proper measures against Cuba.
    a) No Cuban-registered boats or aircraft may transport anything from Cuba
    to the United States.
    b) No Cuban-registered boats or aircraft may transport anything from the
    United States to Cuba. [20]

Additionally, the Secretary of the Treasury and the Secretary of Commerce were
authorized to implement the embargo measures contained in the 1961 Amendments to Section 620 (a) of the Control of Exports Act of 1949. Almost immediately, all of the legal mechanisms began to take form and new measures were
added to guarantee a total embargo. Thus, on March 24, Section 5 (b) of the
Trading with the Enemy Act of 1917 was amended, prohibiting any product
totally or partially manufactured with Cuban materials from entering the United
States, even if it was produced in a third country.[21]

In May, 1962, the U.S. government unilaterally cancelled Cuba's Most Favored Nation trading status, which was a violation of the agreements between
the countries with respect to GATT ordinances.[22] The U.S. government wanted
the world, not just Latin American countries, to follow its policy toward Cuba,
and subsequently sent Secretary of State Dean Rusk to engage in talks with
other countries in an attempt to convince them not to import Cuban products.
Countries that refused were "black-listed," preventing them and their vessels
from entering any American port or from receiving any economic assistance
from the United States.[23]

The United States was progressively attempting to strangle the Cuban
Revolution, especially after the Bay of Pigs invasion. A political-military, diplomatic, and propaganda plan against Cuba was designed, which included the
possibility of direct intervention of U.S. forces. During the second half of 1962,
in an attempt to intimidate the Cuban government, military exercises were carried out by the United States in the Caribbean, the Atlantic Ocean, along the
coasts facing Cuba and at the Naval Base at Guantanamo. During that period,
U.S. support to counter-revolutionary groups in the Escambray Mountains increased. In addition, the anti-Cuba propaganda in Latin America increased, and
a second "white book"[24] with reports about alleged Cuban human rights abuses

was distributed.

Cuba sought a pro-active position in response to already imminent aggression, and thus decided to sign a military agreement with the USSR: "Our firm conviction that Yankee imperialism would, under any pretext, launch its military forces directly against our country, and our idea that proposed measures to prevent it would help strengthen the Socialist bloc as a whole, determined our decision to sign the Cuban-Soviet agreement regarding the deployment of nuclear weapons in our territory."[25]

According to the previous quotation, the aim of such an agreement was to defend the revolution by preventing U.S. aggression. However, the United States would not tolerate the idea of having a free socialist country as a neighbor, and on October 22, decreed a naval blockade of Cuba while announcing its decision to use all its power to stop vessels from transporting armament to Cuba. As a result, the October Crisis or the Cuban Missile Crisis put the world on the brink of a nuclear war.

Notes

1. Compared with others underdeveloped countries of Asia, Africa, and some Latin America, Cuba's economic performance was superior.

2. José Luis Rodriguez and George Carriazo, *Erradicacion de la pobreza en Cuba (Eradicating poverty in Cuba)*, (Havana: Editorial de Ciencias Sociales, 1987), 33.

3. Fidel Castro Ruz, "History Will Absolve Me," 27-29

4. Quoted by: Nicanor Leon Cotayo, *El bloqueo a Cuba (The Blockade to Cuba)*, (Havana: Editorial de Ciencias Sociales, 1983), 21.

5. Fidel Castro Ruz, 22.

6. Fidel Castro Ruz, 26.

7. *Hoy* newspaper, February 5, 1959, 1 and 4.

8. Piero Gleijeses, *Conflicting Missions: Havana, Washington, and Africa 1959-1976.* (Chapel Hill: University of North Carolina Press, 2002), 18.

9. For a thoughtful discussion of Fidel's visit, see Herbert Matthews *Revolution in Cuba* (Charles Schribner's Son, New York, 1975).

10. *Hoy* newspaper, April 17, 1959, 3.

11. Nicanor Leon Cotayo, 39.

12. *Revolución* newspaper, September 27, 1960, 4.

13. For the latest detailing of CIA activities directed against Cuba, especially in the 1960s and 1970s, see Thomas Blanton, ed. *The CIA's Family Jewels* (National Security Archive Electronic Briefing Book number 222) Washington, DC 2007). Accessed at www.gwu.edu/~nsarchiv/cuba.

14. For further information, see: Presidential Proclamation No.3355, July 6, 1960 (25 FR 6414).

15. For further information, see: Ley 851 of July 6, 1960 and *Obra revolu-*

cionaria, No.6, July 1960.

16. For further information, see: *Revolución* newspaper, September 18, 1960 and *Obra revolucionaria,* No. 6, September 1960.

17. For further information, see: *Obra Revolucionaria,* No.6, October 25, 1960 and Fidel Castro Ruz: Press Conference, October 15, 1960. *Hoy* newspaper, October 16, 1969, 1.

18. For further information, see: Presidential Proclamation No. 3383 of December 16, 1960 *(25* FR13131).

19. For further information, see: Presidential Proclamation No. 3440 of December 1, 1961 (26 FR 11714).

20. For further information, see: Presidential Proclamation No. 3447 of February 4, 1962. According to Foreign Assistance Act of 1961 (75 Stat. 444: C 2370).

21. 50 C App. *5* (a); 27 FR 1116.

22. Treasury Department Decision 55638, May 24, 1962 (76 Stat.78; 19 C 1351 note).

23. These measures were included in Public Law 87-565, Section 301(d) of September 16, 1962 (76 Stat. 261).

24. A first White Book was published by the CIA in 1960 regarding alleged Cuban crimes against political prisoners.

25. Fidel Castro Ruz, *Informe central: Primer Congreso del PCC,* 40-41.

Chapter Three

The Missile Crisis Or The October Crisis?

Without any doubts, the so-called Missile Crisis or October Crisis was, within the long-time historical confrontation between Cuba and the United States, the most dangerous incident endured by both countries during the Cold War period. Prior to the aforementioned incident, the invasion of mercenary troops at Playa Girón, also known as the Bay of Pigs, had occupied the top place within the history of the United States aggressions against Cuba. Nevertheless, during the October Crisis, there was neither such a warlike confrontation as in Girón, nor were conventional or nuclear weapons used on a large scale. What is it that makes the October Crisis an incident of such dramatic meaning within Cuba-United States confrontation?[1]

We can understand the October Crisis only by placing it within the wider plans that the United States had against Cuba. It is historically inaccurate to characterize the October crisis as representing events where Cuba was primarily responsible for bringing the world to the brink of nuclear war.[2] The plotters of the aggression against Cuba in U.S. policy making circles have never been able to accept the Girón failure. Nevertheless, it seems that they found relief in accusing Cuba of placing the world at the edge of a nuclear holocaust, when actually that historical responsibility should be allocated primarily to the U.S. administrations and their obsession to overturn the Cuban revolution.

In general, it has been considered that there are three important questions to answer when analyzing the October Crisis:[3]

- Why did Khrushchev decide to send offensive missiles to Cuba?
- Why did Kennedy respond to this action in the way he did?
- Why did Khrushchev decide to surrender under North American pressure and send the missiles back to Soviet territory?

But, the way of asking is also influenced by the general conception that the person has of the event in question. Asking about something is far from being an innocent action, nor is it simply looking only for unknown information. In this case, the questions aim at guiding the reader from the perspective of the interviewer's conceptions. On the other hand, we would not say that the formulated questions lack importance, but that they are not the only important ones. There are other questions and other ways of asking the ones listed above that answer to a broader, multilateral and complex conception of what was the so-called Missile Crisis. The additional questions are as follows:

- Did Khrushchev decide by himself to send nuclear missiles to Cuba?
- Were the nuclear missiles in Cuba offensive weapons?
- Was Khrushchev's decision to remove the nuclear rockets from Cuba a capitulation before the North American pressures?
- What was it that essentially caused the so-called Missile Crisis?
- Was the so-called Missile Crisis only a confrontation between the United States and the USSR?
- Can we affirm that the so-called Missile Crisis was solved?

Our hypothesis to answer the previous questions is framed by the following: the crisis was not only or essentially between the USSR and the United States, but it was also between Cuba and the United States. In the context of the Cold War, the alliances served as transmission channels that caused the crisis to adopt a global character. That's why the crisis adopted a strategic character for the nations involved in it. At the end of October, 1962, the crisis was solved for the United States and the USSR, but not for Cuba, because its essential concerns were not addressed adequately in such a context. Once Cuba was excluded from the negotiations during the crisis, her interests were not taken into account although the missiles had been installed in Cuba and the real cause for their installation (not their acceptance by Cuba) came from the threat of an invasion from the United States. Such issues must be addressed in order to achieve a clear vision about what actually happened during the October Crisis.

Historical Background to the October Crisis

Dwight Eisenhower had supported dictator Fulgencio Batista since he had assumed the U.S. Presidency in 1953 and had little inclination of getting along with the revolutionary Cuba, government that assumed on January 1, 1959.[4] Therefore, the Eisenhower administration did not produce a new policy toward Cuba, but instead continued the efforts that had begun during 1958 to find an alternative to the July 26th Movement. The aggressive policy previously pursued in order to replace Batista by "a plausible candidate" who would avoid the taking of power by a triumphant revolution, was now used to challenge revolutionary power. The main core of that policy was, "If we cannot avoid that they take hold of the power, we can avoid that they consolidate it, and finally we can overthrow them."

The 1959-1961 period, which was well-described in the previous chapter, was characterized by the design and the implementation of a group of actions aimed at avoiding at any cost the consolidation of the political power by the revolutionary forces in Cuba. Such aggressive actions comprised the widest spectrum. Thus, more than 40 years later, there is almost nothing new to invent in order to attack Cuba that was not already done by the Eisenhower administration during those years.

A series of events took place that were designed and supported by the Eisenhower administration against Cuba. First, a group of individuals who formed part of the revolutionary government at the beginning were used within the context of a fierce anticommunist campaign: first from inside, as a fifth column, and then, some of them were used as leaders of the first counterrevolutionary organizations; among these leaders, we could mention Manuel Díaz Lans, Manuel Artime, Tony Varona, and Miro Cardona.[5] Second, the work of the CIA and of the U.S. government inside and outside Cuba was characterized by an intense activity to organize counterrevolution. They tried to get all those individuals, locally or from abroad and who were willing to attack the Revolutionary Government, involved in counterrevolutionary activities.

Third, from the early days of 1959 there were sabotage actions, destruction of economic goods, plans to assassinate the leaders of the revolution, raids, pirate attacks, murders, bombing of Havana and social and economic targets, among others.[6] Fourth, it is extremely interesting to observe how the economic aggression was carried out through a systematic combination of tools. That is to say, while the sugar supply from Cuba was reduced or eliminated in the U.S. market, U.S. operatives were also bombing and burning the sugar cane crops, the sugar mills, and the facilities for sugar transportation.[7] Fifth, the highest levels of the U.S. government arrived at the conclusion that the only way to "solve" the Cuban issue was through killing Fidel Castro and invading the island.

Kennedy Administration and the Danger of an Invasion to Cuba

By the beginning of the Kennedy administration, U.S. policy toward Cuba was already obvious. The new President, during his campaign, had asked for support from those he called "fighters for freedom," so he did not take long to renew the invasion plans that he inherited from Eisenhower. Once Kennedy was elected, on November 18, 1960, the CIA Director, Allen Dulles, and his Deputy Director, Richard Bissell, held a meeting with the new President and informed him on the invasion plans for Cuba. From then on, the CIA carried out a shrewd game in order to get Kennedy deeply involved in the plans of invasion. They sought the President-elect's approval, but without giving him all the information on the risks of the plans. These were risks that even Dulles and Bissell were not, in many occasions, able to estimate. The CIA presented everything in such a way that JFK saw little choice but to launch the U.S. troops against Cuba in the invasion of Girón.

As a matter of fact, it must be stated that Kennedy always had doubts regarding the operation, but it was almost impossible for him to disregard the heritage that his predecessor had left him. His statements on Cuba during the presidential campaign, his reputation as an intellectual President, Allen Dulles' strong personality and Kennedy's immeasurable respect for the CIA made it impossible for him to take his doubts to the level of an absolute distrust of what was being proposed.

The U.S. government broke relations with Cuba on January 3, 1961, thus fulfilling the stated aspirations of President Eisenhower.[8] When John F. Kennedy reached the U.S. Presidency on January 20, 1961, he inherited a plan of invasion against Cuba and a policy towards the island with a rigid design that pressed him not to change anything of what his predecessor had done. There were many people who benefited by and were committed to that policy that were also inserted within an institutional structure that Kennedy inherited. The same plotters of Eisenhower's policy towards Cuba (Allen Dulles among others) were at the head of the CIA. Besides, it was a policy where Eisenhower did nothing but to follow the line imposed by the Cold War and the confrontation to communism, which on the other hand, Kennedy himself shared.[9] Perhaps that was the uneasiness that overwhelmed Kennedy, when having been faithful to the course of that policy against the Cuban Revolution for almost three years, in November 1963, it seemed that he was looking for a negotiating approach with Cuba.[10] But with Kennedy, everything started very differently from how it ended. In his first press conference, the President stated that the United States did not have a plan to reestablish relations with Cuba.[11]

In a message to the nation in 1961, Kennedy launched his project of the so-called "Alliance for Progress." The Alliance for Progress was a direct response to the triumph of the Cuban Revolution and it represented a nuanced response to the challenge presented by the events in Cuba. The initiative operated on the premise that if U.S. policies in the region made peaceful change impossible, then violent revolution would be inevitable. To this end, U.S. policy in the region would become more enlightened, stressing three principles—democracy, land reform, and industrialization. The policy acknowledged that long term support for regimes that did not allow for broad-based economic growth were vulnerable to being overthrown by revolutionary groups like the July 26th Movement promising social reforms and a better life for the urban masses. In hindsight, the Alliance for Progress was quite perceptive of the Latin American reality, but it never became the actual centerpiece of U.S. policy toward Latin America. The Alliance policies came to be seen only as long term vision, and in the short term, the focus was a Cold War driven perspective that shaped U.S. policy toward Cuba and would later be present in U.S. support for the 1964 Brazilian military coup and the 1965 invasion of the Dominican Republic. In any case, U.S. policy toward Cuba practiced by Kennedy was in no way enlightened. The Alliance for Progress was meant to prevent future Cubans, and in the meantime, the Cuban revolutionary reality was to be overturned. He stated that the communist agents had a base in Cuba. At the same time, he stated, ". . . our objection with Cuba is not that the people want a better life. Our objection is her dominance for the external and the internal tyranny . . . we will never be able to negotiate with the communist dominance in this hemisphere. . ."[12]

The President's early actions were not limited to the Giron invasion. On March 31, 1961, following the policy already started by Eisenhower, he lowered the quota of Cuban sugar in the U.S. market to zero for the rest of 1961. Kennedy not only followed the political actions designed by his predecessor, he also put his intellectual advisors to work on anti-Cuban plans. Arthur Schlesinger, under his supervision, wrote the so-called "White Book," in which Cuba was characterized as the USSR's satellite, as a betrayed revolution, and was proclaimed as a present danger for the hemisphere.[13]

As a result, Kennedy pursued the policy of sabotages, military raids, and plans to kill the leaders of the Revolution. At the same time, in the middle of April 1961, there was still a debate concerning how far they should go to help the Cuban counterrevolutionaries in order to overthrow Fidel Castro. There is evidence that the Giron plan caused him great concern, but we cannot say that he opposed such an action or that he considered it incompatible with the policy he wanted to follow towards Cuba. Kennedy's doubts, in spite of his declaration of support to the so-called "freedom fighters," were evident later, when in the middle of the defeat of the mercenary brigade, he did not allow the direct use of the U.S. armed forces.[14]

Girón and the October Crisis

Amid last minute corrections, the President's concerns, the maneuvers of the CIA, and the uncertainties of whether the support of the U.S. army would be used or not, the Girón days arrived. For Cuba, the prelude to Girón was the sabotage to the "El Encanto" store on April 13 and the bombings at the airports on April 15, these latter ones with the objective of destroying the incipient air force of the Rebel Army. Cuba, on the other hand, had ignored when and where she would be attacked, but the bombings on April 15 were correctly interpreted by the Cuban leadership as a preamble of a coming invasion. In general, Cuba had mobilized against an attack but with no intelligence as to where it would occur. As a result, the surprise factor was in favor of the mercenary troops led by the CIA.[15]

Once the mercenary landing started, the order from Castro, made as Commander in Chief and given to the air force to attack the ships, proved decisive. It did great damage to the invaders, affecting their supplies and cutting their retreat. At the same time, it was a psychological factor that played, not in the least, a significant role in the defeat of the mercenary brigade.[16] The plan projected for the invasion was very clear for those that formulated it: to take a beach head, to keep it, and to bring in the counterrevolutionary government that they had created in Florida. Afterward, the plan was to obtain the recognition from the United States and its allies in the OAS and to establish a "republiqueta" (small republic) in Cuba, with the intention of enlarging it later with the help of the

U.S. army. However, the immense majority of the mercenaries came with the idea that it would be an easy victory, by means of which they would take the power directly in Cuba. They believed that the militias would not fight or that they would surrender easily, and therefore, they would be acclaimed as heroes at their entrance in Havana some hours later. If the situation turned difficult, the troops of the North American army would come to their help, although President Kennedy had several times tried to deny that possibility.[17]

The idea that the U.S. army would intervene was simply something that the CIA allowed to spread—first, because the whole time they had worked for that purpose; second, because they never believed that Kennedy would have to be pressured to rush the marines into the combat if it was necessary; and third, because it was a variant that filled the mercenary brigade with confidence and that made the work less difficult. In reality, none of that happened and their frustration was of immeasurable proportions. That frustration over the failure at Playa Girón is something that has remained in the history of the U.S. policy up to the present. Frustration was followed by justifications, some more sophisticated than others. In the explanations, given mainly by the CIA, it was stated that there supposedly had been so many mistakes in the conception, organization, and implementation of the Girón operation, that Cuba had not won the confrontation, but rather, the CIA had lost it, trying at any price to deny victory to the revolutionary government and its supporters.[18] However, it is actually necessary to say that the mercenary brigade was well-prepared because they brought equipment and enough armaments for what they intended to do. There were ex-military people at the head of the battalions that received significant support from the North American government. The landing place was well-selected, and by chance, it was not sufficiently protected. The only thing that they never had in their favor was the ethical-moral factor and the stimulus of fighting for a just cause, apart from the possible idealism of some of them that came to recover their estates and privileges under the flag of an annexionist project.

Kennedy accepted the defeat when he said "victory has many parents, defeat is orphan."[19] Girón was a categorical failure for the Kennedy administration. It was an event through which the President could confirm that his concerns were not groundless, and also, to what extent he had not been well advised and even deceived by part of his closest collaborators. But it is also advisable to specify that Girón was not only a military failure, but also a total defeat for the United States in its confrontation with the Cuban Revolution. It was a defeat for U.S. institutional structures, especially for the defense establishment, magnified by the idyllic vision that Kennedy had of the CIA. It cannot be ignored either that Girón was not only a humiliation for the empire, but also for the Kennedy brothers, in their intimate personal conception. Therefore, Cuba[20] acquired, from then on, a special connotation for the administration, especially for the President who from subsequently had almost uncontrollable desires to avenge the humiliation they had undergone.

Girón Failure and the Danger of an Invasion to Cuba

After Girón, the Kennedy administration designed a series of aggressive measures and actions against Cuba and they quickly began the arrangements for an invasion to the island on a large scale. Such a situation explains, as we will see later, the fact that during October, 1962, the plans of direct aggression to Cuba that were being developed and the presence of the nuclear armament in the island coincided.[21]

All of this allows us to affirm that the October Crisis can be best explained and finally understood as primarily a confrontation between Cuba and the United States that had already been able to generate an invasion of the island, which they sought to repeat at a level that would ensure success. [22] At the same time, after the bitter defeat suffered in Girón, Kennedy intended to carry out a strict control of the political actions against Cuba, an experience that he subsequently applied during the October Crisis.

After Girón, Kennedy no longer carried forward any commitment from the previous administration. From then on, he would follow his "own policy," although, in short, the latter did not represent any essential change compared to the previous one, but at least it would be a policy for "his whole pleasure and responsibility." On April 20, 1961 he declared, ". . . A nation of Cuba's size is not much of a threat to our survival, but it is so as a base for the subversion of other free nations in the whole hemisphere. It is not our security interest which is in greater danger, but theirs."[23]

Kennedy, acting in accordance with what happened in Girón, assigned General Maxwell Taylor to lead a commission that would thoroughly study the causes of the defeat at Playa Giron. He also assigned the Assistant Secretary to the Defense for International Security affairs, Paul H. Nitze, to preside over a taskforce, formed by representatives from the State, Defense, and Justice Departments, and from USIA and the CIA, with the mission of recommending the policy to immediately follow towards Cuba.

From then on, Kennedy also intended to reconsider the non-participation of the U.S. armed forces in the activities against Cuba, in such a way that, only ten days after the Girón invasion ended, the President, together with McNamara and Admiral Burke, revised a contingency plan for the deployment of American troops in Cuba. According to this plan, the number of required soldiers necessary to obtain the complete control of the island in eight days was seen to be 60,000 men. According to McNamara, such an assessment was not equivalent to deciding to invade, but should that option be chosen, effective plans were in place for successful implementation. The Kennedy administration denied on many occasions his intentions of invading Cuba on a large scale, that is to say, using the U.S. army.[24]

On the other hand, the Cuban leadership, especially Fidel Castro, was always convinced, mainly after Girón, that invasion was completely possible and that it was being prepared. The U.S. administration did not even acknowledge this as a reason for Cuba to accept the Soviet rockets. They preferred to judge such a Cuban decision on Cuba's willingness to be an alleged satellite of the USSR. Today, the existing documentation clarifies that situation. The Kennedy administration made arrangements for invading Cuba and the dates of that possible invasion coincided with the final days of October, 1962.[25]

In accordance with the hemispheric form in which Kennedy focused the policy toward Cuba, Paul Nitze, fulfilling the objectives of the aforementioned Task Force, presented a document entitled, "Cuba and the Communism in the Hemisphere." In addition, the President met with a group of Cuban exiles, headed once more by José Miro Cardona, then President of the Cuban Revolutionary Council, the same one that had hoped to disembark in Cuba as a government in arms at Playa Giron. Miro Cardona later declared that Kennedy had formalized a pact with them for a new invasion of Cuba.[26] President Kennedy continued to regard the participation of the Cuban counterrevolutionaries as important in the plans against the Island. [27]

In a National Security Council meeting held on May 5, 1961, the policy to follow towards Cuba after Girón was discussed. The President expressed that the policy toward Cuba should ultimately be aimed to cause Castro's fall. He would not intervene in Cuba in that moment, but he would not take any measure that would avoid the possibility of a military intervention in the future.[28] The primary change made by Kennedy following the Nitze report was that any future invasion of Cuba would be coordinated by the Pentagon, not the CIA. Such a shift was logical given the failure of the CIA plan at Giron and the choice of the Pentagon underscored the seriousness of the administration's commitment against Cuba.[29]

Cuba's Response

As the preparations for an invasion of Cuba continued, Cuba continued increasing her relations with the socialist countries, especially the USSR. In September, 1961, a second agreement was signed with the USSR, by means of which Cuba received supply of conventional armament for an amount of $149 million. From this figure, Cuba would have to pay $67,550,000 and would have ten years to liquidate the rest of the bill, paying a two percent interest fee per a year.[30] Thus, the USSR reaffirmed its willingness to help the Island.

The U.S. answer to closer Cuban-Soviet ties did not take long. McGeorge Bundy presented the 100 Memorandum of National Security Action entitled "Emergency Plan for Cuba" on October 5, 1962, through which the State Department committed itself ". . . to value the ways of potential action opened to the United States if Castro should be eliminated from the Cuban scene, and to prepare an emergency plan with the Defense Department for the military intervention, if such was the case."[31] The United States, with enough reasons to invade Cuba after the defeat of Girón, added to these the capacity that Cuba was acquiring for her defense. From the Cuban perspective the sabotage of the "La

Coubre" ship in 1960 by the CIA had already given more than enough indication of how far the U.S. government was ready to go in order to prevent Cuba from acquiring an adequate defensive capacity. Together with the arrangements that the Kennedy administration was already carrying out, they deployed a harassment campaign against Cuba in the OAS. The United States leaned on some Latin American governments, particularly in Argentina and Venezuela, to achieve Cuba's complete isolation and to avoid at any price that there would be dissident voices in the hemisphere once the island was finally invaded.

Operation Mongoose

In November, 1961, the administration hastened the preparations for the operation that was going to be the biggest subversive operation implemented against Cuba. On November 30, President Kennedy made the Special Augmented Group (SAG) official within the National Security Council, presided over by General Maxwell Taylor and the Attorney General Robert Kennedy. The so-called Mongoose Operation was officially created, although it was kept secret until recently.[32] Operation Mongoose had a singular objective to overthrow the Revolutionary Government using all the necessary means.[33] U.S. plans against Cuba, broadly reactivated after Girón, had as their main political objective to make world public opinion believe, especially to the hemispheric opinion, that there was a civil war in Cuba between the government supporters and an organized opposition, all with the purpose of endowing genuineness to the internal armed counterrevolution. In fact, the counterrevolution had been organized by the North American government that supported and financed it. Therefore, they never had legitimacy because also, the objectives of these groups were only to sow terror in the areas where they operated, for their members to win favor with the CIA and the U.S. government, and to escape later to the United States where they could live the rest of their lives off of the actions they had carried out in Cuba.[34]

United States' plans of invasion, once the Mongoose Operation was designed, had a destabilizing and a "softening" arm until the moment came for the invasion on a large scale with the U.S. army, which was conceived as the last step inside the Mongoose Plan itself.[35] By November, 1961, there were three basic factors articulated within the policy of Kennedy administration towards Cuba: a process of preparation of the invasion of the island using the American army; the detailed follow up of the whole process by means of which Cuba increased and strengthened her defensive capacity; and the development of the Mongoose Plan, addressed to destabilize the island internally, with all types of military and para-military subversive actions led from the United States by the CIA.

Expulsion from OAS

This last plan, intended as a culmination, was the execution of the invasion if the subversive actions were not enough to overthrow the revolutionary government. In any case, the measures of economic aggression continued with the characteristics already mentioned before that were strengthened that same year 1962. Because of these reasons, Cuba was developing a defensive campaign in Latin America and in the United Nations, where the actions against the island undertaken by the Kennedy administration had the precise objective to present Cuba as a pariah of international relationships and as a nation incompatible with the rules of the intra-hemispheric coexistence. When the U.S. Secretary of State at that time Deán Rusk took the floor at the Chancellors meeting of the OAS on January 25, 1962, he pointed out,

> First, we should recognize that the alignment of the Cuban communist government in this hemisphere is incompatible with the purposes and principles of the interamerican system, and that her activities are always an ever-present and common danger to the continent's peace and security. In the second place, now we should make effective the decision of excluding Castro's régime from all participation in the structures and bodies the interamerican system and to order the Organization Council to determine how to give a better and quicker execution of this decision.[36]

The United States carried out its plan to gain Cuba's expulsion from the OAS. This represented such a violation of the principles of the Constituent Charter of the OAS organization that Senator Hickenlooper, in the Congressional session on January 29, 1962, stated, "We are faced with a real juridical problem. Seemingly there is no way to expel Cuba from the OAS, unless another meeting is summoned to modify the Charter."[37] Another meeting was not summoned, nor was the OAS Charter was changed. The solution to this dilemma was "to suspend" Cuba on the basis of "the incompatibility of the Marxist-Leninist régime in Cuba with the interamerican system." Consequently, there arose the paradoxical situation, that the seat and the Cuban flag remain in the OAS but Cuba remains absent, a situation that still exists today. In fact, the objective of this meeting had in fact been to unleash the rupture of diplomatic relations with Cuba, to reinforce the commercial blockade, and to create a hemispheric military bloc against Cuba. Thus, three basic external variants were put into operation in order to define the design of the invasion.

Prior to its moves at the OAS, Kennedy gave definitive form to the blockade policy towards Cuba that had already been developing since Eisenhower, by means of the 3447 Presidential Proclaim that he enforced on January 7, 1962; this defined the fourth lever of pressure with which the administration sought to isolate Cuba. From then on, the United States began a process on a large scale through the black list that pointed with force toward the changing of the commercial embargo, into a transnational mechanism designed to close off to Cuba all the possible roads of her economic survival in the international arena.

Intensifying the siege of Cuba even more, a meeting of the Caribbean Command took place in the area of Panama Canal with the participation of Robert MacNamara and other military chiefs, where it was stated that the security of the hemisphere countries was threatened by the communist subversion, particularly from Cuba.[38] In addition, there was a conference in the headquarters of the Atlantic Command in Norfolk, Virginia on February 7 and 8 to analyze the operation plans 314 and 316 in 1961 (OPLANs 314 / 316 - 61) directed to carry out a military aggression of the United States armed forces against Cuba.[39] Going on with the warlike preparations for the invasion of Cuba, a document for debate prepared by the Joint Chiefs of Staff on March 13, 1962 was submitted to the Defense Department. It was entitled, "Pretexts to Justify a Military Intervention of the United States in Cuba" and contained a group of harassment measures that had an objective to create the conditions to justify a direct military action. This document pointed out: 1) Due to the fact that it would be profitable to use legitimate provocations as a bases for the military intervention of the United States in Cuba, a plan could be executed that raises the Cuban reaction... 2) A series of well-coordinated incidents would be designed that would take place inside and in the vicinity of Guantánamo Naval Base. These would be conceived so that they were seemed to have been carried out by hostile Cuban forces. This last document was considered as useful and careful material that was necessary to keep in mind.[40]

They were not simple plans. In April, 1962, the Cuban government submitted a diplomatic note of protest where they listed provocative actions carried out in Guantánamo Naval Base and its surroundings during twelve days. The provocation, a tool very frequently used by the CIA, entered fully into the game, and on April 3, the U.S. naval exercise, well-known as "Quick Kick" started. Some days later, President Kennedy met again with the contrarrevolutionary leader José Miro Cardona and reaffirmed the willingness of the United States government to solve the Cuban problem through armed means. For that purpose, it was necessary to prepare six divisions.[41] It can be assumed that this was Kennedy's call to look for the participation of those that supposedly held a grudge against Girón action.[42]

October Crisis

These warlike preparations, the Mongoose Plan, the worsening of the blockade with the Presidential proclamations, together with the plans of direct invasion, fed the concerns that gave Khrushchev the idea of suggesting to the Cuban leadership to install the nuclear missiles in Cuba.[43] That is to say, apart from the reason that Khrushchev might have proposed Cuba's installation of nuclear rockets in her territory, the actual issue was that the Island was continually ha-

rassed by the counterrevolution and it was under the imminent threat of an invasion from the U.S. Army. All of these factors were seen by Khrushchev as a
legitimate justification to make such a proposal to the Cuban leadership.

The nuclear missiles would never have emerged as a defense alternative for
Cuba if they had not been preceded by mortal dangers that hung over the Cuban
Revolution. The political cost and the danger of the presence of the nuclear
missiles in Cuba were only understood on the basis that they served to improve
the nuclear strategic power of the socialist camp, and at the same time, to play a
strong persuasive role to deter the United States from invading Cuba.

As we have demonstrated the crisis did not begin with the installation of the
rockets in Cuba, but much earlier. The true crisis between the Cuban revolution
and the U.S. administrations existed since 1959. The October Crisis reached the
level of danger that it did because Cuba made the decision to accept the Soviet
offer of nuclear weapons with the reasonable certainty that if they did not do so,
the United States would be undeterred to carry out the invasion plans that it was
clearly formulating following the failure of the Girón invasion. Beyond the
misconception that Cuba was solely responsible for the crisis is the idea that the
event lasted for only thirteen days. In reality it lasted from around October 14-
16, 1962, when Kennedy officially learned about the existence of the nuclear
weapons in Cuba until approximately November 30, 1962, when the interview
between Mikoyan and Kennedy took place and the positions regarding the final
agreements of the crisis were fixed.[44] The thirteen day framing is just another
incorrect way of stating that the presence of the missiles in Cuba alone caused
the confrontation, when in fact, as we have demonstrated, the October confron-
tations grew out of U.S. provocations toward the island over the previous three
years. From our perspective, it was the warlike measures outlined by President
Kennedy on October 22 in his speech to the U.S. people that served to escalate
the crisis to its potentially catastrophic consequences.[45] However, it is also important to note that there were other factors in this crisis that must be laid primarily at the feet of the Soviet leadership. Certain Soviet behavior served to first
escalate the crisis sharply at the beginning, and then at the end of the crisis, to
place Cuba in an unfavorable position and undermine longer-term Cuban-Soviet
relations. First, the fact that the installation of the nuclear rockets was carried
out secretly and gave the North American side a substantial moral, political, and
strategic advantage because when they discovered the missiles, they had enough
time to design and to plan reply actions. For the USSR and Cuba, who only
suspected the discovery, the only thing left for them was to wait. Besides, the
deceit allowed Kennedy to turn the terms of the confrontation upside down since
he was able to present himself as the attacked side, when actually, they had been
the aggressors. On several occasions, Cuba insisted to the Soviets on the moral
and strategic inconsistency of installing the rockets secretly, but after several
attempts Cuba did not succeed in convincing Khrushchev and finally she accepted to leave the matter in hands of the Soviet leadership. The consequences
of installing the rockets secretly were disastrous; we could dare to affirm that it
is possibly the most dangerous moment Cuba has gone through in her confronta-

tion with the United States.[46] The consequences of this error were also disastrous for the international image of the USSR during the crisis. Cuba, on the other hand, also suffered the negative consequences of this error.

Second, Khrushchev, in his letter to Kennedy on October 26, communicated his disposition to move all the weapons that the United States regarded as "offensive" away from Cuba. This declaration, besides being an unforgivable moral withdrawal, from the Cuban perspective also turned out to be a bottomless trap when the negotiation started. Kennedy, clinging to such a statement from Khrushchev, drove the negotiations of the weapon withdrawal as he pleased, making more demands at each step, both in the conversations for the removal of the missiles and their verification, as well as in the pressures, even through an ultimatum to achieve the retreat of the IL-28 bombers before November 20, 1962.[47] Other additional errors from Khrushchev were the following:

- To communicate to the United States, during the negotiating process for the retreat of the missiles, that all the steps that he was taking were in common agreement with Cuba—an allusion that was not true.

- To try to make Cuba allow the inspection of her territory in the process of the missile withdrawal, which meant a disregard of the Cuban sovereignty.

- To ignore Cuba during the negotiating process, although they tried to include her later, without any practical effectiveness, whereas the key decisions had already been agreed by Kennedy and Khrushchev behind Cuba's back.

- To jeopardize Cuba's national security by accepting a promise from the United States of non invasion to the Island, which in the context of the Cuba-United States conflict, had a very relative and little value. The United States in the absence of a formal treaty could make the commitment of not invading Cuba and go on attacking her, such as they have done until today.

- To negotiate the retreat of the missiles from Cuba for those of Turkey's was a process that had nothing to do with the situation and it got Cuba involved in another country's interests over which she had no control. Besides, the Soviets had not informed Cuba about this step. Khrushchev deceived Kennedy, and Cuba as well, when he negotiated behind Cuba's back and hid information from her on its dealings with the North American government. Cuba turned out to be the most damaged party in the whole process.[48] Then, in practice, in spite of everything that the USSR, especially Khrushchev, had positively done for Cuba up to that moment and later on, during the October Crisis he took strategically erroneous and non-consulted steps that seriously jeopardized the Cuban national security and the prestige of the Revolution. Besides, it destroyed the only real opportunity that Cuba would have had of seriously influencing the course of her future relationships with the United States. It is evident that neither Khrushchev nor the Soviet policy strategists were acquainted with the political and practical details of the confrontation between Cuba and the United States. They, apparently, saw the framework and the strategic connection of a conflict in the Caribbean with the nuclear confrontation, but they lost the essential content regarding the real and integral solution to the problem and the way of negotiating it.

The solution to the crisis was only for the United States and the USSR because both limited themselves to negotiate from their logic as superior powers. For Cuba, there was no solution; it was only about a lost opportunity. In fact, Kennedy did not commit formally to anything. Everything remained in words. The only thing that was fulfilled was the retreat of Jupiter rockets from Turkey, although they were replaced by the mounted Polaris in the submarines, thus going from a fixed to a mobile one, which is without any doubt, merely formal, and was even more dangerous to the USSR. The promise of not invading Cuba was even more relative, because the United States continued harassing her, invading her on a small scale, and continually submitting her to all kinds of aggressions, to the present day. In fact, the United States, during these more than forty years, has not invaded Cuba on a large scale, not because they care about the 1962 agreement, but because the political, and even the military cost would be practically unpayable. U.S. leaders may have learned valuable lessons from the October Crisis about the danger of nuclear war but it was not those lessons alone or the commitments made to the USSR at the time that have primarily protected Cuba from invasion by the United States. Today there are many people, institutions, and reasonable politicians in the United States that would oppose with determination a plan like that.

However, an important damage that Khrushchev caused to Cuba is that, when the Soviet Prime Minister negotiated with the United States to withdraw the rockets without consulting Cuba, he did nothing but to reaffirm Kennedy on his thesis, already stated in the "White Book," that supposedly the island was but a USSR satellite. Such a confirmation of the hypothesis had lasting and very negative consequences for Cuba, although it also had the same effect for the North American foreign policy.[49] Only the uncompromising position of the Cuban leadership, to prevent the inspection, to demand the Five Points, to work against the reconnaissance flights, and to prevent coercion at any price, together with resolved attitude of the people, was the thing that saved the prestige of the Revolution face to such events. When speaking about the Five Points, we refer to the demands that Cuba considered she should make to the United States during the negotiation for the withdrawal of the strategic armaments installed in the Island. Such demands were the following ones: First, stop the economic blockade and all the commercial and economic pressing measures that the United States exercise all over the world against Cuba. Second, stop all the subversive activities, launchings and landings of weapons and explosive materials from air and sea, the organization of mercenary invasions, infiltration of spies and sabotages, all those actions that are carried out from the territory of the United States and from some accomplice countries. Third, stop the attacks that are carried out from the existing bases in the United States and in Puerto Rico. Fourth, stop all the violations of the air and naval space by North American war airplanes and ships. Fifth, withdraw the Guantánamo Naval Base and return the territory occupied by the United States.[50] The United States could not impose their conditions upon Cuba, at least what depended on their will, and such a sample of ethical—political strength cannot be forgotten.

Notes

1. This event is also known as the Caribbean Crisis, name given by the Soviets. The latter would rather answer to the attitude of given an external projection to the conflict. Though it later became global, it mainly involved three nations: Cuba, the United States and the USSR.

2. The film "Thirteen Days," under the direction of actor Kevin Costner, regardless of the fact that it was not an anti-Communist seeking to attack Cuba, is nevertheless trapped within the superficial perspective of showing the United States as a victim and Cuba and the USSR as simple aggressors that jeopardized the lives of the peaceful North American people and the world.

3. Mark L. Haas. Virginia University, "Prospect Theory and the Cuban Missile Crisis," *International Studies Quarterly* (International Studies Association, Blackwell Publisher, USA, 1991), 243.

4. For more information on this issue, see the author's: "United States' Policy Towards Cuba 1959-1961," (CESEU Library, Havana University), (Publication in Progress). See also: Carlos Alzugaray's, "Chronicle of an Imperial Failure," (Social Science Editorial, Havana, 2000), 71-193.

5. See also: Carlos Alzugaray's, "Chronicle of an Imperial Failure" (Social Science Editorial, Havana, 2000), 71-193.

6. Coronel J.C. King, chief of the Western Hemisphere Section in the CIA, had already tried, since 1958, to find an alternative solution within the dictatorship army, to replace Batista. On December 11, 1959, Mr. King, had already suggested a project to assassinate Fidel Castro. See: Oscar Pinos Santos', "The Complot," "Nuestro Tiempo" Editorial, S.A., Mexico FD, 1992, 43-84.

7. It is interesting to see the tenacity to carry out this part of the aggression. See, *Cuba and the United States, A Chronological History*, (Jane Franklin, Ocean Press, New York, 1997).

8. Jane Franklin, 34.

9. See: Stephen E. Ambrose's *Towards a Global Power* (Latin American Editing Group, New York, 1991) 143-148.

10. J. F. Kennedy had opposed Cuba on the bases of his own conception of believing that "the United States was the last, the best hope of humanity" and maybe by the end of his life, he reached to the conclusion that it was not incompatible with the fact of trying to find a way of understanding with the Island. I certainly believe that the experiences he went through were more than enough to make him reach that conclusion. Such a change in Kennedy, concerning in seeking an approach in order to speak with Cuba, without any doubt, influenced on his murder by the end of November, 1963. Paradoxically, the President that up to the moment had taken part in the two most dangerous events of the relations between both countries was murdered when he was looking for an approach

with Cuba. His two greatest mistakes in the policy towards Cuba face to the hawks: not to have launched the marines in Girón and afterwards to allow, after the October Crisis, that communism went on 90 miles away, cost him his life. (Author's Notes)

11. In general, it has been imposed as a rule, that during the battles for the Presidency, although Cuba is not a subject of the campaign itself, the different interested political forces move themselves stating their alternatives and forcing the candidate to speak on the subject. (Author's Notes)

12. The Alliance for the Progress was an important distinguishing element of Kennedy's policy towards Latin America in relation with the policy followed by Eisenhower, as well as a more intelligent understanding on, not only how to attack Cuba, but also how to avoid more future Cubas. (Author's Notes)

13. Especially Kennedy's consideration of "Cuba as satellite of the USSR," survived for a long time, causing an invaluable damage to the North American foreign policy in order to have a clear view of the real role of Cuba in the international field. From then on, the United States actually never understood the Cuban foreign policy and for that reason they have always smashed against it. (Author's Notes)

14. We have the impression that for supporting a plan that he had inherited, it was already enough. Kennedy wanted to develop his own policy, no different from the previous one, but under his own rules and principles. (Author's Notes)

15. In the conference "Girón; Forty year later," Fidel Castro narrated how the place of the landing was not in fact the most protected one, thus confirming that Cuba did not know specifically where the attack would be. (Author's Note)

16. See: Fidel Castro's speeches. Recorded versions of the Conference, Girón 40 years later, taken place in the Convention Center, on March 23 and 24, 2001, Havana, Cuba.

17. It is astonishing to see the result that can produce the combination of constantly repeated lies, the always negative propaganda, the hate to the revolution, forgetfulness, ignorance and as a result of all that, self-deceiving. Not a few persons, during these 40 years, have been victims of that ideological phenomenon, characteristic of the contrarrevolutionary atmosphere, particularly in Miami. (Author's Notes)

18. To get more information about this conception of the failure of Girón see: Lyman Kirkpatrick's, Report from the General Inspector of the CIA on the Bay of Pigs operation, New Heráld, 1997. Published on March 1, 1998.

19. Also see, the Official Press Statement from April 24, 1961, where the Press Secretary from the White House informed that the United States President accepted "the full responsibility of the last days' events." See *Chronology on the October Crisis* by Tomas Diez, History Institute, Havana, Cuba.

20. The United States would only suffer a defeat of similar political proportions some years later in Vietnam. Girón defeat was good to show the United States that if they wanted to defeat the Cuban Revolution militarily, they could

only do it by taking the risk of employing themselves thoroughly. (Author's Notes)

21. All kinds of aggressive activities against Cuba were linked to the so-called Mongoose Plan, where October was precisely chosen as the date for carrying out the direct invasion, in case that all the destabilizing actions that were carried out against the Island failed.

22. It is not by chance that on October 28, when an understanding had already been reached between Khrushchev and Kennedy for the retreat of the nuclear rockets, the hawks, among who stood out Admiral George Anderson, Chief of Naval Operations and Curtis LeMay, Major State Chief of the Air force, Kennedy-Khrushchev agreement, was valued as a lost game, because they had lost the opportunity of attacking Cuba. See: Le May Curtis', "The Cuban Experience: Responses and Lessons." Supplement for Commanders 114. Dec. 1962: 2-7.

23. See: Speech in the American Society of Newspapers Directors, April 20, 1961.

24. Both in the Conversations of Vienna with Khrushchev, as well as with Khrushchev's son-in-law, Alexei Azhubei, Kennedy denied systematically that he had intentions of invading Cuba. (Author's Notes)

25. See Mongoose Plan. Document 5: Gen Brig. Edward Lanzadle's, "Cuba Project." February 20, 1962. (program review and basic action plan for Operation Mongoose). Document 6, Special Group Augmented, Guidelines for Operation Mongoose, March 14, 1962 and Document 8, Defense Department / Joint Chiefs Staff, projection of Consequences of U.S. Military Intervention in Cuba. In *The Cuban Missile Crisis* 1962, A National Security File Documents Reader, Edited by Laurence Chang and Peter Kornbluh, The New Press, New York, USA, 1992, 1998, 23–52. Mongoose would unleashed internal uprisings, contrarrevolutionary insurrection that would facilitate the direct intervention, with OAS covering. That ratified the conviction of the Cuban leadership that by the middle of 1962 there was in progress a plan that would lead to the military aggression against Cuba.

26. Diez, *Chronology on the October Crisis.*

27. It is not possible to clarify whether Kennedy agreed that the content of the meeting was disclosed, or if it was a simple exhibition of power on the part of Mister Miro Cardona. (Author's Notes)

28. Diez, *Chronology on the October Crisis.*

29. Memorandum for the Record, "Paramilitary Action Against the Castro Government of Cuba," May.

30. Diez, *Chronology on the October Crisis.*

31. Diez, *Chronology on the October Crisis.*

32. See: document 4. Minutes of First Operation Mongoose meeting with General Attorney Robert Kennedy, December 1, 1961, Work National File, Washington DC, Selection of Giron, 20. See: The White House, "Eyes Only For

The President," Richard N. Goodwin, Giron Selection, Washington AD, Work National Files.

33. During the October Crisis, Mongoose was also very well supported. On October 16, 1962, amid the scenario of the discovery of the rockets in Cuba, President Kennedy "whipped" the leaders of Mongoose demanding more action from them. See: Document: 10, Mongoose Meeting with The General Attorney, October 16, 1962, in *The Cuban Missile Crisis*, 62-63.

34. Mongoose Operation was also good to reactivate outlawry in Cuba since the groups had been strongly beaten before Girón, as many people that had served the bandits as collaborators and food suppliers remained in the areas where those groups operated before, the bands resurged and extended practically to all the provinces of the country, and they managed to survive until the beginnings of 1965, when they were finally annihilated. (Author's Notes)

35. You can find more details on this called Mongoose Plan. Work "The Cuban Missile Crisis" 20-63.

36. Diez, *Chronology on the October Crisis*.

37. Diez, *Chronology on the October Crisis*.

38. Diez, *Chronology on the October Crisis*. It is very important to take into account that already since the so-called White Book, with two versions, that from the beginning of Kennedy administration in 1961, and a second version published on January 1962, Cuba had been regarded as a USSR's satellite. Therefore, all Cuban actions in the hemisphere were given the character of actions from the international communism. That's why the island, was fully inside the so-called East-West confrontation. (Author's Notes)

39. Diez. *Chronology on the October Crisis*.

40. Diez. *Chronology on the October Crisis*.

41. Diez. *Chronology on the October Crisis*.

42. Although many of them, were still in Cuba, waiting to be exchanged by preserved food, they would pass the October Crisis in Cuba. This was a lingering negotiation, until towards the end of December 21, 1962, when the signature of the agreement takes place between Fidel and Donovan. (Author's Notes)

43. The defense of Cuba was an excellent justification to install the rockets in the Island. Khrushchev never used another reason. But, his performance, when not accepting the secret; to negotiate the retreat of the rockets behind Cuba's backs; to hide from Cuba the exchange with the rockets from Turkey and Italy; to consent to move away all the weapons that Kennedy considered as offensive; to seek that Cuba also allowed to be inspected and all the bilateral handlings that Khrushchev made with Kennedy behind Cuba's backs, made it doubt that the priority which motivated Khrushchev to install the rockets in the Island had been the defense of Cuba. (Author's Notes)

44. On November 29, 1962, A. Mikoyan and J.F. Kennedy held an interview to analyze the propositions from both sides in the negotiating process. Here they analyzed once more, the subject on the declaration projects. Mikoyan stated

dissatisfaction for the North American proposal because it annulled the obligations incurred by the U.S. Kennedy said it was not feasible to concert three declarations, because they would not vote for the Cuban project and the Cubans would not agree with the USA; that U Thant should limit himself to taking notes, without reaching any voting in the Security Council. Regarding the flights, Kennedy said that they would execute them from a great height as a verifying way. That in their country there was a strong campaign that questioned the effective execution of the retreat of the offensive armament. Mikoyan on the other hand expressed that these flights, no matter how they were made, they were a violation, acts against the international law; and that if they were suspicious of the nonfulfillment of the agreements, they should accept the multilateral inspection. See: Tomas Diez, *Chronology on the October Crisis*.

45. Actually, there are several indications as if they were made to introduce doubts about whether Kennedy, far before October 16, did or didn't have any elements to presuppose the presence of nuclear rockets in Cuba. But regrettably we cannot step on that issue. Consult, among others, the substantial report from the CIA, Special National Intelligence Estimate, The Military Buildup in Cuba, the Cuban Missile Crisis, 1962, 71-73. In a meeting that took place between McCone, CIA director and President Kennedy, on August 22, 1962, the first one communicates that he suspected that the Soviet government was getting ready to deploy nuclear rockets in Cuba. See: Chronology, Conference 30 Anniversary, 28. On May 24 the USSR had already made the decision of installing the rockets in Cuba. Days later, on May 29 the proposal was made to Cuba. On June 10th, the Soviet Presidium made the final decision. On July 7, 1962, Malinovsky informed Khrushchev that everything was ready to begin the shipment of nuclear rockets to Cuba.

46. See: Record of the Meetings from the Central Committee of the PCC (Cuban Communist Party), on January 25 and 26, 1968, Havana Cuba, 55-62. You can find a very clear expression of Kennedy's advantages in the speech on October 22. See: Document 29: "Radio-TV Address of the President to the Nation from the White House." *The Cuban Missile Crisis*, 160-164.

47. See: Document 53: Work: *The Cuban Missile Crisis*, 1962, 238-242. Also see: *The November Extension*, 244-245. (Author's Notes) To get more information, consult: Work Tripartite Conference, January 11, 1992. Fourth Session, 7-27.

48. There is still an exchange of non-declassified documentation between Kennedy and Khrushchev that can surprise us; regarding many matters handled by Khrushchev with Kennedy that were not informed to Cuba. (Author's Notes)

49. See: Records of the Meeting from the Central Committee of the PCC, on January 25-26, 1968, session January 26th, Havana, Cuba, 1-17. The essence of the policy didn't disappear then nor today, and it is still part of the debate on whether they should or should not keep the aggressiveness, as an essential component of the policy towards Cuba. (Author's Notes)

50. See: Khrushchev's letters from October 27 to 28, 1962. Chronology of the October Crisis. Tripartite meeting, 1992, 82-88. See: Dangers and Principles. The October Crisis from Cuba. "Verde Olivo" Editorial MINFAR, Havana, 1992, 170.

Chapter Four

U.S.-Cuban Relations After The October Crisis (1963-1979)

During the first four years of the Revolution, several economic measures taken by the United States against Cuba posed serious difficulties for the Revolutionary government. Cuba was compelled to re-orient its foreign trade toward distant regions because American pressures resulted in raising the tariffs that Cuba had to pay for transportation, thus making importation and exportation more expensive. Cuba was able to reach the global fleet market only under extremely detrimental conditions and was subject to uncommon contract clauses and interest payments well over prime rates in the world market. The following years were characterized by the United States strictly implementing the embargo and by increased U.S. pressures on capitalist countries trading with Cuba. Internally, counter-revolutionary groups operating in the mountains were given further support in an attempt to destroy the Revolution.

The United States government continued implementing its blockade policy. On July 8, 1963, the Cuban Assets Control Regulations (CACR) were approved as part of the Treasury Department's Office of Foreign Assets Control (OFAC).[1] It prohibited all transactions related to Cuba, affected all financial operations with Cuba and froze all property in U.S. territory owned either by Cuban nationals or by the Cuban Government. The CACR was a necessary measure for those agencies formulating anti-Cuba policy for two reasons. First, the regulations on Cuban exports prohibited trade of products having Cuban or American components, between both countries but it did not prohibit trade between American subsidiaries based in third countries and Cuba. Secondly, these regulations literally prohibited all trade or financial transactions between the United States and Cuba, but left an "open window" in one part of the law, where transactions subject to general licensing could be authorized.

During the Johnson administration, the U.S. policy toward Cuba was marked by aggression and hostility that was aimed at economically isolating the Revolution. Nevertheless, those aggressions were less frequent than in previous administrations, in part, due to their continual failures. Lyndon Johnson stated that: "The use of Cuba as a base for subversion and terror poses an obstacle to our hopes in the Western Hemisphere."[2] Johnson's statement validated his administration's use of vast resources, from diplomatic isolation to military actions, to try to damage Cuba's world standing. On December 16, 1963, the U.S. Congress passed Public Law 88-205 amending the Foreign Assistance Act of 1961, establishing that the United States would not offer any kind of assistance to any current or future government in the island, unless the President determined that seized property from U.S. citizens by the Revolutionary government was properly indemnified. At the beginning of 1964, the Department of Commerce denied general license requests for sending powdered milk to Cuba after the devastation caused by Hurricane Flora. Through CAC Regulations 371-270 and 371-540, amended on May 14, special license requests were permitted for sending food or medicine to Cuba.

On the eve of the July, 1964 OAS Summit, the United States tried to convince countries still having relationships with Cuba to break them because a large deposit of weapons linked with Cuba had been found in Venezuela. According to the United States, Cuba was responsible for encouraging subversion in that country. At the Summit, an agreement was reached to condemn Cuba, citing that the arms issue constituted aggression and an act of Cuban interference in Venezuela's internal affairs. During that 12th OAS Foreign Ministers' meeting, several resolutions proposed by the United States were passed. These resolutions recommended OAS member states not to ship any cargo coming from or to Cuba, and discouraged re-fueling of those ships involved in Cuban trade. Mexico was the only OAS country to definitively reject these measures.

In 1964, the U.S. Supreme Court ruled in Banco Nacional de Cuba vs. Sabbatino[3] that under the Sovereign Power Doctrine, Cuba had the right to nationalize foreign properties. In reaction to the Court's ruling, the U.S. Congress passed the Hickenlooper Amendment to the Section 620 (e)(2) of the Foreign Assistance Act of 1961. This amendment provided a loophole for the judicial system to rule in favor of U.S. businesses having properties which had been nationalized by the Cuban government. In effect, the amendment gave businesses the right to file claims against confiscated Cuban assets in the United States if Cuba did not properly compensate these claims. In addition, through Public Law 89-6 of March 24, 1965, the U.S. government was authorized to increase its participation in the Special Operations Fund of the Inter-American Development Bank. The increased funding gave the United States greater voting power. Though the decision to increase its share of funding to the IDP was done for broader reasons, a consequence of the increased share was to have greater leverage to block IDP projects that could aid Cuba. Although Mexico had been Cuba's only Latin American trading partner, the United States positioned itself to discourage other Latin American countries from engaging in trade with Havana.

The United States was now primarily preoccupied with the escalation of the Vietnam conflict. However, U.S. military and subversive activities against Cuba continued. One such plan included members of the U.S. Armed Forces attacking the U.S. Naval Base located at Guantanamo, on the eastern side of the island, dressed as Cuban guerrillas. Known as "Project Patty," this attack would then justify direct U.S. military action against Cuba. Cuban counter-intelligence ("Project Candela") effectively dismantled the U.S. operation. After the "Patty-Candela" incident, the U.S. government organized secret military bases in Central America and Florida, specifically, to aid contra-revolutionary attacks against Cuban territory.[4]

There is also evidence that at several points during the Kennedy and Johnson presidencies, Fidel Castro and the Cuban leadership put out feelers aimed at achieving a détente with the United States. The reasons for such overtures can be found in Cuban suspicions about the Soviets flowing from the October Crisis. As discussed in the previous chapter, the Cubans had reason to question the Soviets' ultimate commitment to Cuba's defense. Other reasons for the overture may have included the impact of the embargo, especially in prohibiting Cuba's receipt of spare parts. One such initiative came while John Kennedy was still the U.S. President in the fall of 1963 when Cuba signaled its willingness to talk through channels at the United Nations. According to Wayne Smith's account, the plans for arranging a significant meeting were placed on hold with the assassination of President Kennedy in November. There is also evidence that Kennedy had sent a message directly to Castro through private channels exploring the possibility of an accommodation.[5] It is unlikely that the overtures would have substantially changed U.S.-Cuban relations had Kennedy lived, but in any case, it appears that the Johnson administration and its assistant secretary for Latin American affairs, Thomas C. Mann, were not inclined to respond favorably. This was not surprising since Mann had been a staunch proponent of the Bay of Pigs invasion and other counterrevolutionary schemes. In spite of the initial rejection, Castro continued to seek negotiations through a series of newspaper interviews with *New York Times* reporter, Dick Eder. He made certain conciliatory gestures, including a willingness to pull back troops from the Guantanamo naval base perimeter, but the United States categorically rejected the overtures. The U.S. position was that talks could occur only if Cuba first ended its relationship with the Soviet Union and ceased to support Latin American revolutionaries. Castro's campaign for negotiations continued through his July 26, 1964 speech to the Cuban people, where he explained his willingness to speak with the United States as long as the legitimacy of Cuba's revolutionary system was respected. The United States categorically rejected the initiative and pressed ahead with a resolution at the Organization of American States that deepened hemispheric support for the economic embargo against the island.[6] In many ways, the terms stated by Cuba in 1964 for normalized relations remain unacceptable to the United States more than forty years later. For the United States, recognition of the revolutionary government represents surrender, a position that for many historical reasons the United States is not yet prepared to take.

Nixon Presidency

In January, 1969, President Richard Nixon was inaugurated. As Dwight Eisenhower's Vice President, he had been one of the creators of the 1960 embargo
and of the Bay of Pigs invasion. He continued the established policy toward
Cuba which included the economic and diplomatic blockade, support to internal
and external counter-revolutionary movements, and the sabotage of Cuban embassies and trade offices in third countries. The latter was an attempt to hinder
Cuba's growing relations with the rest of the world. Thus, U.S.-Cuban relations
continued to be tense. The United States had become firmly entrenched in its
position to return Cuba to its formal dependency role, including the restoration
of properties seized by the Cuban government. Between 1959 and 1971, the
Cuban-American conflict reached a pinnacle of unilateral and multilateral hostility. During these twelve years, the United States levied all forms of pressure to
return Cuba to hegemonic neocolonial rule.

Also, during the first decade of the Cuban Revolution, the Cuban-American
conflict reached a high level of confrontation as a result of Cuba's foreign policy
directed at weakening U.S. imperial dominance. The basis of Cuba's foreign
policy was international solidarity with Third World forces fighting for their
independence. When Cuba showed its capacity to perform as an independent
nation, internally as well as externally, the conflict between sovereignty and
hegemony reached its highest point. Since then, the conflict has been characterized by hostility in all spheres.[7] Consequently, the components of such conflict
were clearly discernable: military-strategic, economic, political-ideological,
diplomatic, legal, issues related to geographical vicinity, and most recently,
environmental issues.[8] This aspect of Cuba's international relations has infuriated U.S. leaders throughout the years.

A Policy of Constructive Steps in the Context of Détente

During the 1960s, Cuba experienced a significant growth in its socialist construction process, especially with respect to social welfare programs, which
dramatically improved the standard of living for a greater percentage of the
Cuban population. Additionally, Cuba gained a strong reputation in the international arena and managed to strengthen its economic and diplomatic ties with
Latin America, Asia, Europe, and Africa. Even though more than 80 percent of
the island's commerce was conducted with socialist countries after 1970, the
increase in sugar prices in the international market in the mid-1970s made it
possible for Cuba to raise its financial resources in hard currency, thus opening
the door to improved commercial relations with Western European countries as
well as Latin America.

From a global point of view, the 1970s were characterized by détente between the East and the West. This event provided a change from confrontation
to cooperation among countries with different social systems based on principles

of peaceful coexistence. Détente was driven in part by the failures of the United States in Vietnam and the views of Henry Kissinger that both the USSR and China could be convinced to assist the United States in blocking further revolutionary gains against U.S. interests. In Latin America, democratic and progressive forces came to power and sponsored an OAS resolution aimed at revoking the former diplomatic and trade sanctions against Cuba. Accordingly, a consciousness arose among some members of the U.S. Congress within the business community and some academic and public opinion circles that the Cuba policy had been a failure and needed to be changed. As a result, the position of the United States toward Cuba was re-evaluated during this period of détente. This led many people to believe that the embargo would be lifted in the near term because the U.S. government took a group of important measures aimed at softening the embargo.

The measures were the following:

- February 15, 1973: the United States and Cuba signed their first agreement on air piracy. The Department of State, however, announced it would not take any reconciliatory steps toward improving US-Cuba relations. The air piracy agreement between the two countries became necessary because over the years there had been numerous hijackings of planes that were forced to fly to Cuba. Some of the hijackers had been given asylum in Cuba but some of them later wound up in trouble with the Cuban authorities. In addition, the hijackings had increasingly come to be associated with terrorism and Cuba did not wish to be identified with such acts. From the Cuban perspective, they were the victims of numerous acts of terrorism initiated by the United States and the signing of the air piracy agreement with the United States allowed it to take a principled position on the issue. Under the agreement, both sides agreed to prosecute hijackers or return them to the other country for prosecution. Ironically, in recent years, it has been planes and boats hijacked in Cuba and brought to the United States that have resulted in implementation of the agreement.

In spite of the public State Department declaration to the contrary, the United States did make overtures to Cuba in late 1974. Henry Kissinger proposed to Fidel Castro that secret talks be held to explore the possibility of improving the broader relations between the two countries. Kissinger's initiative fit within his larger perspective that the world's communist-led countries could be brought into a broad status quo alliance that would control the revolutionary forces in the world in return for more favorable treatment from the United States and its allies. President Castro responded positively to the Kissinger request and several meetings were held.[9] In January, 1975, Castro made remarks that indicated his pleasure with the tone of the contacts. In March, 1975, in a speech in Houston, Kissinger said that the United States was willing to move in a new direction if Cuba was willing to make some concessions. He added that he saw no virtue in "perpetual antagonism between Cuba and the United States."[10] However, Kissinger did not spell out what concessions Cuba would be required to make.

- July 29, 1975: The United States voted with the majority in the organization of American States to end the multilateral diplomatic and economic sanctions that had been in place against Cuba for eleven years.

- OAS member governments were now free to maintain diplomatic and trade relations with Cuba if they wished. Several Latin American countries did reestablish relations soon after, but the United States did not, instead moving to amend various U.S. regulations that limited U.S. commercial contact with the island.
- August 29, 1975: The Department of Commerce amended the Export Administration Regulations[11] and authorized the re-fueling of vessels from third countries conducting trade with Cuba. However, the prohibition on provisioning Cuban registered, Cuban chartered, or Cuban owned vessels remained.
- October 8, 1975: The Treasury Department's Office of Cuban Foreign Assets Control Regulations (CACR)[12] were amended to establish the approval of licenses for export and import transactions between subsidiaries of U.S. owned or controlled firms, based in a third country and Cuba, under the following conditions:[13]
  - No transactions in U.S. dollars.
  - No citizen of the United States could be involved.
  - A maximum of 20 percent of U.S. manufactured components.
  - No information technology transferal.
  - The subsidiary must be legally registered in the third country.
  - The subsidiary must remain autonomous from the U.S. parent company.
- November 24, 1975: The Department of Commerce amended Section 385 of the Management of Export Regulations[14] to establish a policy of approbation of licenses on a case-by-case basis, provided less than twenty percent of the transaction materials, parts, or components were of U.S. origin on non-strategic products manufactured abroad.

The apparent small steps of progress in U.S.-Cuban relations were broken in the latter part of 1975 by events in Angola. The southern African country was moving toward independence following Portugal's decision to end its colonial control. There had been three major rebel groups in the country, each backed by a different outside power. Holden Roberto's National Front for the Liberation of Angola (FNLA) backed by China, Zaire, and the United States; Agostinho Neto's Popular Movement for the Liberation of Angola (MPLA) backed primarily by Cuba and the Soviet Union; and Jonas Savimbi's National Union for the Total Independence of Angola (UNITA) backed by South Africa and China. U.S. support for UNITA would come only later in 1975. In January, 1975, the three liberation groups met in Portugal and signed the Alvor agreement pledging them to a joint transitional government that would rule until independence in November, 1975. However, the United States did not support the Alvor agreement and stepped up its clandestine support to the FNLA, which began military attacks against the MPLA that shattered the transitional government. In March, 1975 the Soviets, responding to the attacks on the MPLA sanctioned by the

United States, resumed military aid to the MPLA and in June, Cuba sent 230 of
its military advisors to the country to aid the MPLA. By July, the MPLA had
gained the upper hand in expelling the UNITA and FNLA forces from the area
of Angola's capital, Luanda. In response, the United States increased its covert
support for FNLA and began for the first time to support UNITA. On August 9,
South African forces intervened for the first time, occupying a power plant in
southern Angola. Two months later, the South Africans, with no protest from the
Ford administration, launched an all out drive toward Luanda with the intent to
unseat the MPLA from its growing position of power. Cuba responded to MPLA
requests by airlifting additional troops to defend the capital against the South
Africans and the advances of the FNLA. The Cuban actions successfully stabi-
lized the MPLA and angered the American CIA, which sought authority to step
up its assistance to the anti-MPLA forces. However, at that moment, the U.S.
Congress intervened and in December, 1975 passed the Clark Amendment
which forbade assistance to the FNLA and UNITA and ruled out a direct U.S.
troop presence that had been briefly considered. The passage of the Clark
Amendment occurred at the end of the year in which the Vietnam War had finally ended and there were strong sentiments in the U.S. population for non-
intervention reflected in the Congressional vote. It would be a rare moment in
U.S. history when the popular will of the U.S. people thwarted the intentions of
the U.S. defense and intelligence establishment.

Soon after the passage of the Clark Amendment, the South Africans with-
drew claiming betrayal by the United States, and by early 1976, the MPLA was
firmly in control of most of the country, though the FNLA and UNITA did not
end their resistance. The impact of the Angola events on U.S.-Cuban relations
was to slow the momentum for normalizing relations, though none of the measures implemented by the United States in 1975 toward Cuba were repealed. The
Ford administration portrayed Cuba's intervention in Angola as naked aggression and suspended the secret negotiations with the Cuban government, declaring that they would only resume when Cuba removed its troops from Angola. As
the previous narrative indicated, the U.S. attacks on Cuba were questionable
given the role of the United States in the Angolan conflict, but in the mind of
Henry Kissinger, the actions of the Soviets and Cubans were a betrayal of
détente. From Kissinger's point of view the benefit of détente to the United
States was that revolutionary situations like the one that existed in Southern
Africa could be managed in such a way that political forces would come to power that furthered the agenda of U.S. foreign policy, particularly regimes that
were pro-capitalist in nature. Certain elements within the Soviet and Chinese
leaderships may have accepted this premise, but Kissinger's worldview was,
inevitably, going to conflict fiercely with the Cuban worldview. By 1975, Cuba's revolutionary internationalism had been tempered somewhat by the failures
of the Latin American guerrilla movements in the 1960s, but in Angola, the
Cubans saw an extraordinary opportunity to support progressive forces against
the reactionary actions of apartheid South Africa and embraced the Angola op-

erations with enthusiasm. Pragmatic steps were taken in that time period by both sides to improve U.S.-Cuban relations, but the Angola events revealed how far apart the worldview of the two countries remained.

Angola was not the only issue that blocked further movement in U.S.-Cuban relations during 1976. That year saw some particularly significant examples of continued terror attacks against Cuba emanating from organizations that were either sponsored by the U.S. government or tolerated. In April, 1976, two Cuban fishing boats in international waters were attacked by Cuban exiles. On October 6, a Cuban airliner was destroyed in mid-air near Barbados by a bomb planted by an exile group with connections to the CIA. All seventy-three passengers and crew were killed. In a speech following the event, Castro blamed the CIA and announced that the 1973 air piracy agreement would not be renewed because the United States had not honored it. Ironically, the Barbados bombing remains a point of contention to the present time as Cuba has sought unsuccessfully since 2005 the extradition from the United States of Jorge Posada Carriles, an admitted accomplice in the 1976 terror act. As 1976 progressed, Cuba began withdrawing troops from Angola, confident in the dominant position of the MPLA. However, the Ford administration continued its insistence that only full withdrawal would result in a renewal of negotiations. However, the fall, 1976 presidential elections provided the basis for a possible change in U.S. policy. A commission headed by former U.S. ambassador to the OAS, Sal Linowitz, made a series of recommendations for the new administration, among them a proposal that the new U.S. president forcefully seek better U.S.-Cuban relations early in the new term. Candidate Carter embraced the recommendations, though his future transition team, especially National Security Advisor, Zbigniew Brzezinski, was highly skeptical that such a move benefited the United States. Ultimately, Brzezinski acquiesced when he was convinced that U.S. policy toward Cuba was an impediment to better U.S. relations with other countries in the Hemisphere.[15] It is important to note that Brzezinski's acquiescence would prove temporary as he would be a key factor in later retrenchment of the U.S. initiative.

Even before Carter's inauguration, the Secretary of State designate indicated that efforts to improve relations with Cuba would be a priority. At his confirmation hearing on January 10, Cyrus Vance told the senators that better relations with Cuba were possible.[16] Soon after taking his position, Vance formally stated that Cuban troop withdrawal from Angola would not be a precondition for negotiations with Cuba. In another executive action, the U.S. government ceased its regular reconnaissance over flights, which had been in place since 1962.

Immediately after President Carter's inauguration, a group of influential Senators, Congressmen, and journalists visited Cuba. Among them were Democratic Senators Abourezk and Haskell (January 1977), Jonathan Bingham, Chairman of the House Foreign Affairs Committee (February 1977), and the editor and chief writer of *Newsweek* magazine. All of them spoke in favor of lifting the economic embargo against Cuba. Following these visits, Congress debated the issue of monetary expenditures by U.S. citizens in Cuba.[17] In an important step taken between January and March, 1977, the Treasury Department amended the CACR,[18] permitting U.S. citizens traveling to Cuba to pay for their airfares and other expenses during their stay on the island. The purchasing of Cuban products for personal use up to $100 was also authorized, with permission to re-enter the United States with these limited purchases. Academics, researchers, and journalists were also authorized to import publications and other printed materials related to their work without price regulations. Likewise, U.S. enterprises abroad were given authorization to pay for or to reimburse Cuba travel-related expenses of their employees. Also, regulations related to issuing specific licenses for U.S. subsidiaries trading with Cuba were amended, which previously excluded U.S. parent company officers and employees from any negotiation or transaction subject to license petition, specifying that such participation would be reason enough for denying the petition or for canceling a license.

For its part the Cuban government took notice of the U.S. initiatives and proposed through Swiss intermediaries that the two countries meet to discuss maritime boundaries and fishing rights. Such negotiations were essential because of a U.S. decision to establish a 200-mile fishing administration zone. Since the Florida Straits are only 90 miles across, some agreement was needed on that area. As a result, meetings were held between Culver Gleysteen, the U.S. State Department's director of Cuban affairs, and Nestor Garcia, first secretary of the Cuban Mission to the United Nations. Gleysteen had headed the Cuban affairs section since 1975 and had long been convinced that negotiations with Cuba were the best course. With a new policy established from the top, he had the opportunity to implement his long held views.[19] From the U.S. perspective, it would be a step by step process where small agreements might eventually lead to the ending of the embargo. The Cuban government had publicly stated in January that the lifting of the embargo should be a prerequisite for renewed negotiations. The U.S. position was very different, based on the view that a settlement on the issue of U.S. properties nationalized on the island in 1960-61 had to come before a lifting of the embargo was possible. In spite of this possible obstacle, planning for the resumption of negotiations moved forward and the two countries agreed to meet. Cuba did not push its position on the embargo and the United States did not insist on Cuban withdrawal from Angola. Both issues would be essential to future negotiations, but they did not become immediate obstacles to progress.

On March 24, 1977, U.S.-Cuba talks on fishing and other maritime rights began. As a result of such negotiations, the second part of which was held in Havana, on April 27, 1977, an agreement was signed regarding the preliminary maritime boundaries between the United States and Cuba, as well as an agreement on fishing. The latter agreement determined the participation of the Cuban fleet in fishing for abundant species within 200 miles of the U.S. maritime

boundary with prior authorization of the U.S. government. An additional agreement was reached regarding the reciprocal re-fueling of fishing vessels, and by
May 12, 1977, the Treasury Department allowed U.S. tourist agencies to organize trips to Cuba.[20] On April 28, Senator George McGovern introduced an
amendment to the Authorization Bill for the Department of State for 1978 (co-
sponsored by Senator John Sparkman, Chairman of the Senate Foreign Relations
Committee), which called for lifting the trade embargo on food and medicine.
McGovern sponsored this amendment after traveling to Cuba and confirming
that the Cuban government would interpret the partial lifting of the trade embargo as a concrete goodwill measure on behalf of the United States. However, the
Carter administration did not give its definitive support to the legislation since
key State Department officials argued in the summer of 1977 that such a unilateral action by the United States was not warranted at that stage of the negotiations.

Shortly afterward, Senators Stone, Church, and Humphrey, as well as other
senators, raised strong opposition to these measures. In their opinion, a partial
opening of trade with Cuba would negatively affect U.S. sugar producers and
would undermine one of the most important negotiating levers the U.S. Government had for dealing with Cuba. After an extensive debate, an accord was
reached to continue the embargo. Senators Javits and Humphrey designed an
amendment that favored one way commerce to allow U.S. business to sell food,
medicine, and agricultural products to Cuba, but Cuban products could not enter
the U.S. market. Ironically, such legislation previewed policies that would pass
the Congress almost twenty-five years later. On May 10, 1977, the Senate Foreign Relations Committee passed the modified amendment (ten votes against
six). The following day, the Senate passed an additional amendment, proposed
by Senator Javits, that gave the President the power to re-enact the embargo. On
May 12, while the House of Representatives was discussing the 1978 Food Aid
and International Development Bill, Republican Representative John Ashbrook
introduced an amendment entitled: "Prohibition of Assistance to Vietnam and
Cuba,"[21] which cut off aid or commerce with those countries. After passing the
House of Representatives and the Senate, the President signed the amendment
bill, thus becoming public law and effectively ending the efforts to significantly
loosen the embargo. On the same date, the CACR of the Department of Treasury
was revised and the general license allowing travel agencies to assist U.S. travelers in their trips to Cuba, to charter aircraft and vessels to travel to Cuba, and
to facilitate checks, travel checks, and credit cards related to expenses in the
island was approved. [22] However, regular service for national and foreign commercial transportation between both countries was not authorized.

These official contacts led to a series of positive steps on the part of both
governments, one of the most important of which was an agreement reached on
May 30, 1977, to simultaneously open interest sections in the Czechoslovakian
Embassy in Washington and in the Swiss Embassy in Havana to represent both
countries. These interest sections were officially inaugurated on September 1,

1977, and resulted in the first direct diplomatic contacts between both countries since January 3, 1961, when President Eisenhower broke off relations with Cuba. These arrangements have remained in place down to the present day. The interest section arrangement permitted the United States to renew regular formal dialogue with the Cuban government, to monitor more closely developments on the island, and to provide consular services to the tens of thousands of U.S. citizens that were now to be visiting Cuba each year. From the Cuban perspective, the arrangement allowed for a regularization of its relations with its powerful northern neighbor and a presence in Washington, D.C., from which it could directly dialogue with those sections of the U.S. population that favored better relations with the island. Thirty years later these basic diplomatic relations remain in place, largely unchanged.

On June 16, while the Senate was ready to consider the 1978 State Department Authorization Bill, Senator McGovern requested the abrogation of the amendment on one way trade, adducing: "it was useless and needless, and would not help to improve relations with Cuba."[23] Even though Cuba agreed with the partial lifting of the commercial embargo, it always maintained that trade must be equally bilateral and that with a one way trade proposal, the general embargo measures would still be in effect. On November 3, regulations of the Treasury Department's Office of Foreign Assets Control were amended, and as a result, foreign enterprises owned or controlled by U.S. nationals were allowed to resupply Cuban aircraft with fuel and Cuban ships with food and fuel.[24] On December 23, regulations of the Treasury Department's Office of Cuban Foreign Assets Control were amended, and individuals residing in the United States were permitted to send up to $500 quarterly to their close relatives in Cuba and to send additional remittances of $500 at a time for travel related expenses,[25] but funds from frozen accounts were not allowed. This framework for remittances has remained in place until now and today represents an infusion to the Cuban economy that is second only to tourism as an earner of foreign exchange for contemporary Cuba.

As previously noted, there were groups within the United States who were interested in a process of gradual liberalization of policy toward Cuba, while on the other hand, there were groups that opposed the normalization process and considered any gradual approach unfavorable to the interests of the United States. Within the latter group, the most conservative members of Congress from both parties blocked the constructive policy of the Carter administration toward Cuba. The opponents of dialogue promoted Congressional resolutions that established preliminary conditions to be fulfilled by Cuba before the normalization of relations. Those conditions were: appropriate compensation for confiscated assets; liberation of political prisoners in Cuba; withdrawal of Cuban troops from Africa; cooperation in air piracy; safety at Guantánamo Naval Base; and respect for human rights. Actions by U.S. legislators during 1977 demonstrated that significant contradiction and mixed criteria existed regarding U.S.-Cuban policy. Even when pro-normalization positions within Congress were still strong, opposition to the betterment of Cuban-American relations was gaining force. The opponents of normalization of relations within the House of Representatives obstructed the approbation of even the first variant of one way commerce. Consequently, the House decided to continue "the embargo" over trade with Cuba.[26]

On April 1978, the House of Representatives modified a section of the Food Aid and International Development bill, suspending sanctions on aid to countries trading with Cuba. On April 26, the Treasury Department's Office of Foreign Assets Control regulations were amended. These changes permitted limited travel-related business transactions for authorized Cubans visiting the United States, vis-á-vis U.S. travel agents or sponsors of academic or cultural programs. On June 14, the Senate rescinded an amendment that required the United States government to oppose any assistance to Cuba, Cambodia, Laos, and Vietnam. On June 22, while the House of Representatives was discussing a draft resolution for the Foreign Aid Authorization Bill, the House rejected an amendment that included Cuba in the list of countries that could not receive funds directly from the United States.

Cuban Economy Grows

In order to understand the movement in the U.S. Congress toward limited normalization of relations with Cuba, it is necessary to assess what was happening in the Cuban economy and society. During the 1970s, the Cuban economy was growing sheltered from the worst aspects of the rapid rise in oil prices as the result of its position in the CMEA. At the same time, the U.S. economic crisis of 1974-1975 prompted business to seek new markets; therefore, the reestablishment of trade with Cuba was viewed favorably by some in the business community. During the first half of 1977, several American business people visited Cuba. They were interested in evaluating potential trade areas of mutual interest and subsequently signed agreements in anticipation of the re-establishment of commercial relations between both countries. A significant representation of U.S. corporations (Coca-Cola, General Motors, Ford, Caterpillar Tractor, Abbott Laboratories, General Mills, International Harvester, Boeing, Xerox, Pillsbury, Honeywell, Dow Chemical, Control Data, John Deere, First National Bank of Chicago) expressed interest in making contacts with Cuba and voiced concern about the continuation of the commercial embargo.

According to estimates, annual exports to Cuba would have amounted to $390 million, reaching a total import and export volume of $700 million.[27] This, in turn, would have provided a significant number of jobs for the United States. On the other hand, within the United States a considerable number of companies and individuals opposed trade with Cuba unless the Cuban government compensated them for their nationalized properties. Approximately 50 major corporations, including ITT, Borden, Amstar, United Brands, Long Star Industries, Bangar Punta Co., Firestone, Manati Industries, and others formed a powerful lobby known as the Joint Committee on Corporate Claims (JCCC). Under the direction of Robert W. Hutton, they demanded an indemnization of $1.8 billion for their properties nationalized in Cuba, which at an annual interest of 6 percent, would have doubled the original principal amount. Members of the JCCC lobbied Congress against lifting the embargo. It is noteworthy that within the JCCC there were several sugar and citrus producers that feared that their markets would be affected by the re-establishment of relations with Cuba. In contrast with JCCC's position, several other companies (General Mills, Honeywell, Coca-Cola, General Electric, and International Harvester) chose not to make discussions of future trade contingent upon the settlement of property claims. These corporations sent representatives to Cuba to explore future commerce. The role of the business community in pressing for a possible lifting of the embargo on Cuba underscores how Cuban reality perceived within the United States becomes an important part of the bilateral relationship. By the late 1970s, the relative prosperity of the Cuban socialist system was leading some political and economic elites to believe that the Cuban transformation was permanent and therefore the revolutionary regime had to be accommodated to serve long term U.S. interests. However, this perspective did not become the dominant one and U.S.-Cuban relations soon reverted to their previous state.

From 1978 to 1979, during the second half of the Carter administration, U.S.-Cuba relations experienced a dramatic setback. U.S. conservative thinking considered that détente had only contributed to the crisis of weakened U.S. world leadership. They argued that détente had been responsible for the success of the revolutionary New Jewel Movement in Grenada, the Sandinista victory in Nicaragua, the growth of Panamanian nationalism through the signing of the Torrijos-Carter Agreement, and the hostage crisis in Iran. From the conservative point of view, all of these events in a zero-sum game represented the Soviet-Cuban expansion worldwide, especially in Central America and the Caribbean. Wayne Smith, who became head of the U.S. Interests Section in Havana when it reopened in 1977, argues that while President Carter himself and some key advisors such as Cyrus Vance genuinely wanted better relations with Cuba, they did things as early as the summer of 1977 to undermine their own efforts. The previously mentioned lack of administrative support for the lifting of the food and medicine ban was telling. The Cuban and U.S. diplomats responsible for the possible negotiations agreed in principle to a framework for moving forward that proposed simultaneous but separate negotiations over the embargo on the island (Cuba's most important issue) and compensation for seized U.S. properties (the U.S.'s most important issue).[28] The head of Latin American affairs for Latin America, Terrence Todman, approved the approach in September, 1977 but it was never implemented. The White House was focused on gaining support for the Panama Canal treaties, especially from conservative members of the U.S. Senate who did not favor the overtures toward Cuba. Fearing to alienate those forces, the negotiations with Cuba were placed on hold and before the momentum could be regained a series of issues emerged in U.S.-Cuban relations that served to temper the move toward better relations. The U.S. was angered when Cuba continued its insistence that the United Nations pursue active self-determination for Puerto Rico. Cuba has long supported the independence movement in Puerto Rico. Developments in Angola also became an obstacle in mid-1977 when Cuban withdrawals were halted when the MPLA faced new threats from Zaire. However, it would be a November 16, 1977 statement by National Security advisor Brzezinski that would become the most significant problem to advancing a negotiations agenda. In a background briefing to journalists, he stated that a CIA study revealed that there was a significant buildup of Cuban troops in both Ethiopia and Angola and that normalization with Cuba was now "impossible."[29] In reality, there was no change in Cuban support for the governments of Angola and Ethiopia, but the statements from Brzezinski indicated clearly that there were key figures in the National Security Council (NSC), headed by Brzezinski, that had serious reservations about the Cuban initiative and were willing to manipulate intelligence reports in order to further their policy objectives.

The conservatives regarded the MPLA's success in Angola and Cuba's subsequent assistance to Ethiopia as a sign that the U.S. anti-Communist policy in Africa had been a failure, and as unmistakable evidence that the USSR and Cuba availed themselves of the U.S. weakness in foreign policy to advance their interests. The success of revolutionary movements in Ethiopia and Afghanistan, with the support of Cuba and the USSR, the loss of the U.S. ally in the Persian Gulf, the Shah of Iran, and the continuation of tensions with Japan and the European allies made it possible for public opinion and academic circles to give credence to the conservative perception that the foreign policy design of détente had been a total failure. During the 1970s, the U.S. political system's perception about its internal and external weaknesses resulted in the implementation of a political model based on trilateralism. The decade ended with a return to an atmosphere of confrontation between the two superpowers. Thus, the Cold War was reinforced and the liberal model was abandoned.[30] The consequence of this shift in U.S. establishment thinking was that the brief period of thaw in U.S.-Cuban relations, begun in 1975, came to an end.

Notes

1. Federal Register, Section 515.

2. Francisco Lopez Segrera, *De Eisenhower a Reagan* (*From Eisenhower to Reagan Administrations*). (Havana: Editorial de Ciencias Sociales, 1987), 161.

3. For further information, see: Olga Miranda, *Las nacionalizaciones cubanas, las cortes norteamericanas y la enmienda Hickenlooper (Cuban Nationalizations, U.S. Courts and the Hickenlooper Amendment*), (Havana: Biblioteca del Ministerio de Relaciones Exteriores, August, 1971).

4. For further information about aggressions toward Cuba, see: Carlos Batista and Jorge Domínguez, *El costo de las agresiones de Estados Unidos contra Cuba,* 1987.

5. For a more complete discussion of overtures, see Wayne Smith, *The Closest of Enemies* (New York: W.W. Norton, 1987).

6. Smith, *Closest of Enemies*, 88.

7. Graciela Chailloux, 10.

8. Chailloux, 10.

9. Smith, *Closest of Enemies*, 93.

10. Henry Kissinger, quoted in *Toward Improved United States-Cuba Relations*, Report of a Special Study Mission to Cuba, 10-15, February 1977 (Washington, D.C.: U.S. Government Printing Office, 1979).

11. *Export Administration Bulletin,* Number 145, August 29, 1975 (40 CFR 371.9).

12. *Federal Register Bulletin,* Number 196, Vol. 40, October 8, 1975.

13. An Analysis of Licensed Trade with Cuba by Foreign Subsidiaries of U.S. Companies: Special Report, Dept. of Treasury, Washington, D.C., 1992.

14. 40 FR 55314; 15 CFR 385.1 (b) (2).

15. Smith, *Closest of Enemies*, 100.

16. *New York Times*, 11 January 1977, 1.

17. For further information, see: Barry Sklar, *Cuba: Normalization of Relations* (Washington, D.C. Congressional Research Service, 1978).

18. 42 FR 472; Section 5 15.559.

19. Smith, *Closest of Enemies*, 104.

20. Federal Register Number 96, Vol. 42, May 18, 1977.

21. Philip Brenner, *The Limits and Possibilities of Congress,* (New York: Palgrave Macmillan, 1983), 50.

22. 43 FR 19623.

23. Philip Brenner, 37.

24. 43 FR 19852.

25. 43 FR 51762.

26. For further analysis about this period see: Graciela Chailloux, Rosa Lopez and Carlos Batista, *Puede Clinton parecerse a Carter? (Can Clinton be like Carter?)*, (IPS, Havana: February, 1993).

27. *The Potential of US-Cuba Trade*, US-Cuba Bulletin No. 2, (New York, March, 1981).

28. Smith, *Closest of Enemies*, 118.

29. *New York Times*, 17 November 1977, 1.

30. Roberto Gonzalez, "Theory of International Relations," Working Paper, Institute of International Relations, 1983; quoted by Graciela Chailloux, - *Cuba Relations: Conflict or Diferendum?* 34.

Chapter Five

The Renewal Of The Cold War Against Cuba After 1979

By the beginning of the 1980s, Cuba's economy had achieved many of the goals it had proposed, both socially and economically. In social terms, the government was able to assure full employment, a social security system that provided assistance to the entire population, and a free care health system that delivered not only medical treatment, but included a preventative health care maintenance system that was able to eradicate many diseases from the island, such as polio, diphtheria, tetanus, yellow fever, and malaria, which prior to 1959, were rampant among the population.[1] About one third of the population, or 3.5 million people, were enrolled in formal educational programs at various levels, thus creating conditions to empower the labor force with the skills and knowledge necessary to take advantage of new technologies.

In economic terms, the Cuban economy experienced a significant qualitative growth as a result of Cuba's relations with socialist countries, especially with the Soviet Union. This growth was due to the maturation of the industrialization process during the 1970s, particularly in the industrial and sugar sectors. A reflection of this growth was apparent in Cuba's gross national product (GNP), which grew 3.9 percent annually between 1966 and 1970, but in the 1970s, the GNP grew 10 percent per year.[2] In 1972, Cuba became a member of the Council for Mutual Economic Assistance (CMEA) that, virtually, guaranteed the improvement of the Cuban economy through subsidized prices for Cuban exports and soft credits. Machinery, spare parts, and raw materials were supplied at fair prices. Additionally, CMEA provided a stable market for Cuban imports and exports. Cuba's integration into the socialist economic bloc, permitted the development of its productive forces and consolidated socialist relations of production, thus creating the conditions for a more rational productive structure of the Cuban economy.[3] From 1971 to 1975, Cuba experienced a five percent economic growth of its GNP. The construction sector had an exceptional twenty-six percent growth rate. The agricultural sector underwent a sustained growth in all branches, and the labor force had a growth rate of 2.5 percent.[4]

During the entire 1975-85 period, the GNP grew four percent per year,[5] while other underdeveloped countries, with the exception of NICs (Newly Indu-strialized Countries), went through what has been called "the lost decade," with their GNP going back to 1977 levels. Therefore, in the 1980s, the Cuban econ-omy was well ahead of the Latin American economy, although some difficulties appeared that forced the government to implement measures that led to the "process of rectification of errors and negative trends" in 1986.[6]

Table 5.1
Cuba GNP (Current Price) (Thousand pesos)

Year	GNP	Per capita
1981	22,172.5	2,280
1982	23,112.8	2,358
1983	24,336.9	2,459
1984	26,052.7	2,607
1985	26,956.7	2,670
1986	26,515.9	2,600
1987	25,575.9	2,483
1988	26,334.4	2,529
1989	26,652.0	2,533

Sources: *Anuario estadístico de Cuba 1990* (Cuba Statistics Yearbook), Comité Estatal de Estadísticas, Habana,1990.

During the 1980s, Cuba's GNP grew 7.3 percent annually (see Table 5.1.), while industrial production grew 8.8 percent annually. Sugar production grew 12.2 percent, mechanical industry 50 percent, non-sugar agriculture 3.8 percent, citrus production 14 percent, electrical production 4.3 percent, oil production 50 percent, fertilizer production 43 percent and fishery production 4.9 percent.[7]

Total foreign trade exchange grew, 65 percent at current prices, while ex-ports grew 58 percent and imports grew 71 percent. The trade deficit increased 13 percent during this decade (see Table 5.2.). The main products Cuba exported were sugar, which amounted to 73.2 percent of the total; followed by nickel, 9.3 percent; citrus, 2.3 percent; and tobacco, 1.5 percent (see Table 5.3). These four products represented 87.3 percent of the total Cuban exports during the 1980s. By 1990 the total internal investment in the economy, since 1959, was 65,000 million pesos. The industrial sector accounted for 32 percent of this amount. COMECON countries were purchasing 85.4 percent of Cuba's total exports and providing 84 percent of Cuba's total imports.[8] The bottom line of Cuba's eco-nomic developments during the era of CMEA participation in the 1970s and 1980s was that Cuba developed a significantly independent position economi-cally from the capitalist world.

Table 5.2
Cuba Foreign Trade 1981-1988
(Thousands pesos)

Year	Exports	Imports	Balance
1981	4223.8	5114.0	(890.2)
1982	4933.2	5530.6	(597.4)
1983	5534.9	6222.1	(687.2)
1984	5476.5	7227.5	(171.0)
1985	5991.5	8035.0	(203.5)
1986	5321.5	7596.1	(224.6)
1987	5402.1	7583.6	(2181.5)
1988	5518.4	7579.8	(2060.4)

Source: Anuario estadistico de Cuba 1990
(Cuba Statistics Yearbook).

Table 5.3
Cuban Exports by Group of Products Selected Years 1981-1989
(Thousands pesos)

	1981	1983	1985	1987	1989
Total Exports	4223.8	5534.9	5991.5	5400.1	5392.0
Sugar Industry	3339.9	4096.0	4462.8	4012.6	3948.5
Mining Industry	332.6	299.0	307.5	332.2	497.7
Tobacco Industry	55.8	102.9	92.0	90.5	83.6
Fishery Industry	98.2	106.6	119.6	144.3	128.8
Agricultural products	122.7	185.1	203.5	250.9	211.3
Other	274.6	745.3	806.1	571.6	522.1

Source: *Anuario estadistico de Cuba 1990,(Cuba Statistics Yearbook)*
Estadisticas, Havana.

By the late 1980s, prior to the beginning of troubles in the Socialist bloc, there was relatively little incentive on the Cuban side to make any concessions with the United States to gain a change in the embargo. In a 1987 interview with the author, Sanchez-Parodi, the Cuban representative in the United States, stated that he saw little change in Cuba's trade relations, even with the end of the U.S. embargo. At that point, eighty-seven percent of Cuba's trade was with the Soviet bloc on a reasonably favorable basis, so in his view, Cuba had little to gain in a significantly greater economic position vis-á-vis the United States. From the U.S. side, the drive from the business community for an opportunity to do business on the island was muted by the fact that in the 1980s there were few capitalist business opportunities on the island in Cuba's almost fully socialist system.

U.S. Policy in the 80s

Concerning U.S. policy toward Cuba, 1980 Presidential candidate, Ronald Reagan, stated repeatedly that the United States should subject the island to a military blockade as a counter measure against the Soviet invasion of Afghanistan. Likewise, the Republican Party platform noted that "Carter remained indifferent while Cuba trains, arms, and aggressively supports the forces of the opposition and revolution."[9] In January 1981, the new administration assumed an aggressive policy position toward Cuba, derived from the Santa Fe Report and prepared in 1980 by the Santa Fe Committee, a group of Republican analysts. Its author stated that Cuba's support to revolutionary movements in Nicaragua, El Salvador, and Guatemala had generated political instability that would allow the USSR to expand its influence in the Western Hemisphere. This was an intolerable situation for the United States, and thus gave them the need to "go to the source," that is, to take measures against Cuba in its capacity as a USSR satellite."[10]

The following instances were examples of the Reagan administration's policy toward Cuba

- On January 30, 1981, Alexander Haig, Secretary of State, stated: "It is clear that Cubans are seriously involved in El Salvador, and we are finding more and more evidence of their involvement in Nicaragua."[11]

The Cubans had viewed the fluid developments in the Central American/Caribbean region as a unique opportunity to carry out their vision of revolutionary internationalism. In Central America, revolution was clearly on the agenda in the late 1970s. Long standing military dictatorships in Guatemala, El Salvador, and Nicaragua were under serious challenge from revolutionary movements by 1978-1979. The Cubans had long standing relations with the Sandinista National Liberation Movement (FSLN) going back to its founding in 1961. When the revolutionary struggle turned against the Sandinistas in the late 1960s many of its leaders gained exile in Cuba. When there was a rebirth of the revolutionary opportunities in the mid 1970s, the Cubans provided valuable support to the FSLN, but the primary financial and logistical support prior to the FSLN triumph in July 1979 came from anti-Somoza forces throughout the region, especially in Costa Rica and Venezuela. The main Cuban contribution was an agreement hammered out with Castro's mediation in March, 1979 by the contentious factions of the FSLN. This unity was a springboard to the success of the FSLN's final offensive. Once in power, the Cuban reluctance to be front and center as a supporter of the FSLN ended, and Cuba airlifted hundreds of doctors, teachers, military advisors, and technicians to help the Nicaraguans in their revolutionary plans, many of which were modeled on the Cuban experience.

Earlier in 1979, a revolutionary black nationalist organization, the New Jewel Movement, seized power in Grenada and began to move in a socialist direction. New Jewel leader Maurice Bishop sought and received Cuban assistance in plans to upgrade its airport to increase its tourism earnings. The result of these two revolutionary triumphs was an especially joyful July 26, 1979 event in Havana where Fidel stood alongside Bishop and Sandinista leader, Tomas Borge. Coupled with its successes in Africa, Cuba was chosen in 1979 to lead the Non-Aligned Movement for three years. Cuba was no longer supporting revolutionary movements in South America, but they saw the opportunity to promote revolutionary movements in Central America.

El Salvador became the focus of Cuba and progressive movements throughout the hemisphere. Revolutionary movements had steadily gained momentum in the years after the military voided the election victory of Christian Democrat Jose Napoleon Duarte in 1972. By the time of Sandinista triumph in 1979, the revolutionary forces were seriously contending for state power. A progressive military coup in September, 1979 succeeded temporarily in coopting some of the revolutionary forces, but the push for revolution began anew in March, 1980 following the assassination of Archbishop Oscar Romero. During the remainder of that year, the revolutionary forces pressed their advantage in the rural areas of the country, united under the banner of the Farabundo Marti National Liberation Front (FMLN). The Cubans and the Nicaraguans, sensing the possibility of another revolutionary breakthrough on the heels the Sandinista and New Jewel victories, provided material aid to the FMLN. On the eve of President Reagan's January, 1981 inauguration, the FMLN launched a military offensive intending to make a revolutionary Salvadoran regime a reality for the new administration. However, buoyed by aid from the outgoing Carter administration, the Salvadoran government survived and dealt the rebels a serious military defeat.

- On November 5, 1981, Alexander Haig admitted to having requested the Defense Department consider measures against Cuba, among them: naval exercises in Cuban territorial waters, a naval blockade, or stronger actions aimed at cutting the arms supply to El Salvador.

The timing of Secretary Haig's attack on Cuba was interesting because by the end of 1981, the FSLN, sensing that the FMLN was not going to triumph in the near term and that their relationship with the United States was growing especially dangerous, dramatically reduced their arms shipments. Given the close relationship between Cuba and Nicaragua it is likely that the more cautious Sandinista policy had the support of the Cuban government. It was clear that Secretary Haig saw the backing off from the FMLN by Cuba and Nicaragua as evidence that both were vulnerable and acting from a position of weakness. These November actions were the result of recommendations from an interagen-

cy task force that operated from the assumption that the Cuban government
could be intimidated into following U.S. policy directives.

- On August 5, 1983 the U.S. Congress passed the Caribbean Basin Initiative
  Act, which prohibited setting aside federal resources to promote commerce
  with Cuba.
- The United States once again pressured Latin American countries to break
  relations with Cuba. Panama denounced such pressures.
- The U.S. ambassador to the UN in Geneva declared that his country would
  boycott the VI United Nations Conference on Trade and Development
  (UNCTAD), if the summit were held in Havana.
- The U.S. government opposed Cuban participation in the North-South Dialogue Summit to be held in Cancun, Mexico and announced that the CIA
  would re-consider the use of Cuban-American counter-revolutionary troops
  in punitive actions against Cuba.
- The United States renewed its aerial recognizance over Cuban territory
  using SR-71 aircraft.
- In 1982, the United States sharply limited the travel of U.S. citizens to the
  island, ending the possibility for U.S. tourists to visit the island as they had
  done since 1977.

Travel was restricted to Cuban-Americans visiting close relatives, academics,
journalists, diplomats, and U.S. citizens traveling on behalf of non-U.S. organizations like the World Council of Churches. U.S. citizens challenged the travel
restrictions in court, but in 1984, on a 5-4 vote, the Reagan rules were judged to
be constitutional. These restrictive rules have remained the basis for limited U.S.
citizen travel to the island down to the present.

The measures taken in the first eighteen months of the Reagan administration clearly signaled that the U.S. government no longer saw achieving normalized relations with Cuba to be in U.S. interests. Not surprisingly, the head of the
U.S. mission in Havana, Wayne Smith, resigned in protest. The renewed overt
hostility to Cuba represented a shift in worldview that came to the forefront in
the Reagan era. Believing that the U.S. had grown overly timid in the wake of
the Vietnam War, the new administration sought to openly challenge what it
called the Vietnam Syndrome. In addition to directly challenging the Soviet
Union through significant new arms spending, the Reagan administration developed what became known as the Reagan Doctrine, a doctrine that sought to roll
back the gains of Soviet-backed third world revolutions. The main battlegrounds
of these efforts were Nicaragua, Cambodia, Afghanistan, and Angola, where the
U.S. supported active anti-Communist rebels, but Cuba was also in the mix of
this policy, viewed as a country where the hold of the Communist Party was not
accepted as permanent.

Throughout 1982 and 1983, the U.S. Government maintained its threat and
pressure campaign against Cuba, based on alleged Cuban terrorist activities in
Africa, Cuban support to subversion in Central America, and Cuba's participation in an international coalition lead by the Soviet Union. In addition, Cuban

officials were accused of trafficking drugs in the Caribbean that were to be sent to the United States. On September 23, 1983, the U.S. Government announced the creation of Radio Marti, aimed at broadcasting information to Cuba regarding "what is really happening in the Communist island."[12]

Although ideological warfare was the principal instrument the United States used against Cuba during the Reagan administration, vis-á-vis Radio Marti, economic and military instruments were also used. During the U.S. invasion of Grenada in October 1983, there were 784 Cuban civilian workers building an airport in Grenada and they were used as a pretext for the U.S. intervention and overthrow of the New Jewel government. Also, during 1983 and 1984, the United States continued carrying out naval and air exercises aimed to provoke a conflict between the two countries near Cuban jurisdictional waters. Aerial recognizance flights over Cuban territory continued as a normal procedure for U.S. intelligence operations. In the economic field, the Reagan administration reinforced the U.S. travel ban to Cuba, prohibited Cubana Airlines to use air paths over U.S. territory, and reinforced the prohibition of any ship transporting Cuba merchandise or entering Cuban ports to dock in any U.S. port. Another economic measure lowered the quarterly remittances Cuban-American could send to relatives in Cuba to $500.

The Reagan policy in Central America and Cuba was based on the aforementioned Santa Fe Report and the Caribbean Basin Initiative (CBI). These two documents were included in the National Bipartisan Commission on Central America. The Commission, under the direction of Henry Kissinger, was responsible for formulating a bipartisan consensus on U.S. policy toward Central America, which argued that Cuba and Nicaragua, under the direction of the Soviet Union, represented a threat to U.S. national security. The report emphasized Cuba's military capacity as the second most powerful military power in Latin America and that the Cuban-Soviet axis supported Latin American guerrillas. On February 17, 1984, Reagan sent the Initiative for Development, Peace, and Democracy in Central America bill to Congress as part of the implementation of the Kissinger Commission's proposals. He asked for $8 billion over the next 5 years.[13]

After several rounds of negotiations held between July and December, 1984, immigration agreements between Cuba and the United States were finally signed on December 14 with the purpose of normalizing the immigration procedures between both countries. The migratory agreements between Cuba and the United States had become a priority of U.S. foreign policy after the 1980 mass migration known as the "Mariel Exodus," as a result of which more than 135,000 Cubans left Cuba for the United States.

Both parties signed the following agreements:

- The United States agreed to an immigration quota of up to 20,000 immigrants each year. Additionally, the United States would continue issuing visas to Cuban residents (spouses, parents, and unmarried minor children of a legal permanent resident or citizen of the United States). The United States would issue these visas in addition to the original quota.

- In 1985, the United States would issue immigrant visas to 30,000 political refugees (ex-prisoners) and their immediate families.
- Cuba would accept the repatriation of 2,746 people from the Mariel Exodus found ineligible to reside in the United States.[14]

The signing of the immigration agreements by both countries took place on the eve of global negotiations on strategic matters between the United States and the USSR. There were talks about the Angolan conflict in which Cuba also took part, talks held in Central America led by the Contadora Group, talks between the United States and Nicaragua, and talks between the FMLN rebels and the Duarte Government in El Salvador. The successful negotiation of the migratory agreements in a time of intense hostility toward Cuba by the U.S. government followed a long-standing pattern of U.S.-Cuban relations where events on the ground in Cuba virtually demanded U.S. attention. The Cuban government realized that if it allowed its citizens to migrate to the United States without restriction, enough of them would choose that option and cause problems for U.S. authorities in Florida. The "Mariel Exodus" had demonstrated that reality. As a consequence, much like with the agreement on air piracy years earlier, it was in U.S. national interests to normalize immigration between the two countries. Such an agreement was also in Cuba's interest because it provided an orderly way for Cubans who were discontented with their lives on the island to leave and therefore potential future political dissidents.

Notes

1. José Luis Rodriguez and George Carriazo, *Erradicación de la pobreza en Cuba* (Eradicating Poverty in Cuba), (Havana: Editorial de Ciencias Sociales, 1987), 33.

2. Rodríguez and Carriazo, 68, 93 and 134.

3. Fidel Castro Ruz, *Informe central: Primer Congreso del Partido Comunista de Cuba (Report to the First Congress of Cuba's Communist Party)*, (Havana: Editora Politica, 1975), 75.

4. Castro Ruz, 84.

5. Gerardo Trueba, "Principales características de la economía cubana: panorama histórico y situación actual (Main characteristics of Cuban Economy: Historical Overview and Current Issues)," *Cuba en transición* (Dossier No 3, 1992), 38.

6. For more Information, see: Fidel Castro Ruz, Speech at 25th Anniversary of Playa Giron Victory, Granma newspaper, April 20, 1986, 1, 3, 4 and 5.

7. Gerardo Trueba, "Principales características de la economía cubana: panorama histórico y situación actual," 56.

8. José Luis Rodriguez and George Carriazo Moreno, *Erradicación de la pobreza en Cuba*, 98 and *Informe central al III con greso del PCC (Main Report*

to 11th Congress of Cuba's Communist Party), Havana: Editora Politica, 1987, 81-87.

9. 1980 Electoral Platform, Grand Old Party, Republican National Convention, USIA, News Service, August 1980.

10. For further information, see: Lynn Francis Boucher, Roger W. Fontaine, David C. Jordan and Gordon Sumner, *The Santa Fe Report: A New Inter-American Policy for the Eighties*, prepared by the Committee of Santa Fe, New Mexico: for the Council for Inter-American Security, Inc. (CIS), Washington, D.C., 1980.

11. Quoted in Francisco Lopez Segrera, *De Eisenhower a Reagan (From Eisenhower to Reagan Administrations)*, (Havana: Editorial de Ciencias Sociales, 1987), 172.

12. Ronald Reagan announcement creates Radio Marti, USIA News Information, U.S. Interests Section, Havana: Sept. 27, 1983.

13. After one year of negotiations, Congress passed an Act authorizing only 800 million USD for Central America.

14. For further information, see: Rafael Hernhndez, "La politica de los Estados Unidos hacia, Cuba y las cuestion de la migración," (US-Cuba Agreement), Cuadernos de nuestra America, Vol. 2, No,8, January-March, 1985, Habana., *El costo de las agresiones de Estados Unidos contra Cuba (The Cost of Aggressions against Cuba)*, Centro de Estudios sobre Estados Unidos, Universidad de La Habana (CESEU-UH,) Working Paper, July, 1987.

Chapter Six

U.S.-Cuban Relations After The Collapse Of The USSR (1989-1999)

A great deal of speculation preceded George H.W. Bush's inauguration regarding his future policy toward Cuba. There was some indication that it would be more pragmatic and therefore, less ideological than that of his predecessor. But, a few days after his inauguration, the Baker Memorandum was leaked to the press. The memorandum stated that U.S. policy toward Cuba would remain the same. Such a policy was not surprising given that Bush had served as Reagan's vice-president for eight years and there had also been no significant changes on the Cuban side. As 1989 began, Cuba's economy remained firmly in the socialist camp, and in spite of the ferment surrounding Mikail Gorbachev's reform programs in the Soviet Union, there were few people in Havana or Washington who would have predicted the dramatic events that would unfold in Eastern Europe in the fall of 1989. As a result, the U.S. embargo against Cuba remained firmly in place, and on the Cuban side, a series of adjustments had been made as Gorbachev hinted at changes in the Soviets' trading relations. Otherwise, the Cubans were confident that their position within the socialist camp would continue to protect them. During the 1988-89 period CMEA provided a market for eight-five percent of its exports and approximately seventy-five percent of its imports. In many ways Cuba's situation had been largely unchanged since the early 1970s when it accepted its position within the socialist economic bloc. Cuba's leaders had expressed some concerns about the effects of Gorbachev's reforms on Cuba, but no one predicted the rapidity with which events would move.

In the summer of 1989, Mikail Gorbachev renounced the Breshnev Doctrine that had committed the Soviet Union to come to the rescue of Communist Party regimes in Eastern Europe as they had done in Hungary in 1956. Soon after, the Eastern Europeans began uprisings across the region in the fall of 1989 that one by one brought political revolution from Poland to Romania. The Berlin Wall was torn down and the process of reunification began in Germany. The economic effect on Cuba was immediate as all of the newly non-Communist governments in Eastern Europe walked away from CMEA and unilaterally abrogated their trade deals with Cuba. Overnight, Cuba underwent a soap shortage because the island had received all of the raw material to make soap from East Germany. Most of Cuba's buses came from Hungary and immediately no spare parts were available. Most of the buses would be gone from Cuba's streets within four years. However, as surprising as the collapse of CMEA was, there was not initial panic in Havana. Few analysts in the East or the West anticipated that the events in Eastern Europe would also engulf the Soviet Union. Cuba was reassured by Soviet leaders that the basic structure of Cuba's socialist trade would remain in place, albeit almost exclusively with the USSR. Most importantly, the favorable exchange of Soviet oil for Cuban sugar would remain intact. However, even the loss of Eastern Europe was significant. In 1989, Cuba's foreign trade with Eastern Europe (not including the USSR) was 1.952 billion pesos in 1989, 1.162.5 billion pesos in 1990, and only 235.9 million pesos in 1991. After 1991, foreign trade with these countries went almost to zero (see Table 6.2).

In spite of Soviet assurances, and with Eastern Europe largely going away as a trading partner, 1990 and the first half of 1991 were the beginning of the deep Cuban economic crisis. Then, in August 1991, the surprising events surrounding the attempted coup against Mikail Gorbachev brought the Soviet Union to its end. The result of these events were immediate, and Cuban trade with the USSR for the full year of 1991 was cut nearly in half, from imports in 1990 of $5.1 billion to $2.7 billion in 1991 and a cut in exports from $3.6 billion to $1.8 billion. In 1990, Cuba received more than seven-hundred different kinds of products from the USSR, including thirty-five percent of Cuba's industrial machinery needs, ninety-five percent of its fuel, eighty percent of its leather, and seventy percent of its raw materials to domestically produce clothing. After the demise of the Soviet Union, Cuba's trade with Russia was basically a barter system of sugar for oil as illustrated in Table 6.5. The amount of oil that Cuba received for its sugar was set at the world price for both commodities, thus reducing Cuba's oil supplies by more than sixty percent. The lack of oil and industrial inputs had a devastating impact on Cuba's economy. The country's GNP dropped 36.4 percent between 1990 and 1993 as industrial operations were sharply curtailed, and agricultural output was slowed by the lack of fuel for tractors. Almost overnight, the country's mass transit system came to a halt and 750,000 bicycles were imported from China to provide alternative transportation. Oxen were imported to replace many of the tractors.

U.S. Response to Cuba's Troubles

Cuba's deep economic crisis resulted in a shift in U.S. policy toward the island with the intent of bringing down the revolutionary government. Such a goal had always been the purpose of U.S. policy since the early months of 1959, but now policymakers saw a real opportunity as a result of the events in Eastern Europe and the fall of the revolutionary Sandinistas in Nicaragua in 1990.

As a result, the Bush administration and certain forces in the U.S. Congress gave more emphasis to embargo measures. What would eventually emerge in

twelve European countries, and in Australia and Japan. Because of the opposition to the bill among these allies who would be affected, the Bush administration initially opposed the legislation. As the Deputy Assistant Secretary of State
for Interamerican Affairs said in a testimony before the House Foreign Affairs
Committee, "The proposed legislation would remove the focus on Cuba and
shift the burden to the United States." He added, "our attempt would be rejected
. . . few nations want to impose an embargo against Cuba."[4] The U.S. business
community also opposed the legislation as being a restraint on free trade. However, 1992 was an election year and George Bush changed his position, apparently out of fear of losing Cuban American votes in Florida to William Clinton.
The Act was signed by Bush on October 26, 1992 after William Clinton attended a political fundraiser in Little Havana in Miami, where he came out in
favor of the Torricelli legislation. The leader of the Cuban-American National
Foundation (CANF), Jorge Mas Canosa maneuvered skillfully to play off the
two candidates against each other to achieve the passage of the bill. However,
not too much power should be ascribed to the Cuban American community in
Florida. The Torricelli legislation would never have been made law had there
not been strong thinking at the highest levels in Washington that renewed economic pressure on a weakened Cuba could have the desired effect of bringing
down the revolutionary government, a long standing goal of U.S. foreign policy.

Clinton Administration

George Bush lost the 1992 election, and for the first time in twelve years there
was a Democrat in the White House. President William Clinton expressed his
intentions to put into practice the best of the legacy of his Democratic predecessor, James Carter.[5] Many of Clinton's Cabinet members had served in the Carter
administration. The presence of new cabinet members who had formed part of
Carter's Cabinet caused some speculation that there would be a Cuban policy
similar to that of Carter. However, a change in the policy toward Cuba would
have implied an abandonment of the former well-entrenched policy. Change was
also not likely in 1993 because at that time, policy makers in Washington believed that the deep economic crisis in Cuba might yet bring down the revolutionary government. The strategic goal of U.S. policy toward Cuba had remained the same for three decades: to regain its control over Cuba.
    Clinton's position on Cuba came to be known as the "two-track" policy. On
the one hand was the continuation of the economic embargo, strengthened by
the addition of the Torricelli legislation and unrelenting political and ideological
attack on the Cuban system. Therefore, the first track of Clinton's Cuba policy
was a full-scale continuation of Washington's policies begun during the Eisenhower administration. The first track would later be amplified by the addition of
the Helms-Burton legislation in 1996. However, the Clinton administration did
not limit its policies to the tightening of the embargo; it also pursued additional

1992 as the Cuba Democracy Act (Torricelli Bill) began in 1990 as the Cc
Mack Amendments I, II, and III, which sought to suppress licensing for ‹
mercial relations between Cuba and subsidiaries of U.S. companies base
third countries. By 1990, this third country activity had become a major tr
totaling as much as $750 million and providing U.S. companies with an im]
tant opportunity to participate in Cuba's commerce with the capitalist wc
Eventually, the Mack Amendments materialized as the Cuban Democracy
of 1992,[1] proposed by Robert Torricelli (D-New Jersey), which widened
spectrum of pressures on Cuba with the manifest goal of speeding up the det‹
oration of the Cuban economy, already depressed by the collapse of the forn
socialist countries. The authors recognized that Cuba would be forced to s‹
new markets in the capitalist world and that this legislation was designed
reduce their opportunity to do so. From the beginning of the proposals in 199
some of the closest U.S. allies—Canada, the United Kingdom, Belgium, and t
European Community—objected to the legislation because it was aimed at cc
porations chartered in their countries and they were not in support of the U.
embargo against Cuba.[2]

According to its main advocate Robert Toricelli: "In the course of this ver
year the bill would have a definitive impact on Fidel Castro's downfall an
would promote democracy and liberty in Cuba."[3] The law was designed to pu
intense pressure on Havana and to establish a variety of links between Washing
ton and Cuba after what was hoped to be Fidel Castro's overthrow.

The five basic points of the *Cuban Democracy Act* were:

1. It would be necessary for the President to request the cooperation of othei
countries on the embargo issue, subsequently all economic support and benefits would be denied to any nation dealing with Castro's government.

2. The President would ease the existing restrictions to Cuba by allowing the
exportation of medicine.

3. The President would permit improvements in telephone communications
between the two countries.

4. The President would increase the economic pressures over "Castro" by
prohibiting subsidiaries of U.S. companies to conduct trade with Cuba. U.S.
companies would be prohibited from declaring tax deduction for expenses
derived from commercial operations with Cuba. The law would prohibit
vessels from entering U.S. ports, vessels that have previously entered Cuba
to engage trade with the United States. It would limit the amount of money
to finance trips of Cubans to the United States.

5. It would maintain economic pressure through the embargo administered by
the U.S. Treasury Department's Office of Foreign Assets Control.

Also, the Act stated that the President would promote a democratic transition on the island by guaranteeing food and medical supplies to a transitional
government, and normal diplomatic relations would be restored upon the establishment of democracy in Cuba. The Torricelli Act made these regulations ap-
plicable outside U.S. borders, that is, in fourteen Latin American countries, in

programs that came to be known as the "second track." The "second track" followed naturally from the logic of the Torricelli legislation, which details the process by which the United States will support a "democratic transition" in Cuba. The concept of support to a "democratic transition" in Cuba is now at the center of U.S. policy toward Cuba, beginning with Torricelli and then continuing with the Helms-Burton legislation and more recently in the 2004 Powell Commission report.

The target of the "second track" was the reconstitution of Cuba's civil society, the pro-capitalist social life, and organizations that had disappeared during the long years of rule by the revolutionary government. Washington wanted to rebuild it anew and in the process create an alternative political force to Fidel Castro and the Cuban Communist Party. Robert Torricelli argued that the purpose of the Cuba Democracy Act was "to wreak havoc" in Cuba and to spur the creation of anti-government organizations. The Clinton administration came to the conclusion that if there were not to be pure chaos on the island as the result of the tightened embargo, it had to engage in increased humanitarian aid that would also strengthen anti-government forces on the island. The administration also theorized that more direct contact between the Cuban people and U.S. citizens would infuse more pro-capitalist and pro-democracy ideas to the island creating more Cuban citizens who would be willing to support movements to remove the revolutionary government from power.

To pursue the use of humanitarian aid to undermine the Cuban government, the administration amended the rules on travel and doing business with the island to allow Catholic Charities and other mainstream humanitarian aid organizations to provide assistance to the island. By doing so, the Clinton administration was seeking to bolster the political position of the Roman Catholic Church on the island, one of the few institutions operating with some independence of the Cuban government. The Cuban government was aware of the U.S. intentions and ultimately placed limits on the work of such U.S.-based charities, but it was also maneuvering with the Vatican to gain a papal visit to the island, which came in January 1998. These humanitarian aid programs have continued in a limited way but with little relative impact on the island. Ironically, one of the most important humanitarian aid efforts is mounted each year by Pastors for Peace, a New York-based organization that stands opposed to the U.S. embargo and is in general sympathy to the Cuban system. While never seeking official sanction from the U.S. government for its work, the group has generally been permitted to carry out its activities since they fall within the guidelines of humanitarian aid permissible under U.S. law. In the last two years U.S. citizens traveling with the caravan have received threatening letters from the U.S. Treasury Department but so far no one has been prosecuted for traveling to the island with humanitarian aid.

In 1995, the Clinton administration made a subtle but important change in the Treasury Department rules for legal travel to Cuba by expanding the category of permissible research activities in Cuba to include undergraduate and high school students. Prior to 1995, only graduate students and faculty could apply for licenses to travel to Cuba for research purposes. Under the new rule, undergraduate students could go to Cuba as long as they were enrolled in a formal course of study that included travel to the island. Almost immediately, scores of U.S. universities and some high schools developed such courses and by the beginning of the second Bush administration in 2001, thousands of U.S. students were traveling annually to the island for courses ranging from two weeks to a semester. By 1999, new rules were developed that allowed U.S. universities to gain general licenses for a two-year period to conduct a variety of research and study programs on the island. The U.S. government saw these students as ambassadors for capitalist and democratic ideas. By 2004, hundreds of U.S. universities had such licenses and were sending thousands of students to Cuba each on programs ranging from two weeks to an entire school year.

Simultaneous to the growth of the formal educational programs, another category of travel was created as part of "track two" that proved even larger. Under the rubric of "people to people" travel, many U.S. institutions, including college and university programs of lifelong learning, began organizing trips to Cuba that were, in reality, open to just about any U.S. citizen who had the time and money to make the trip. Organizations such as Global Exchange in San Francisco and the Center for Cuban Studies in New York expanded their previously targeted educational trips to include most any U.S. citizen who was interested to visit the island. Social justice organizations such as Witness for Peace, Madre, and the Women's International League for Peace and Freedom received licenses from the U.S. Office of Foreign Assets Control and began to organize short term trips to the island. By 2003, close to 40,000 people were traveling to the island under this rubric.

However, for the renewed U.S. influence on the island to have any practical effect on the politics of the island, it was necessary for the U.S. government to identify pro-U.S. political forces on the island, to work with them, and to strengthen them to be in a position where they could assume power in a post-communist political order back under the control of the United States. As a result, the U.S. government began a process of funding political groups on the island using funds from the United States Agency for International Development (USAID). This program began under Clinton and expanded to a $26 million-a-year program under the Bush administration.

Helms-Burton

As Cuba's economic situation continued to worsen in 1993 and well into 1994, political forces in Washington continued to develop plans to step up the pressure on Cuba even more. Since at that time Cuba was moving to reintegrate itself into the world's market economy and especially gain significant foreign direct investment into its tourist sector, the policymakers were looking for ways to thwart Cuba's efforts. Such a strategy was crucial because if Cuba could find a way through its economic crisis, then the revolutionary government would be strengthened and therefore not subject to easy removal. The bill would be motivated by the $1.5 billion in international investment that came to the island in 1994, and later by the $2.3 billion in 1995.

On March 12, 1996, President Clinton signed the Cuban Liberty and Democratic Solidarity Act of 1996 into law, better known as the *Helms-Burton Act* (named on behalf of its main sponsors, Republican-Senator Jesse Helms from North Carolina and Republican-Representative Dan Burton from Indiana). This act strengthened the U.S. economic blockade against Cuba, using strong international mechanisms of pressure against third countries having economic relations with Cuba, and closing at least temporarily the possibility of U.S. businesses dealing with the island. Helms-Burton was consistent with U.S. perceptions, beginning in 1991, (after the demise of Soviet Union) and coinciding with the difficult economic crisis that Cuba was submerged into, known as "the special period in peace time."[6] From the U.S. Congress' point of view, the Cuban internal situation operated in favor of strengthening the traditional U.S. hostile policy toward Havana in the hopes of bringing an end to the revolutionary government.

The Cuban Liberty and Democratic Solidarity Act of 1996 was actually a compilation of several resolutions proposed in the House of Representatives, which were:

- HR-611 entitled the "Cuban Free and Independent Assistance Act"
- HR-81 . . . the opposition of Cuban membership into international financial institutions.
- HR-82 . . . the denial of U.S. visas to aliens, involved in business with Cuba and using U.S. claimed properties.
- HR-83 . . . withholding U.S. payments to any international organization that provided assistance to Cuba, Iraq, Iran and Libya.
- HR-84 . . . forbidding any country that imported Cuban sugar to export sugar into the United States.
- H. Conc. Res. 24 . . . asking for an international embargo against Cuba before the United Nations.

Republican-Representative Lincoln Diaz-Balart[7] from Florida sponsored all of these resolutions.

To fully comprehend the current dynamics of the U.S.-Cuban conflict, it was necessary to understand the Cuban Liberty and Democratic Solidarity Act of 1996 and its implications since most of the former and near term U.S. policies toward Cuba were concentrated within it. This act contains an introduction and four chapters (or titles). The introduction explains U.S. congressional perceptions about the Cuban Government, the goals of the act, and includes definitions of terms, such as property, confiscation, and traffic, in a broadened context that negates internationally defined principles. A prime example is the definition of trafficking. A person "traffics" in confiscated property if that person knowingly and intentionally sells, transfers, distributes, dispenses, brokers, manages, or otherwise disposes of confiscated property, or purchases, leases, receives, possesses, obtains control of, manages, uses, or otherwise acquires or holds an interest in confiscated property; engages in a commercial activity using or otherwise benefiting from confiscated property, or causes, directs, participates in, or profits from, trafficking by another person, or otherwise engages in trafficking through another person.[8]

Title I, entitled: "Strengthening International Sanctions against the Castro Government," proposed a series of measures directed to internationalize U.S. economic, commercial, and financial sanctions against Cuba, such as:

1. Internationalization of U.S. economic sanctions toward Cuba through the UN Security Council by imposing an obligatory international embargo of Cuba.[9]

This proposal, presented in H. Conc. Resolution No.24 by Lincoln Diaz-Balart, ignored a preponderance of the international community's opinion against the blockade. Cuba has presented resolutions condemning the US blockade before the UN General Assembly since 1991. In 1995, the resolution had received the support of 157 nations with seventeen abstentions. Only the United States and Israel opposed.

2. Urging the US Executive Branch to request third countries to restructure their trade and financial relations with Cuba.[10]

The strong extra-territorial character of this section was aimed at cutting the economic links of ninety-five countries with Cuba by imposing an international cease and desist order on foreign investment by companies in Cuba. Those countries accepting these rules would, in effect, be forfeiting their sovereignty. This was precisely why the Helms-Burton represented a test case.

As referenced in Chapter Two, Secretary of State Dean Rusk traveled throughout Latin American and Western European countries in 1962 to try to convince them to terminate their economic and diplomatic relations with Cuba. Following the approval of the Torricelli Act, the U.S. government had sent letters to those countries having economic relations with Havana to advise them of the difficulties they could face with the United States in the event of continued business relations with Cuba. The Cuban-American National Foundation (CANF) also sent letters, especially to Latin American and Caribbean countries, to discourage their relations with Cuba.

3. Strengthening the Cuban Assets Control Regulations and imposing fines and jail penalties for those persons violating the Trading with the Enemy Act of 1997 and giving the Treasury Department the right to issue or deny specific licenses to travel to Cuba, to impose fines up to $50,000, and to confiscate the assets involved in any violation of the CAC Regulations.[11]

4. Codifying the "commercial embargo" (as it had been up to March 1, 1996) in order to consolidate and include all Presidential Proclamations, Executives Orders, and departmental resolutions. In doing so, Congress took away any prerogatives the Executive Branch had with regard to U.S. policy toward Cuba.

5. Prohibiting any U.S. citizen or agency to issue credits, bonds, or any direct

or indirect funding of a foreign person or company involved in "trafficking" U.S. property confiscated by the Cuban government.[12]

As noted in Chapter Four, the Cuban Assets Control Regulations (CACR) were modified in 1975 to allow U.S. subsidiaries based in third countries to trade with Cuba. The Cuban Democracy Act of 1992 (Torricelli Act) ended these authorizations and reinstated the more stringent CACR regulations established in 1963. Under Helms-Burton, this indirect trade prohibition was enforced.

In many ways Helms-Burton took for granted the failure of the Torricelli Act because the primitive measures included in the latter were too weak to overthrow socialism in Cuba. Section 103 (a) was additionally designed to impede the development of Cuba's new economic relations, especially related with investment and joint ventures. During the years before 1996, Cuba was forging new economic and trade relations with non-traditional partners and, by the end of 1998, had more than 340 joint ventures with foreign capital that had supplied more than $2.5 billion to the Cuban economy. Those joint ventures, linked with the re-adaptation of the Cuban economy, had allowed the GDP to grow more than eleven percent since 1994.

Section 103 contained measures primarily aimed at threatening Canada and Mexico. These two countries were among Cuba's most important trading partners, from which significant amounts of financial resources were flowing to the island. However, Canada and Mexico represent the first and third largest trade partners of the United States. As a result of this close economic relationship, the United States used its economic clout to actively discourage Canadian and Mexican businesses from investing in Cuba. A noteworthy example of this extraterritorial influence was evidenced in the Mexican cement corporation (CEMEX)'s, abandonment of a profitable joint venture with Cuba. Faced with significant economic losses, CEMEX removed itself from Cuba. In this case, CEMEX, the fourth largest cement corporation in the world, was producing and exporting cement from Mexico. Washington prohibited US businesses, which represent CEMEX's most important customers, from importing any CEMEX product into the United States as long as CEMEX was involved in a joint venture in Cuba. Taking into account that Cuba needed a large amount of investment to continue its present economic improvement, and that current foreign investment represents only seven percent of the total economy, Helms-Burton was intended to undermine future foreign investments.

6. Instructing U.S. delegates to oppose Cuban membership in international financial organizations such as the World Bank, the International Monetary Fund, the International Financial Corporation, the Inter-American Development Bank, etc. should these institutions provide Cuba any financial support, the United States would reduce an equal amount from its funding from that organization.[13]

This was not a new measure. U.S. opposition to Cuban membership in international financial institutions has been a part of the U.S. policy since 1963.

What changed is that, in past years, the United States was capable of imposing such a policy. However, considering the current global political climate and the possibility of Cuba gaining membership in some of these organizations, the United States relies on the weight of withholding its funding quota to oppose Cuba's entrance.

7. Instructing the U.S. Permanent Representative before the Organization of American States to oppose Cuba's reentrance until the island holds free and democratic elections.[14]

Again, this was not a new policy as Cuba has been suspended from the OAS for more than forty years, but this restatement was necessary because by the 1990s, Cuba was actively participating in other regional forums, such as the Ibero-American Summits and the Association of Caribbean States.

8. Proportionately reducing U.S. financial assistance to former USSR republics equivalent to the assistance they are offering Cuba: no interest or low interest loans, soft credits, or prices lower than the international market. The United States would also proportionately reduce its financial assistance to any country financing the nuclear power facility at Juragua, Cienfuegos Province, or any other installation used for military intelligence such as the Lourdes facilities in East Havana.[15]

It is evident that the U.S. Congress was trying to halt once and for all Cuba's development of nuclear power generation, which would allow Cuba to save of millions of dollars in oil imports. Russia and Cuba has continued work on the project in the early 1990s but the Cubans remained eager to restart the project and the U.S. government was equally committed to stopping it. The strategy has been successful because as of 2005, Cuba has been unable to complete work on this over twenty-year old project. Additionally, any developing country, primarily former USSR republics, requesting institutional funding to improve its economy, was blackmailed from open market trade if that trade involved Cuba.

The global U.S. "anti-Cuba aid" position, as expressed in Helms-Burton, presented an interesting paradox in the case of Russia. First, Washington recognized the gravity of the destabilization of the Russian economic crisis because this situation impeded Russia's transformation. However, Russia's transformation or any other ex-Soviet bloc country's transformation into an open market economy was a process that the United States needed to continue to support even if it meant accepting continued Russian trade with Cuba.

9. Orders the President of the United States to provide to Congress a detailed annual report containing Cuba's foreign trade and economic relations. This report must include:
   a) a description of all bilateral assistance to Cuba, including humanitarian assistance
   b) Cuban trade partners and the amount of their trade
   c) a description of all established or proposed joint-ventures
   d) a report including joint-venture facilities claimed by U.S. citizens or corporations

e)   amount of Cuban indebtedness by country, including financial and commercial debt

f)   measures taken to assure that no product, made totally or partially in Cuba, is entering the United States.

This focus on the state of Cuba's economy and its international economic relations was very revealing about the focus of U.S. policy. By tracking Cuba's economic activity, Washington was looking for ways in which to sabotage Cuba's economic recovery programs. By identifying Cuba's trading partners, Washington sought to pressure other countries not to do business with the island while always seeking to track the success or failure of its policies.

10. Prohibiting the importation of sugar or molasses made in any country that imported those products from Cuba.[16]

This section attempted to impede indirect subsidization of the Cuban economy via third countries, which have U.S. sugar import quotas, and buy Cuban sugar for their domestic consumption.

Title II, entitled: "Assistance to a Free and Independent Cuba,"[17] specified how the Cuban society must design a "transitional government" without Fidel and Raul Castro and described how to have a "democratically elected government" within the following eighteen months in order to receive Washington's seal of approval. Then and only then would the President of the United States consider lifting the embargo. This approach was first spelled out in the Torricelli bill and more recently in the Powell Commission report.

Title III, entitled: "Protection Property Rights of U.S. Nationals" established the judiciary procedures U.S. citizens must follow to file legal claims for nationalized property, and it determined the criteria for the eligibility of a legal claim.[18] Any person who traffics in property that was confiscated by the Cuban Government on or after January 1, 1959, shall be liable to any U.S. national who has a legal claim to such property for money damages, interests, court costs, and attorney's fees.

An interesting aspect of this section is that it provided for ex-post facto claims against Cuba twenty-four years after the U.S. Foreign Claims Settlement Commission had completed their investigations. The provision allowed any person becoming a U.S. citizen by March, 1996, the date of the passage of this law, to file a U.S. claim against Cuba. This third title has not been enacted because U.S. Presidents have the right to delay its implementation for six months intervals. Both Clinton and Bush have exercised this right since July, 1996. This waiver has been carried out to appease U.S. allies who argued that its execution would violate international law. However, the continued existence of the laws can still serve the purpose of discouraging investment.

Title IV, entitled: "Exclusion of Certain Aliens."[19] obligated the Secretary of State, in consultation with the Attorney General, to exclude any alien from entering into the United States who has acquired, managed, or used any property claimed by a U.S. citizen or corporation. Furthermore, executives and shareholders of these corporations are included in the ban, as well as their wives and children under twenty-one years old. This is yet another attempt to pressure Cuba's foreign trade partners that have relations with the United States, especially Canada and Mexico.

In many ways, at the beginning of 1996 Clinton faced some of the same dilemmas that confronted George Bush in 1992 over the Torricelli bill. Overall, President Clinton supported the intent of the bill and the overthrow of the Cuban Socialist system. However, like the elder Bush, he was concerned about how the European governments would view a bill that clearly sought to impose the views that U.S. leaders had for the embargoing of Cuba on other countries. As a result, Clinton expressed serious reservations about the clauses in the bill that would adversely affect U.S. allies.

Brothers to the Rescue Incident

On February 24, 1996, Cuban Air Force MIGs shot down two Cessna aircraft belonging to Brothers to the Rescue (BTTR), the Miami-based Cuban American group opposed to the revolutionary government. All four persons on board the planes perished. A third plane containing BTTR leader, José Basulto was not attacked. The Cuban government has always maintained that the planes were making their second incursion of the day into Cuban airspace and that its pilots acted properly. U.S. officials have insisted that the shoot-downs occurred outside of Cuban airspace. Whether it happened over Cuban territorial waters or international waters has not been settled, though the International Civilian Aviation Organization (ICAO) did issue a finding, disputed by the Cuban government, that the planes were over international waters, when shot down. To understand Havana's actions, it was necessary to examine the events that lead to the incident. Prior to February 24, Cuba had protested to international authorities that airplanes departing from Southern Florida had violated its territorial air space on nine occasions between May, 1994 and January, 1996. The Cuban government viewed these violations as serious and were compounded by the fact that on several of the occasions anti-government leaflets were dropped. On July 13, 1995, Havana protested that a Cuban exile flotilla of several boats and airplanes had entered Cuban waters and airspace until stopped by Cuban naval forces. Following incursions in January, 1996, the Cuban government temporarily closed the Giron corridor normally used by civilian aircraft from the United States. In spite of the fact that aircraft flying from U.S. territory were clearly in violation of Federal Aviation Authority (FAA) rules, no actions were taken prior to February 24, 1996 by the U.S. government against the BTTR organization that was carrying out the flights. In hindsight, it was clear that the exile organization was pushing the limits in challenging the Cuban government and may have been seeking to provoke a confrontation between the two governments. The BTTR had been particularly upset by the 1994 immigration agreement that had largely ended illegal immigration from Cuba to the United States. BTTR had been active in retrieving Cubans who had set out in rafts during 1993 and

1994, but that work had largely ended by 1995 because the U.S. Coast Guard and Cuban authorities were cooperating in returning the rafters to Cuba, a policy that the BTTR vehemently opposed.

Regardless of the specifics of the shoot-down, the Clinton administration, by not preventing the flights in the first place, put itself into a difficult position. Clinton judged that to placate the Miami community that was leaning Democratic for the 1996 elections he had to react strongly. As a result Clinton adopted several measures:

- Suspension of all charter air travel from the United States to Cuba
- Request to Congress for legislation providing compensation to the families of the victims using frozen Cuban assets in the United States
- Expansion of the services and range of Radio Marti
- Tightening of travel restrictions on Cuban officials living in or visiting the United States
- A compromise with Republican lawmakers on the Helms-Burton sanctions bill.

The most important measure was the last one, given Clinton's skepticism over Helms-Burton. In many ways the most important presidential concession was that with the approval of Helms-Burton, Clinton agreed that henceforth anti-Cuban executive decisions could be terminated only with congressional approval. Ultimately, the compromise that was crafted allowing President Clinton to sign Helms-Burton was highly skillful. The controversial third title of the bill that allows the suing in U.S. courts of foreign companies doing business in Cuba was left in the bill. However, a provision was added allowing the president to suspend the provision every six months if it was judged to be in U.S. national interest. This provision proved crucial because the controversial measure has been suspended by both Presidents Clinton and Bush every time it has come up for review. However, the very existence of the provision has had the result of discouraging certain investments from entering Cuba. The ability of the president to suspend the provision allowed the United States to at least partially reassure the Europeans and Latin Americans. There is also evidence that the Clinton administration considered even stronger, potentially military, sanctions against Cuba. However, these ideas were ultimately rejected as both impractical and an overreaction. Many analysts in the United States tended to place the entire burden for the outcome of the shoot-down on the Cuban government, arguing that it ended a developing reapproachment with Cuba by the Clinton administration. In our view, this perspective is inaccurate as there is no real evidence that Clinton was in any serious way contemplating a breakthrough in Cuba policy. The second track was correctly viewed by the Cuban leadership as seeking no less than the overthrow of the revolutionary leadership. In the minds of the Cuban government, the decision to shoot down the airplanes was almost definitely linked to the provocative U.S. government support for dissident groups on the island and its tolerance of the unlawful flights of the BTTR. In many ways, this incident typified the fundamentally distrustful positions of both governments.

The shoot-down of the airplanes and the signing of Helms-Burton served to perpetuate the long-standing confrontation in U.S.-Cuban relations.

United States policy toward Cuba did not undergo any fundamental changes during Clinton's term even though the U.S. policies toward Cuba had few supporters in the world. Though Clinton did suspend the controversial Title III every six months, he supported 1997 amendments to Helms-Burton that furthered efforts to deny new investments on the island. However, even Clinton himself admitted during a visit with Canadian Prime Minister Jaques Chretien in 1997 that U.S. policy toward Cuba had failed. Of course, Clinton defined failure as the inability to unseat Fidel Castro from power. In March, 1998, two months after an historic visit of Pope John Paul II to Cuba where he called upon the United States to lift its embargo against the island, the White House issued new regulations toward Cuba, partially lifting some of the sanctions for declared humanitarian reasons. The changes affected four areas:

- Allowance of the resumption of direct charter flights from Miami and other U.S. cities
- Renewed permission for Cuban-American families to send money to their relatives in Cuba, up to $1,200 per year
- Increased facilitation for licensing of non-governmental organizations to deliver medical supplies to Cuba
- Support for Congressional efforts to craft a law permitting shipment of food to the Cuban people.

In announcing the measures, Secretary of State Madeline Albright correctly pointed out that these were not fundamental policy changes and that the basics of the embargo remained in place. The actual reasoning behind the first two changes is interesting. The cancellation of the Miami-Havana flights had not stopped Cuban-Americans from traveling to Cuba since they could legally do so under U.S. Treasury regulations. Most of their travel was now through third countries like Mexico and the Bahamas where their airfare payments went directly to the Cuban national airline, Cubana, rather than the Cuban American owned charter companies in Miami. Full legalization of the remittances, which by 1998 were probably reaching over $500 million, was simply bowing to the reality that Cuban American families were aiding their relatives in Cuba at a time of economic hardship on the island. When all travel to Cuba was going through a third country, these remittances were totally out of the control of the U.S. government. By restarting the Miami flights and later adding Los Angeles and New York together with multiple destinations in Cuba, the U.S. government was simply trying to regain control of activity that was probably inevitable.

Elian Gonzalez

The final year of the Clinton administration was marked by an exchange with Cuba that was curious in many aspects. In late November, 1999, a speedboat

carrying refugees from Cuba capsized near Florida with all but one of its occu-
pants perishing. The lone survivor was a small boy, Elian Gonzalez. His mother
died in the accident, but his father had remained in Cuba unaware that his son
was being taken to the United States. Initially, the U.S. government, for stated
humanitarian reasons, allowed Elian to be cared for by distant relatives in Miami. Because he was rescued at sea, this decision was not automatic as he could
have been returned to Cuba since the boat did not reach U.S. soil, normally
needed for an asylum request. Almost immediately, the Cuban government and
the boy's father requested his immediate repatriation to Cuba. What unfolded
until Elian's eventual return to Cuba in April, 2000, demonstrated some interesting aspects to U.S. policy. After initially allowing the temporary residency of
Elian in the United States, the U.S. government sided with the Cuban father in
his request to have the boy returned to him. The U.S. position did not reflect any
sympathy toward Cuba, but rather, there were several international custody
cases pending where the U.S. government was arguing for the primacy of the
rights of the father. As a result, the Clinton administration ultimately demanded
that the child be returned after U.S. courts ruled in favor of Elian's father. The
case was instructive because the Cuban community in Miami made Elian into a
poster child for their ongoing campaign against the Cuban government and
assumed that Washington would stand behind them as they usually did on any
matter related to Cuban policy. However, in the end, the Cuban community
learned that they do not control U.S. Cuban policy as many analysts argue. It is
true that the policies in Washington toward Cuba usually dovetail with those of
the hard-line Miami Cubans, but when wider U.S. national interests are at stake,
they can be bypassed and taught a bitter lesson. The events that unfolded in
Miami when Elian was taken by force from his relatives who were holding him
against the wishes of the U.S. courts also proved to be an embarrassment to the
leadership of the hard-line Cuban Americans. These events hastened the divisions within the Miami community and have emboldened those Cuban Americans who advocate an end to the embargo and better relations with the island. If
the Clinton administration had wished to utilize the return of Elian Gonzalez as
a moment to change basic U.S. policy toward the island, it could have done so.
However, when no such initiative emerged, it was clear that Clinton had never
intended to change Cuban policy in any basic way. As he passed on the Presidency to George Bush, United States-Cuba policy remained little changed from
what it had been when he took office eight years earlier.

Table 6.1
Cuba's Foreign Trade 1988-1997
(Million pesos)

Year	Export	Import	Total Ex-change	Deficit or Sur-plus
1988	5,518.3	7,579.8	13,098.1	-2,071.5
1989	5,399.2	8,139.7	13,538.9	-2,740.5
1990	5,415.0	7,416.6	12,831.6	-2,001.6
1991	2,961.5	4,149.0	7,110.5	-1,187.5
1992	1,784.0	2,315.0	4,099.0	-531.0
1993	1,156.7	2,008.2	3,164.9	- 851.5
1994	1,314.2	1,956.1	3,270.3	- 641.9
1995	1,478.5	2,772.0	4,250.5	-1,293.5
1996	1,966.4	3,695.1	5,661.5	-1,728.7
1997	2,202.4	4,120.1	6,322.5	-1,917.7

Sources: Comité Estatal de EstadIsticas,Anuario *estadIstico de Cuba 1989.* Oficina Nacional de EstadIstica, *La economIa Cubana en 1994,* June 1995. José Luis Rodriguez. "Informe sobre los resultados economicos de 1996 y los lineamientos para el plan economico y social de 1997," *Granma,* Decemeber 27, 1996. Quoted by Hiram Marquetti in: *Cuba: Reformas y transformaciones en el comercio exterior 1990-97,* Centro de Estudos sobre Economia Cubana (CEEC), Havana, January 1998.

Table 6.2
Cuba: Exports to Former European Socialist Countries
1990-1996
(Million USD)

Country	1990	1991	1992	1993	1994	1995	1996
Belarus	--	--	3.8	5.4	9.3	--	--
Bulgaria	82.9	11.7	11.0	19.4	19.4	36.4	24.8
Poland	5.1	--	0.7	0.03	0.02	0.01	0.03
Czech Republic	--	--	--	0.06	0.3	1.0	0.2
Czechoslovakia	80.6	7.8	5.8	--	--	--	--
Hungary	5.2	2.8	--	--	--	--	0.04
Latvia	--	--	2.5	3.5	5.8	13.3	7.1
Yugoslavia	3.2	0.02	5.6	--	--	3.5	--
Romania	99.1	2.8	4.5	6.5	19.6	27.1	60.3
Russia	--	--	607.3	400.7	278.9	194.4	457.5
Slovakia Repub.	--	--	--	0.5	0.7	--	--
Ukraine	--	--	58.9	64.7	0.02	0.5	42.1
USSR	3596.6	1803.9	--	--	--	--	--

Source: IMF, *Direction of Trade Statistics Quarterly,* March 1998 and *IMF Yearbook 1996,* Washington, D.C.

Table 6.3
Cuba: Import from Former Socialist Countries
1990-1996
(Million USD)

Country	1990	1991	1992	1993	1994	1995	1996
Belarus	---	---	4.3	5.3	1.6	---	0.05
Bulgaria	98.0	26.5	1.9	3.4	1.9	12.7	11.6
Czechoslovakia	198.2	83.1	5.2	---	---	---	---
Czech Republic	---	---	---	3.6	---	---	---
Hungary	31.2	12.6	10.5	3.1	1.9	0.0	0.08
Latvia	---	---	2.4	0.07	0.0	---	6.5
Poland	44.6	4.3	4.5	3.9	0.9	0.5	13.0
Romania	103.8	9.1	---	0.2	5.2	29.0	28.5
Russia	---	----	534.5	86.3	41.8	56.8	113.8
Slovakia Republic	----	---	---	4.0	1.7	1.5	9.5
Ukraine	---	---	0.6	4.7	1.9	4.0	1.8
USSR	5,114.4	2,717.6	---	---	---	---	---
Yugoslavia	9.6	7.6	0.7	0.01	---	0.5	5.5

Source: IMF, *Direction of Trade Statistics Quarterly,* March 1998 and *IMF Yearbook 1996,*Washington, D.C.

Table 6.4
Cuba-USSR (Russia) Commercial Exchange
(Million USD)

	1989	1990	1991	1992	1993	1994	1995
Total foreign exchange	8,153.5	8,711.4	4,428.3	757.0	710.8	509.0	408.0
Exports	3,231.2	3,597.0	1,794.7	191.0	311.5	200.0	200.0
Imports	5,522.3	5,114.4	2,633.6	566.0	399.1	309.0	208.0
Deficit or surplus	(2,291.1)	(1,517.4)	(838.9)	(375.0)	(87.6)	(209.0)	(8.0)

Sources: Comité Estatal de Estadistica, *Anuario estadIstico de 1989.* Other periodical informations of United Nations. *Granma internacional,* March 29, 1995, p.10. Quoted by Hiram Marquetti in: *Cuba: Reformas y transformaciones en el comercio exterior 1990-95,* CEEC, Havana: January 1997.

Table 6.5
Cuba-Russia: Barter Trade

Year	Total [1]	Sugar-Fuel [2] Barter Rate		
		Sugar	Fuel	Rate
1992	656	1	1.8	1.8
1993	618	0.9196	2.3	2.5
1994	509	0.5680	1.6	1.1
1995	405	0.5000	1.0	1.5
1996	570	0.4500	1.15	2.5
1997	---	1.5	3.8	2.5

Note: (1) In million USD.
(2) In million metric tons.
Sources: Russia's and international organizations periodical information. Prensa Latina, Moscow, January 17, 1997. *Semanario opciones,* February 2, 1997, 12. Quoted by Hiram Marquetti in *Cuba: Reformas y transformaciones en el comercio exterior 1990-97,* CEEC, Havana, January, 1998.

Notes

1. Cuban Democracy Act of 1992 (Public Law 102-484; 1701 et. seq. 106 Stat. 2575). This Act was signed by President George Bush on October 26, 1992.

2. For further information regarding European Community disagreement with The Torricelli Act, see: Michael Krinsky and David Golove, *United States Economic Measures against Cuba: Proceedings in the United Nations and International Law Issues* (Northampton: Alethea Press, 1993).

3. Findings: *Cuban Democracy Act of 1992,* Public Law 102-484 (1701 et. Seq.; 106 Stat. 2575.)

4. Quoted in Carla Anne Robbins, "Dateline Washington: Cuban American Clout" *Foreign Policy* (Fall 1992) 166-67.

5. For further information, see: Graciela Chailloux, Rosa Lopez and Carlos Batista, *Puede Clinton parecerse a Carter? (Can Clinton be like Carter?),* 1993.

6. Special period. This was a name given by President Fidel Castro to designate the difficult situation Cuba would face after the collapse of the European Socialist bloc. For further information, see: Fidel Castro Ruz, Speech before the 4th Congress of Cuba's Communist Party. *Granma* newspaper, Havana, February 25, 1991.

7. Lincoln Diaz-Balart is a nephew of Fidel Castro's ex-wife Mirtha Diaz-Balart.

8. *The Cuban Liberty and Democratic Solidarity Act of 1996,* Sections, 104-114.

9. *The Cuban Liberty and Democratic Solidarity Act of 1996,* Sections 101 (2).

10. *The Cuban Liberty and Democratic Solidarity Act of 1996,* Section 102 (a).

11. *The Cuban Liberty and Democratic Solidarity Act of 1996,* Section 102 (C) (D).

12. *The Cuban Liberty and Democratic Solidarity Act of 1996,* Section 103 (a).

13. *The Cuban Liberty and Democratic Solidarity Act of 1996,* Section 104 (a) (b).

14. *The Cuban Liberty and Democratic Solidarity Act of 1996,* Section 105.

15. *The Cuban Liberty and Democratic Solidarity Act of 1996,* Section 101 (3) and Section 106 (a) (d) (2).

16. *The Cuban Liberty and Democratic Solidarity Act of 1996,* Section 110.

17. *The Cuban Liberty and Democratic Solidarity Act of 1996,* Title II.

18. *The Cuban Liberty and Democratic Solidarity Act of 1996,* Title III.

19. *The Cuban Liberty and Democratic Solidarity Act of 1996.* Title IV.

Chapter Seven

U.S. Economic Interests in Cuba

One aspect of United States-Cuban relations that needs a separate analysis is the growing interest during the past ten years, for U.S. companies to do business with Cuba. Political relations between the two governments have changed very little during the past ten years and this unchanging aspect of the relationship is well documented elsewhere in the book. However, during that same period, a significant one-way trade of U.S. medical and agricultural products to Cuba has begun. In 2006, Cuba bought close to $400 million in goods from the United States and the country now ranks in the top thirty nations receiving U.S. agriculture products. This chapter will explain how this development occurred, with particular attention to the congressionally mandated U.S. law change from 2000 that permitted certain U.S. companies to do business with Cuba.

U.S. Economic Interest in Cuba

Until 1994 when the Cuban economy began to grow, no U.S. companies had shown any special interest in having economic relationships with Cuba due to the perception that the economic collapse of the island was a fact and that few profits were to be made in a primarily socialist economy. Following domestic unrest in August, 1994, Cuba initiated economic measures, including the liberalization of agricultural and industrial markets, to increase the availability of domestic consumer goods and food. The resulting excess liquidity was reduced and the black market dollar per peso exchange rate adjusted from a peak of 150 pesos to a dollar to thirty pesos to a dollar in the first trimester of 1995. Cuba's GNP increased by 0.7 percent in 1994, and although the figure was not significant in volume, it marked the end of the Cuban economic decline. This was apparently the reason that several U.S. companies began to show an economic interest in the island, as early as 1994, and to sign letters of intention to engage in commercial transactions with Cuba.

For the first time since 1960, a growing number of American businesses began to press Washington to reconsider the economic embargo against Cuba.

They argued that the embargo policy shut them out of a growing market located ninety miles from U.S. shores while other countries were gaining a share of Cuba's market openings. This interest was demonstrated in articles and statements from high-ranking executives of U.S. companies, as well as in testimonies presented in congressional hearings that began in March, 1994 and continued in 1995. Several articles appearing in the U.S. press, especially in the second half of 1994 and in the first half of 1995, confirm this renewed interest by the U.S. private sector.

On August 27, 1995, the front page of the *New York Times* contained an article written by Sam Diellon that read:

> The emergence of a lobby in the private enterprise sector opposed to the embargo against Cuba is an influential new element in the debate, in which economic interests are putting aside political ideology . . . "Pressures are growing"—stated an anonymous official of the Administration. Businesspeople are showing interest in the transition in Cuba and complain that all business possibilities are covered by foreign competitors. U.S. businesses are highly interested in Cuba.[1]

Another article in *Time* magazine, dated September 4 of the same year, pointed out:

> An authentic example of the former took place during a meeting of the Department of State, with high executives of U.S. corporations to talk about commerce in the hemisphere. During the meeting, Alexander Watson, Assistant Secretary for Latin American Affairs, stated that, "Europeans and Asians are knocking at Latin American doors. The game is open and we can be good contenders; it would be unpardonable if we let them play by themselves."[2]

When Assistant Secretary Watson was questioned about the double standard policy that the United States followed, with respect to permitting trade relations between the United States and other socialist countries, Watson simply stated that "Cuba was a special case."[3]

Many influential U.S. executives favored a change in policy and speculated about the possibility of lifting the blockade, even partially. In a televised interview on CNN, D. Wayne O. Andreas, President of Archer Daniels Midland, said: "Our embargo has been a failure for thirty years. We should have all citizens doing business with Cuba. The time for a change has come."[4] It is important to note that Andreas was the main contributor to the presidential campaign of Senator Robert Dole. The Cuban American National Foundation has even admitted that there was a growing interest in Cuba on the part of the U.S. business community, although the organization tried to minimize business' impact in terms of political pressure.

In an interview appearing in *Cigar Aficionado,* Ron Perelman, the head of Revlon and Consolidated Cigar Corporation, anticipated that the embargo would be lifted within five years. Similarly, Thomas I. Polski, representing the Carlson

Companies (a travel and cruise conglomerate) and Radisson Hotels, noted: "We view Cuba as an exciting new opportunity, the Caribbean forbidden fruit. The lifting of the embargo is inevitable."[5] Carlson was one of the first major companies to oppose the embargo against Cuba. In Congressional hearings held on March 17, 1994, and in subsequent hearings related to Cuba, representatives of these companies repeatedly pointed out the cost of the embargo in terms of financial losses to their companies. Another important criticism of the embargo came from Otis Elevator. They regretted the considerable profit loss represented by simple replacement contracts for their 40-year-old equipment in Cuba.[6]

During March, 1995, House Ways and Means Committee hearings on U.S.-Cuba relations, Keith Broussard, the Vice-President of the U.S. Planter's Federation, said: "U.S. rice industry views the Cuban market as one with great potential once the embargo is over."[7] Before the same hearing, Sandra M. Alfonso, representing the Governor of Louisiana, stated that prior to 1960, Cuba was Louisiana's biggest commercial partner and that as a result of the embargo, the state had lost 6,000 jobs that could only be recovered with a change in current sanctions.[8]

Business representatives publicly expressed their opposition to the embargo, but the impetus for change remained with the White House. In several interviews, Richard Nuccio, President Clinton's former Special Assistant for Cuban Affairs, acknowledged that the business opportunity lost argument presented by various U.S. businesses. However, he pointed out that current foreign investments in the island were short-term and highly risky and that they could easily be replaced by U.S. capital in the future.[9] In an interview with the author in August, 1995, Mr. Nuccio said that even though pressures on the Executive Branch were real, they are not that strong, as was in the case of Vietnam, and, therefore, he did not regard them as an effective pressure factor to warrant a change of policy toward Cuba. Vietnam was a potential market of 100 million people, while Cuba was only one-tenth of that.

In 1995, Fidel Castro attended the 50th anniversary of the United Nations in New York and David Rockefeller offered a lunch in his honor. Among the guests were Fortune 500 and Fortune 100 business leaders interested in conducting business with Cuba. However, in March, 1996, the Cuban Liberty and Democratic Solidarity Act, commonly known as Helms-Burton, was put into effect. This law was designed to strengthen the U.S. embargo against Cuba, thus closing any possibilities for U.S. companies to conduct business with Cuba. In the author's opinion, Helms-Burton constituted a hostile response to the incipient process of investment and joint ventures with foreign capital, as a result of which $1.5 billion entered the island in 1994 and $2.3 billion in 1995.

The Helms-Burton Act: Dynamics and Perspectives in the Context of U.S. Economic Interests

There is no doubt that the intense economic crisis that Cuba faced since the demise of the Soviet Union gave the U.S. establishment the long-awaited opportunity to terminate the Cuban socialist project using first the Torricelli Act and later the Helms-Burton Act. However, the Cuban capacity for survival created concern among the most aggressive anti-Castro circles because the implementation of these instruments against Cuba has not sufficiently achieved its goal. Their perception of the blockade was that it has been partially effective but needed to be reinforced. During 1993 and 1994, Cuba began to adopt small economic changes, which stopped its spiraling economic decline and began to restructure its international economic relations. In response to these changes within Cuba, the U.S. political scenario related to Cuba also changed. Although the Cuban Democracy Act became an obstacle to Cuba's internal economic growth and restructuring of external economic relations, it did not impede this process. U.S. mainstream media, represented by the *New York Times,* the *Washington Post,* the *Wall Street Journal,* and others, played an important role in broadening the scope of the U.S.-Cuba debate and has contained the influence of the anti-Castro Cuban-American community, especially in Southern Florida. Inside the U.S. political class there was a growing concern about the blockade as an effective mechanism to achieve U.S. goals because the Cuban Government continued to survive. In spite of the difficulties the island was facing, it was creating a new, singularly identified model, which presented Cuba from a different perspective. Socialism as a system had appeared to be dead, but Cuba presented its own socialist model of social justice.

Because of the aforementioned events, U.S. policy towards Cuba was confronting the reality of the survival of a social project that the United States declared dead at the beginning of the 1990s. This situation created different perceptions within U.S. society, and then as never before, a trend of solidarity toward Cuba was growing inside the United States. This change of perception is based on the reality that Cuba is no longer viewed as a threat to U.S. national security. The new political thought was looking for new ways to deal with the Cuba problem. At the same time, the hard-liners were trying to reinforce the blockade, and through Helms-Burton, the old guard imposed its views.

While Cuba searched for its niche in international economic relations it allowed direct foreign investment. The U.S. establishment saw the necessity to stop this process and applied sanctions, via the Helms-Burton Act, against those countries investing in Cuba, to force U.S. allies and the rest of the world to follow its blockade policy and ultimately force the collapse of the Cuban economy. The main objective of Helms-Burton was to stop the new directions of Cuban reform in order to create such a difficult economic situation inside Cuba that the Cuban people would provoke a political change resulting in a liberal democracy. In its effort to overthrow the Cuban Government, it attempted to impose U.S. global domination. This transnational character is exactly what made Helms-Burton so objectionable to U.S. allies. With passage of the Helms-Burton law, the contradiction between the United States' Cuban policy and the sovereign rights of nations became clearly visible. There have been many instances involving U.S. allies that have required an avoidance of direct confrontation. Negotiations have been necessary whenever sensitive issues arose as the European Union and Canadian interests confronted U.S. economic pressure. But, from the perspective of the economic reintegration of Cuba, the confrontation at the international level takes a triangular shape on the following stages:

- Cuba—Latin American—United States
- Cuba—Caribbean—United States
- Cuba—European Union—United States
- Cuba—Asia—United States

Within Europe, more specifically the European Union, it is important to highlight Russia and the former Socialist countries of Eastern Europe. Russia was a primary U.S. concern due to its continuing relationship with Cuba, to the point that it received special attention in the Helms-Burton law. The Eastern European nations were also of particular interest to Washington, which made significant efforts to prevent their establishing economic rapprochement with Cuba. As far as the Asian triangle is concerned, China, Vietnam, and Korea require special consideration for their position vis-à-vis Cuba since they did not heed U.S. pressure aimed at isolating them from Havana. China, above all, is a special case because of its complex relations with the United States. It is within this context of contrasting and conflicting views that negotiations became unavoidable. The White House sought to abate the problems Helms-Burton created with U.S. allies. In practice, however, negotiating Helms-Burton's international acceptance was Washington's tool to forge a worldwide consensus aimed at subverting Cuba's national interests.

Several stages of confrontation and negotiations ensued in the late 1990s and have repeated themselves under current President Bush. At first, the Helms-Burton bill was not viewed as a proper U.S. policy, but once Clinton found himself "forced" to sign it, he used the new law as an instrument to pressure American allies and other international actors. The President's special envoy, Stuart Eizenstat, played an essential role in explaining Helms-Burton to skeptical allies in an attempt to make U.S.-Cuba policy acceptable at the international level. It must be pointed out that U.S. allies do not grant Cuba any priority in their foreign policy, except basically for their desire to prevent Washington from using Cuba to demonstrate its ability to impose its own interests (as was manifested in the Iraq war). The bottom line here is whether sovereign nations can exercise and defend their own rights, and whether their business communities can develop economic relations with Cuba or with anyone else for that matter. In addition, the stage where these negotiations have been carried out has been dominated by the interests of the United States and its allies. The dispute is taking place within a complex political space that includes the following components:

- The interest of the United States in pressuring Cuba into accepting a "democratic-liberal market" modality, which dominant economic powers are trying to impose on the world by means of a process of globalization that they aim to control.

- The interest of U.S. allies in maintaining a strategic agreement with the United States, although they oppose an ineffective political method that hurts them as competitors at the international level.

It is within this framework, riddled with contradictions between the United States and its allies that Cuba finds an opportunity to move forward with its international economic integration. Still, while these pressures to impose a particular policy approach against Cuba have not been fruitful on the economic front, the United States and its allies still maintain strategies that do not differ markedly on the political front. The allies share with the United States the strategic objective of returning Cuba to capitalism. The difference lies in the strategy, whether to demand it overtly, negotiate it discreetly, or seek it merely as a desirable goal. Hence, the contradictions lie mainly in the methods, not the desired ends.

The methods used to further the goal of returning Cuba to capitalism differ in the various arenas: the United States, Latin America and the Caribbean, the European Union, and Asia.[10] The U.S.-Cuba policy has been conceived as an amalgam of blockade pressures, the absence of economic relations (notwithstanding the paid-in-cash American food trade initiated in late 2001, and continued since), and setting political obstacles to the acceptance of Cuban socialism and characterizing it as incompatible with peaceful hemispheric and international coexistence. U.S. pressure to move Cuba toward "liberal democracy" really seeks to forge the internal conditions that would destroy Cuba's political system. This includes creating the domestic circumstances that could precipitate and justify U.S. military intervention. The conditions have been pragmatically stated (and repeated by President Bush): Havana must carry out free elections, certified by an international team of observers, as a demonstration of its willingness to promote a transition to democracy and capitalism. Cuba's current political leadership is to be excluded from such transition, as defined in Helms-Burton and the "common position" that was agreed upon with the European Union in 1996. But the U.S.-EU negotiating process on Cuba has remained mostly stagnant: after several sessions, only two meetings led to concrete agreements.

The fundamental difference between the European Union's position and that of the United States is that the former maintains economic relations with Cuba and has not accepted the dictates of Title III of the Helms-Burton law because of its extraterritorial reach and its insensitivity toward other nations' sovereignty. The dispute even led to the selection of a panel of judges to review charges brought by the European Union against the United States at the World Trade Organization (WTO). After much negotiation, a standoff remained. Even though all have been willing to use Cuba as a negotiating piece, the unmistakable transnational scope of Helms-Burton gets in the way of any settlement.[11] European hostility to U.S. policies toward Cuba are significant because generally the European governments have the same long term goal as the United States, elimination of the revolutionary government.

One issue that should not be overlooked has been Cuba's participation as an observer in the African, Caribbean, and Pacific (ACP) group of states during the Lomé Convention negotiations, which had the potential of opening the door for alternative relations with the European Union. (Lomé was replaced later by the Cotonou Agreement.) The White House was standing with the extreme Right demanding a stronger hard line against Cuba on one side while the U.S. allies were on the other. However, it was a weak performance indeed since the United States remained in favor of maintaining the blockade and pressure against Cuba, a position supported by President Bush.

In the Latin American and Caribbean area, what stands out is Cuba's progress in its economic relations with the region, the gradual reestablishment of diplomatic relations, and the cooperation the island has promoted with Central America, especially in its provision of medical aid and its willingness to train specialists from and for the region. Also, Cuba has become a participant in such organizations as the Association of Caribbean States (ACS), ALADI (Latin American Integration Association), SELA (Latin American Economic System), CARIFORUM (Caribbean Forum), and others. This has taken place in spite of Washington's attempt to exclude Cuba from hemispheric, economic dynamics. The linkage against the obstacles caused by the blockade could open so-called windows of vulnerability. A most interesting case is Canada, a Western country that has maintained a permanent political dialogue with Cuba while also expanding economic relations with it.[12]

Such Cuban foreign policy initiatives as its membership in ALADI, its observer status in the negotiating group for Lomé, its numerous United Nations resolutions against the U.S. blockade, its role hosting the Iberian-American Summit in November, 1999, its medical aid to Central America, its presentations at the Group of 77 meetings, as well as the speeches by Cuba's foreign minister at the United Nations on numerous occasions, provide factual indication that the island has recovered the international activism for which it was noted prior to 1989.

This recovery process is not only economic but also political and includes Cuba's new image in the hemisphere. The positive emerging image has diluted any lingering animosity from previous times. Thus, such issues as Havana's participation in the Organization of American States (OAS) and its transition to liberal democracy have lost their urgency under the political reality of a new century (demonstrated by the newly elected leftist and center-left presidents in Latin America). Cuba is repeatedly maintaining its personality as a nation in the hemisphere and on the world stage. In turn, the United States has been continuously condemned by the General Assembly of the United Nations for its blockade against Cuba. Although Washington keeps its pressure over the hemisphere and internationally to enforce discriminatory practices against Cuba, the policy has lost support and suffered numerous defeats. Asia, China, Vietnam, and Korea ignore U.S. pressure against doing business with Cuba and proceed to provide the island with a wide range of food and manufactured products. Japan responds to American pressure by maintaining a degree of independence in its relations with Cuba and has looked for ways of widening its economic links with the island.[13]

Havana has been steadily recovering its international links. Today, the country has more than 360 joint ventures with foreign capital, 170 of which were created after the signing of the Helms-Burton law. Marketing and investment agreements have been signed with forty countries. In the last five years new economic relations, especially with Venezuela and China, have raised higher the prospects for the recovery of the Cuban economy in the coming years to a point of prosperity that Cuba enjoyed in the mid-1980s. It has been elected or appointed to twenty governing bodies of the United Nations, and currently has 118 diplomatic, consular, or interest offices abroad, ninety-eight of them are embassies, the highest number in the history of Cuba.[14] Furthermore, Cuba has commercial relations with 1700 companies from 150 nations, hosts seventy-nine nine embassies representing countries from all continents, and has accredited 138 foreign correspondents from 104 media organizations and thirty-one countries, compared with ninety-three correspondents from sixty-two media organizations a decade ago. Faced with this reality, it is not proper to speak of Cuba's isolation, it is more accurate to speak of the growing international opposition to U.S. policy, particularly the blockade against Cuba.

Notes

1. *New York Times,* August 27, 1995, 1.

2. *Time*, September 4, 1995, 73.

3. Donna Rich, Julia Sweig, Sophia Lynn and others ed., *Cuba Info,* School of Advanced International Studies (SAIS), The Johns Hopkins University, Washington, D.C., Volume 7, No. 4, March 27, 1995, 6.

4. Quoted in Rich, Sweig, and Lynn.

5. Quoted in Rich, Sweig, and Lynn.

6. Quoted in Rich, Sweig, and Lynn.

7. House Ways and Means Committee, Hearings on U.S.-Cuban relations, March 17-18, 1995.

8. House Ways and Means Committee, Hearings on U.S.-Cuban relations, March 17-18, 1995.

9. Donna Rich, Julia Sweig, Sophia Lynn and others ed., *Cuba Info,* School of Advanced International Studies (SAIS), The Johns Hopkins University, Washington, D.C., Volume 7, No. 4, March 27, 1995, 7.

10. See Esteban Morales Dominguez, Carlos Batista, and Kanaki Yamaoka, *The United States and Cuba's International Economy Reinsertion,* Joint Research Program Series no. 126 (Tokyo: Institute of Developing Economies, 1999).

11. See for example, "José Maria Aznar's, Spain President," statement in *Granma,* September 11, 1999.

12. Morales Domínguez, Batista, and Yamaoka, *Reinsertion,* 139-44.

13. Morales Dominguez, Batista, and Yamaoka, *Reinsertion,* 152-77.

14. "Informe del Ministro de Relaciones Exteriores," *Granma,* September 15, 1999.

Chapter Eight

Contemporary U.S.-Cuban Policy (2000-Present)

In many ways, Helms-Burton represented a hardening of U.S. policy toward Cuba, but it did not represent the only face of U.S. policy toward the island, especially during the Clinton years. As a part of its two-track approach and under pressure from advocates of Cuban-American trade, the Clinton administration signaled its support for the developing Congressional legislation that permitted the sales of U.S. medicines and agricultural products for the first time in forty years. Sponsored by Senator Chris Dodd (D-Conn.) and Representative Esteban Torres (D-Calif.) with the support of Representative Charles Rangel (D-NY) and 135 other legislators, the Dodd-Torres bill proposed lifting the ban on sales of food and medicine to Cuba. It had been first proposed in Congress in the early 90s with little chance of passage given the political climate at that time, but by 1998, sentiment was changing on a number of fronts. In January, 1998, the U.S. Chamber of Commerce, under pressure from the business community, launched a public campaign opposing the trade embargo and favoring the passage of the Dodd-Torres bill. In the same month, Pope John Paul II made his historic visit to Cuba, condemning the U.S. embargo and calling for more humanitarian aid to the island. After gaining an impressive number of co-signers, on March 21, 1998, on the National Day of Education and Advocacy for Food and Medicine Sales to Cuba, hundreds of Cuban-Americans converged on Capitol Hill to support the legislation. Max Azicri has argued that this unprecedented opposition to the embargo from Miami Cubans was the result of the Pope's visit to the island and his call for aid.[1] The support from Miami Cubans for the new legislation represented significant new divisions within the Cuban-American community over what policy to pursue toward the island. In reality, this shift in perspective was already happening as thousands of Cubans began regularly sending financial assistance to their relatives on the island in defiance of the hard-line community leaders who viewed such payments as only strengthening the Cuban government.

The Cuban American National Foundation was forced to react and proposed sending up to $100 million in food and medical aid to the "Cuban people directly." Fearing the complete end of the embargo, CANF supported this plan as an alternative to the Dodds-Torres legislation. Two months after the Pope's visit to Cuba, the White House announced the partial lifting of some of the sanctions for humanitarian reasons. Within these measures, Clinton also expressed his formal support for the legislation pending in Congress. However, in spite of pleas from Cuban Cardinal Jaime Cardinal Ortega that the Clinton measures did not go far enough to alleviate the situation on the island, the Clinton administration did not move to significantly change the embargo. Support from the President for the sale of food and medicine was crucial to its success, but a bipartisan majority was needed to bring it to passage. To understand how this came to passage in the fall of 2000, it is necessary to study the Congressional dynamic and the organizations lobbying for the bill.

AHTC

The central lobbying organization in the fight to allow the sale of food and medicines to Cuba was the Americans for Humanitarian Trade with Cuba (AHTC). The AHTC was founded in January 1998, under the auspices of the U.S. Chamber of Commerce. The Chamber made the political decision at the time of Pope John Paul's visit to Cuba that the time was right to press for the U.S. business community's entrance into the Cuban marketplace. In 1998, the Cuban economic recovery was well underway and non-U.S. entrepreneurs were reaping significant profits by participating in Cuba's reinsertion into the world's capitalist markets. By 1998, Cuba was importing nearly $1 billion a year in agricultural products, mainly from Asia. The political context in the United States Midwest agriculture regions was the negative impact of falling agricultural commodity prices on the region's farmers. Cuban need for agricultural imports and needs of U.S. agricultural companies and farmers combined to create the opportunity for the promotion of legislation allowing for the sales.

In that context, the AHTC constructed a nationwide organization to foster its efforts. State councils are the core of the AHTC's grassroots political strength. There are twenty-two state councils, primarily in the Midwest, that bring together physicians, farmers, church and business leaders, Cuban Americans, and labor officials. The coalition of forces was based on shared interests for a change in the embargo. Eliciting church support was relatively easy because of long-standing positions in opposition to the embargo. The U.S. Catholic Conference condemned the embargo well before Pope John Paul's visit, as did most Protestant churches, Quakers, and various Jewish organizations. Labor support was gained through a unanimous resolution of the AFL-CIO in favor of the medical and food sales. This vote followed a 2000 report of the World Policy Institute that the partial lifting of the embargo would create 20,000 jobs in the United States. The political breadth of the AHTC is manifested in its Advisory Council, which includes David Rockefeller, former U.S. Trade Representative Carla Hills, President Reagan's National Security Adviser Frank Carlucci, former U.S. Federal Reserve Chair Paul Volcker, former U.S. Surgeon General Julius Richmond, Pete Coors of Coors Brewing Company, film director Francis Ford Coppola, and Craig Fuller, former Chief of Staff for Vice President George Bush. The group is clearly bipartisan, but its particular emphasis was on gaining the support of prominent Republicans since that party had not been sympathetic in the past toward any change in Cuba policy.[2]

Farm state Republican Senators took the lead in supporting the Trade Sanctions Reform and Export Enhancement Act of 2000. A key champion of the law, then Senator John Ashcroft of Missouri (later U.S. Attorney General), explained why he supported the law that would allow trade with Cuba at a World Policy Institute conference in Washington in June, 2000, by stating: "We've seen the failures over and over again of the attempts to withhold food and medicine as a means of shaping international diplomatic relations and I think it's time for us to understand that there is a better way."[3] Like many others, Ashcroft's position was a hypocritical one because he continued to support the embargo on Iraq that was having far more devastating consequences for Iraq than the Cuban embargo. However, 2000 was an election year and the farm state Senators were desperate to secure votes from struggling farmers, so they backed this legislation to bolster their reelection prospects. In 2000, the Senate approved a version of the Agricultural Appropriations bill by a vote of 79-13 to a proposal by Democratic Senator Byron Dorgan of North Dakota to lift all sanctions on the sale of food and medicines to Cuba. The House Appropriations Committee approved similar language submitted by Republican Congressman George Nethercutt of Washington and the Senate Foreign Relations Committee approved similar language offered by Senator Ashcroft. Most significantly, on July 20, 2000, the House of Representatives voted 301-116 to ban Treasury Department funding for enforcement of U.S. restrictions on the sale of food and medicines, an amendment offered by Republican Congressman Jerry Moran of Kansas. Following these votes, the measures went to a conference committee and eventually to the desk of President Clinton. By the fall of 2000, it was clear that an overwhelming bipartisan majority wanted the sales to go forward. On October 27, 2000, President Clinton signed into law the Agriculture Appropriations Bill (HR 4461) that had been previously passed by the Congress. The passage and signing of the legislation was a major victory for anti-embargo forces, but it was not a complete victory. Cuba's continued presence on the U.S. government's list of "nations that sponsor terrorism" meant that each sale between Cuba and the United States must be licensed, a bureaucratic hurdle that some U.S. companies are unwilling to confront. In addition, all purchases by Cuba must be in cash, no U.S. government or U.S. private financing of the sales is permitted. However, the opponents of the overall TSRA bill, who successfully inserted this provision in the final bill in the expectation that it would seriously deter U.S. companies from participating in the trade, must be disappointed by the way in which the agricultural sales on a cash basis have moved forward. Initially following passage of the legislation in 2000, there were no sales because the Cuban government refused to buy under the restrictive provisions. However, in the fall of 2001, following the devastation of Hurricane Michelle, the Cuban government made $30 million in "emergency" purchases that became the start of a very significant trade.

However, in the medical arena the restrictive provisions of the law have been more successful in preventing meaningful trade. U.S. medical products companies interested in selling to Cuba still face the 1992 Cuban Democracy Act's insurmountable licensing hurdles. The small to midsize medical companies most interested in such sales do not have the legal counsel necessary to overcome these hurdles. The end result has been few Cuban purchases of U.S. medicines and no progress on gaining a U.S. market for Cuban bio-medical products, such as the Hepatitis B vaccine.

However, in July, 2004, there was a small breakthrough that may prove important in the long run. CancerVax Corporation received the U.S. government's approval to license three experimental cancer drugs from Cuba. The agreement, made with the Cuban state medical company CIMAB, is the first such authorization. The agreement comes after three years of work by CancerVax and CIMAD following a presentation of the product at a major U.S. oncology meeting. The timing of the deal was significant because it came after the announcement of new hard-line measures against Cuba by the Bush administration in May. Because of the U.S. embargo, CIMAD cannot receive cash payments in the $6 million deals, but CancerVax will pay in goods, foods, and medicines. If the drugs are successfully developed and commercialized in the United States and other countries, the Cuban company can earn up to an additional $35 million, part in cash.[4] Cuba has spent hundreds of millions of dollars to develop its bio-tech industry and is primarily selling its products in Latin America.

U.S.-Cuba Trade and Economic Council

The most important U.S. civic organization involved in promoting the new trading relations between the United States and Cuba is the United States-Cuba Trade and Economic Council. Established in 1994 as an official non-profit organization, the group "provides an efficient and sustainable educational structure in which the United States business community may access accurate, consistent, and timely information and analysis on matters and issues of interest regarding United States—Republic of Cuba commercial, economic, and political relations."[5]

As an official non-profit organization it does not engage directly in lobbying Congress, but the organization does provide a voice for progressive Cubans in the United States as it did in May, 2004 when it sharply criticized the new Cuban travel measures announced by the Bush administration. The main theme of their criticisms was that the new measures punished the very people that they were supposed to be assisting. In the three years since the new measures were enacted further political division in the Cuban-American community has surfaced over the new regulations. Older Cuban-Americans have supported the tightening of travel ban but those in the younger generation of Cuban-Americans were more likely to visit and, as a result, have protested the changes.

The Council is the first U.S. business organization to establish relations with a wide range of organizations within Cuba, including the Cuban Chamber of Commerce, the Ministry of Foreign Trade, the Ministry of Tourism, and the Cuban National Assembly. The Council publishes a weekly journal, *Economic Eye on Cuba*, that has a readership of 10,000 in the business and academic communities, and the organization also maintains a website, www.cubatrade.org. The organization has been a prime facilitator of the contracts for the sale of agricultural products that began in November, 2001. A key event in the development of this trade was the U.S. Food and Agribusiness Exhibition held in Havana in September, 2002. The exhibition had 923 representatives from 293 exhibitors (located in thirty-two states, the District of Columbia, and Puerto Rico). The event was attended by one U.S. governor, Jesse Ventura of Minnesota, and 16,000 Cuban nationals. Decatur, Illinois-based Archer Daniels Midland Company ($22 billion in annual revenue) was the primary sponsor of the event.[6] This agricultural gathering was preceded in 2000 by a U.S. Health Care Exhibition attended by 8,000 Cuban citizens. This conference permitted some of the first significant purchases of U.S. medicines by the Cuban state. In the ensuing years numerous state-level trade delegations have visited the island often headed by the state's governor. Some of the most significant trips have been made by the contingents from Illinois, Idaho, and Nebraska. Such state-by-state activity has contributed to the building political sentiment in Washington for scrapping the embargo entirely.

The most important Cuban-American organization, formed in 1995 to present an alternative voice in the Cuban community to the CANF, is the Cuban American Alliance Education Fund, a national non-profit network of Cuban Americans "that educates on issues related to hardships caused by current United States-Cuba relations." The organization has focused its efforts primarily on maintaining family ties and offering assistance to Cubans through a Cuban NGO in charge of assisting people with various forms of disabilities across the island. An important aspect of the work of the Alliance is the promotion of sister-city relationships between U.S. and Cuban cities. The Alliance spearheaded the founding in 2000 of the U.S.-Cuba Sisters City Association (USCSCA) in Pittsburgh for the "purpose of fostering exchanges between individuals, community groups, organizations and institutions in the United States with counterparts in Cuba."[7] The conference was held in Pittsburgh because one year earlier it established a sister city project with Matanzas and sent six hundred students to Cuba in March, 2000 as part of the University of Pittsburgh's Semester at Sea program. Other significant sister city relationships include Madison, Wisconsin and Camaguey, Mobile, Alabama and Havana (founded in 1993), and Bloomington, Indiana and Santa Clara, California. The activities of the Mobile-Havana exchange have been typical. Several exchanges of delegations have taken place, including artists, religious figures, and musicians. Several ministers, the Bishop of Havana, Cuba's representative in Washington, and Havana's official historian, Eusebio Leal, have visited Mobile. The mayor of Mobile, along with other city officials, has visited Cuba. This sistering relationship is a natural one as the port of Mobile is a key shipping point for the developing U.S.-Cuba agricultural trade. Following the passage of the food and medicine law in 2000, the political focus of the anti-embargo forces in the United States has primarily turned to a campaign to end the ban on travel for most non-Cuban Americans to the island. This campaign to end the travel ban has occurred in the context of the general hardening of U.S. policy toward Cuba conducted by the Bush administration. Rep. Jeff Flake, an Arizona Republican and former executive director of the Barry Goldwater Institute, has led the fight in the House. He has argued: "At some point we need to concede that our current approach has failed and try something new. . . . If we are serious about undermining Castro and bringing freedom and democracy to the island, why not let Americans travel there with that message?"[8] This quote underscores a reality about the core of the movement in Congress to lift the travel ban. They share the goals of the U.S. administrations for four decades to overthrow the current Cuban government—they simply have a different tactic for achieving the same objective. In 2007, Representative Flake and New York Democrat Charles Rangel have introduced HF 654 to end the embargo in its entirely. As of this writing, the legislation has over one-hundred co-sponsors drawn from members of Congress from both sides of the aisle.

Prior to 2007, legislative action on Cuba by the House was blocked by the Republican leadership. Former majority leader Tom DeLay knew that he could count on the four Cuban Americans, including one Democrat, Robert Menendez of New Jersey, to support him in a closely divided House. Henry Hyde (R-Illinois), chair of the House Committee on Foreign Affairs, blocked committee votes that would result in a change in the embargo. Thus, those seeking change moved their bills forward through floor amendments on appropriation bills. The 2000 legislation on food and medicine came about through an amendment to an agricultural appropriations bill. Restrictions on American travel to Cuba are enforced by the Treasury Department's Office of Foreign Assets Control (OFAC). This agency spends as much as one-quarter of its time enforcing the ban. As a result, legislative efforts focused on weakening the Treasury's effort to enforce the ban on the grounds that it should be spending more of its time on other matters, especially its responsibility for tracking al-Qaeda's financial network. President Bush annually threatened to veto the entire Treasury appropriations bill if it contains language that would loosen the travel ban. Nevertheless, in 2003, for the fourth year running, the House passed amendments by overwhelming majorities that would impinge on the Treasury's ability to enforce the travel ban. In 2003, the Senate Foreign Relations Committee went one step further by approving 14-5 S.950, the Freedom to Travel to Cuba Act, which had thirty-three sponsors, that would completely lift the ban. Despite the votes, Congressman DeLay and Senate Majority Leader Bill Frist (R-Tennessee) stripped the Cuba language to spare the president from having to carry out his veto threat. With the Democrats now in control of both houses, it is not clear how long the Congress can continue to block the will of a majority of its members and the growing national sentiment for an end to the travel ban. Congress has been influenced by the strong regional economic support for more trade and travel with Cuba as reflected by unanimous passage of resolutions to that end in the legislatures of California (2002), Texas (2001), Illinois (house, 1999), and Louisiana (2000), among others. Economic studies commissioned by groups favoring a change in policy have also driven the efforts. A 2002 study by former Department of Transportation economists at the Washington-based Brattle Group found that the total impact on the U.S. economy of unrestricted travel to Cuba would generate up to $1.6 billion annually and somewhere between 17,000 and 23,000 jobs. The potential positive impact on Florida has begun to change the political dynamic in that state in favor of reducing or ending the embargo. Kenneth Lipner, a University of Miami economist, estimates that Florida's economy loses between $750 million and $1 billion annually due to the embargo. A Florida-Cuba Business Council has been formed to press for further lifting of trade restrictions and to promote ties with the island. The mayors of St. Augustine and Tampa have supported increased engagement, and with the exception of the *Miami Herald*, all of the states' leading newspapers support a change in U.S. policy. This change has come in part because Florida companies like Crower Lines Services in Jacksonville are servicing the increasingly lucrative agricultural trade with the island.

It is now clear, nine years after the launching of the U.S. Chamber of Commerce campaign against the Cuban embargo, that the U.S. business community is now a crucial part of the political coalition that is seeking to change U.S. policy toward Cuba. Without their involvement, it would have been highly unlikely that key Republican members of Congress would have joined the anti-embargo coalition. Of course, the long-standing forces in the religious and labor movement remain a key element, but the clout and funding of the business community made the difference.

The Second Bush Administration

When George Bush assumed office in January, 2001, he inherited a policy toward Cuba that had been honed by nine previous administrations, a hard line policy that sought the overthrow of the Cuban revolutionary government by a variety of means. However, it was also a policy that had failed miserably in its primary objectives. By 2001, the Cuban government had clearly survived the harsh economic times of the early 1990s and was moving forward with considerable success in reintegrating itself into the world capitalist economy, primarily through a dramatic increase in tourism and a skillful capturing of the remittance dollars that were flowing into the country from Cubans living abroad.

Cuba's success had the potential to drive a move for change in U.S. policy since it did not appear likely that the Cuban government was going to change anytime soon. It had been the success of the new Cuban economy, which was buying hundreds of millions of dollars of food abroad, that had motivated Congress in fall, 2000 to allow U.S. companies to sell food to the island as described earlier in this chapter. However, as Bush took office there were no sales because the Cuban government had refused to buy under the conditions imposed by the Congressional legislation. While Cuba's successes might have propelled the United States to reconsider its policies, there were other factors working against change. Bush had won the Presidency by a narrow margin, ultimately carrying Florida by only 537 votes. The Cuban American vote had been crucial in that victory as he carried close to eight percent of that community, outdoing Republican candidate Robert Dole's support from 1996 by more than ten percent. Bush's debt to the Cuban American community was quickly demonstrated by the appointment of Mel Martinez, a Cuban American from Orlando, to head the Department of Housing and Urban Development (HUD) and the appointment of Otto Reich, a Cuban American with close ties to CANF, to be Assistant Secretary of State for Latin American Affairs. The latter appointment would prove to highly controversial and was ultimately blocked of its permanent application by Congress in late 2002, but it signaled the approach of the Bush administration toward Cuba. Reich was subsequently moved to the National Security Council (NSA) where he likely retained important influence on U.S. policy toward the island. Another hard line Cuban American, Colonel Emilio Gonzalez, was appointed to the Western Hemisphere post at the National Security Agency. The situation that ensued after the attack on the Twin Towers and the Pentagon on September 11, 2001, turned tense due to Cuba's opposition to the way the war against terrorism was being pursued. In his address to the United States Congress, President Bush had dichotomized the world into countries "supporting the United States or supporting terrorism," which posed a hegemonic challenge to the international community. Cuba reacted, making public its opposition to the war in Afghanistan. Havana had offered earlier its sincere condolences and deepest sympathy for the horrific attack against the American people and had expressed its willingness to share intelligence and to permit its airports and airspace to be used as needed to fight terrorism. Finding it of little value, Washington dismissed Havana's good-faith offer.

Pleasing the hard-line Cuban Americans that made up the audience, Bush used a Miami political rally celebrating a Cuban holiday on May 20, 2002, to announce his Cuban policy. Repeating issues raised earlier, he demanded that Havana allow internationally supervised free and democratic elections, freedom of expression, and freedom for all political prisoners, before an end to such punitive measures as trade and travel restrictions could be considered. By then, the White House had welcomed the 2001 UN Human Rights Commission's condemnation of Cuba by a majority of one vote. (The close decision was made possible by the relentless campaign of the United States seeking support for the anti-Cuba resolution, including arm twisting of reluctant delegations whenever necessary). The diplomatic situation was appraised by the head of the Cuban Interests Section in Washington, Dagoberto Rodríguez: "What we hear from the American public is that there is a great desire to have normal and civilized rela- tions . . . [But] what we hear from government officials is that there are no great possibilities that it could ever happen." And yet, "we are always ready to sit down to discuss in a civilized fashion any bilateral issue, but never our internal affairs," added Rodríguez. [9]

The strategy of the Bush administration to deepen its pressure on Cuba def- initely predated the measures announced in May, 2004. In October, 2003, before a gathering of Cuban Americans at the White House, George Bush restated that it was intended policy of his administration to bring down the Cuban govern- ment. Bush officially directed Secretary of State Colin Powell and Cuban-born Housing Secretary Mel Martinez to chair a panel that would "plan for the happy days when Castro's regime is no more." Bush's announcement, which came on the 135th anniversary of the beginning of the Cuban war of independence from Spain, declared that the overthrow of the Cuban government was necessary because Cuban President Fidel Castro had acted in "defiance and contempt with a new round of brutal repression that outraged world conscience." The latter was in reference to boat hijackers that were executed and seventy-five political dissi- dents jailed earlier in 2003. At that time, Bush also aired a forty second long radio message in Spanish to the population on the island. The message, aired on Radio Marti on May 20, the anniversary of Cuban "independence" (1902), stated in part that "Dictatorships have no place in the Americas; may God bless the Cuban people who are struggling for freedom."

Colin Powell also stepped up his focus on Cuba during 2003. Speaking in Santiago, Chile in June, at a meeting of the OAS, Powell classified the Cuban government as the "only totalitarian dictatorship existing in the hemisphere" and called on the OAS to play a key role in a "democratic transition" in Cuba. In part, the aggressive stand toward Cuba at the OAS was designed to fend off efforts by some to reconsider Cuba's position as a suspended member of the organization, a status they have been in since 1962. Not surprisingly, Latin American countries that have normal trade and diplomatic relations with Cuba were not moved by Powell's comments. Other Bush initiatives toward Cuba announced in October, 2003 included commitments to tighten travel to Cuba (carried out in July, 2004) and to crack down on illegal cash transfers to the island. Bush also announced plans to increase the number of visas for Cuban immigrants to the United States and said that aggressive campaigns would be undertaken to inform Cubans about safer routes to the U.S. mainland and that his administration would increase U.S. radio, television, satellite, and Internet broadcasts to Cuba to break what Bush called "Castro's information embargo."

Bush followed the fall, 2003 announcements with further measures an- nounced in February, 2004 on the eve of the Florida presidential primary. Bush declared that the Cuban government had used, at times, deadly force against

American and Cuban citizens over the past decade and might do so again. Such an incident "could threaten a disturbance of international relations." Bush's action expanded the government's authority to prevent unauthorized departure of Cuban-bound ships from U.S. waters. Just prior to this announcement, the U.S. State Department cancelled talks on migration issues that are normally held every six months. U.S. officials claimed that Cuba had not been cooperating in achieving the goal of safe, orderly, and legal immigration. In his order regarding that stoppage of ships, Bush claimed that over the course of the previous year Cuba had taken a series of steps to destabilize relations with the United States, such as threatening to rescind migration accords and to close the U.S. interest section in Havana. Furthermore, he said top Cuban officials had said repeatedly that the United States intended to invade Cuba, despite explicit denials from the United States. The February, 2004 edict came less than one year after a May, 2003 declaration by the Bush administration that any actions by Cuba that resulted in significant migration across the Florida Straits would be viewed as a hostile act. Such statements by U.S. officials, made often in the first part of 2003, during a time of several boat and plane hijackings from Cuba to the United States, contributed to the Cuban government's decision to deal with the hijackers in a harsh measure, including the carrying out of the death penalty against three men in the spring of 2003. In spite of the inevitable international criticism for the executions, the Cuban government feared that if it did not deter the hijackings in the strongest manner, their continuation would provide the U.S. government with the provocation for armed action against the island. From the Cuban perspective, the executions served their purpose as the hijackings quickly ended and the pretext for U.S. action was removed.

In issuing the order on U.S. boat traffic to the island, Bush referred to the potential use of Cuban deadly force against such boats and the danger to the passengers. This line of argument without any evidence to support it was probably a cover for the real reason for the order: the desire of the U.S. government to shut down unauthorized U.S. tourism to the island. By 2004 scores, probably hundreds of yachts were sailing to Cuba from the United States without permission annually, most of them docking at Marina Hemingway in western Havana. The sailing corridor had clearly become a small, but important vehicle for U.S. tourism to the island. There had even been an annual race, operating with a humanitarian aid license, from Key West to Havana. However, in June, 2004, the race organizers were threatened with criminal prosecution and the project was terminated. The new rules governing American boats' movement to Cuba expanded restrictions that have been in place for years. Those rules covered vessels originating in Florida, but the new regulations apply to boats leaving from anywhere in the United States. The new regulations appear to have had their intended effect as U.S.-based vessels have virtually disappeared from the Marina Hemingway. Ironically, while this tourist activity has been all but shut down, the ports of Jacksonville, Mobile, and New Orleans remain very active in processing the now flourishing agricultural commerce between the United States and Cuba. This shipping, which benefits U.S. agribusiness interests, is exempted from the regulations.

In the early months of 2004, the United States also stepped up its efforts to crack down on unauthorized travel to Cuba by U.S. citizens using third countries as points of transit. The Bush administration launched a special program for U.S. customs agents who prescreen travelers headed to the United States from Canada, Aruba, Bahamas, and Bermuda. These agents have been specially trained to ferret out those U.S. citizens who may have used one of those four countries as point of departure to Cuba. In describing the program to Cuban-American leaders in Miami, Treasury Secretary John Snow declared, "we must not and we can not have American dollars lining Fidel Castro's pockets and those who would perpetuate his oppressive regime." The edict on boat travel and the focus on third country travel were part of measures that were enhanced later under the Powell Commission report to stem the tide of tens of thousands of U.S. citizens who were traveling to the island illegally. From the Cuban perspective, these measures are unfortunate, but unauthorized U.S. tourism represented less than five percent of the island's total tourism sector.

USAID Programs

The Bush Administration, as a part of its program to undermine the Cuban government through the Cuban dissident community on the island, stepped up the use of U.S. Agency for International Development (USAID) programs on the island. A fact sheet released by USAID in January, 2004 provided an overview of the enhanced program. The program's agenda was stated as follows: "To increase the flow of accurate information of democracy, human rights, and free enterprise to, from, and within the island.[10] The fact sheet reported that USAID had distributed a total of $26 million to twenty-eight non-governmental organizations. Some of the projects funded by USAID included delivery of food and medicines to persons in Cuban prisons judged by the United States to be political prisoners. Another important and high profile campaign carried out personally by U.S. charge d'affairs James Cason was the delivery to anti-government activists on island of books, newsletters, videos, and other informational materials, as well as office equipment. Another key USAID program has been what the U.S. government has called the "independent journalist program." According to USAID, grantees have published more than ten-thousand reports, via the Internet, from Cuba's dissident community and have disseminated them in hard-copy newsletters on the island. More than one-hundred "independent journalists" have received training under the program. Under what the USAID calls direct outreach to the Cuban people, the U.S. government claims the following achievements: distribution of ten thousand short wave radios, distribution of two million books, newsletters, and other informational materials, a multi-media and internet access program for Cuban citizens, and provision of scholarships for

Cuban students to study in the United States. There is no evidence that the latter program has actually been implemented. Various U.S. based institutions have been utilized by USAID to carry out these programs, including Rutgers University, University of Miami, International Foundation for Election Systems (IFES), and the U.S.-Cuba Business Council.

The contemporary USAID program is only the latest incarnation of a U.S. government policy that goes back to the early days of the Reagan administration. That administration decided that additional tools were needed to achieve the long-standing goal of overthrowing the Cuban government. The Bay of Pigs had not worked, the bombing of the Cuban airliner in 1976 had not worked, nor had attempts to isolate Cuba diplomatically. The long standing economic embargo had also failed since by the 1980s it was no longer multilateral and Cuba was doing most of its trade with the Eastern bloc. Cuba became one of many countries that would be included in a new program to finance non-governmental and voluntary organizations, an arena that later became known as civil society. The program was built around two existing organizations, the CIA and USAID, and a new organization, the National Endowment for Democracy, founded in 1983. In many ways, the new initiative was the repackaging of long-standing U.S. tactics. For many years the CIA had been involved in the funding of foreign organizations from trade unions to civic organizations that were willing to do the bidding of U.S. foreign policy. Such work was instrumental in many prominent CIA operations in countries like Chile, Guyana, and Jamaica, where left-leaning leaders like Salvador Allende, Cheddi Jagan, and Michael Manley were targeted with the assistance of internal opposition groups.

The Cuban American National Foundation (CANF) and its leader Jorge Mas Canosa was one of the first beneficiaries of NED funding. From 1983 to 1988 CANF received $390,000 for activities targeting the Cuban government. The funding helped CANF to become the most prominent Cuban exile organization and to raise its political profile in U.S. politics to a very high level. The National Endowment for Democracy presents itself as a private, non-governmental, non-profit foundation, but it receives an annual appropriation from the U.S. Congress. The non-profit front is maintained by the fact that is monies are channeled through four foundations with official non-profit status, National Democratic Institute for International Affairs, The International Republican Institute, The American Center for International Labor Solidarity, and The Center for International Private Enterprise. Each of the four is linked to a prominent U.S. organization, Democratic Party, Republican Party, AFL-CIO, and U.S. Chamber of Commerce, respectively. The elaborate charade to make the NED appear to be non-governmental may seem unimportant but many countries, including the United States and Cuba, have laws that prohibit their citizens from carrying out the work of a foreign government unless it is done under strict permission.

As stated earlier, work to support Cuban opposition groups began in the 1980s under CANF, but these efforts received a significant boost with the passage in 1992 of the Cuban Democracy Act (Torricelli Bill). Support of Cuban NGOs as part of a declared strategy of engineering a political transition in Cuba was a key part of the legislation. The Cuban Liberty and Solidarity Act (Helms-Burton) of 1996 deepened the commitment. According to Philip Agee, it is very difficult to put a definitive dollar amount on the spending for opposition activities in Cuba in large measure because there is no public reporting of CIA spending and their role in the work is significant. However, some evidence does emerge on both NED and USAID. From 1996 to 2001, USAID reported a total of $12 million in spending. However, the renewed commitment of the Bush administration was seen in the 2002 budget of $5 million and the 2003 commitment of $6 million.

Powell Commission Report

However, the full force of the Bush hard line toward Cuba would not be revealed until the Powell Commission Report was unveiled in May, 2004 near the end of his first term. This document reaffirmed the basic outlines of U.S. policy ever since 1959 and undertook a new series of measures aimed at reversing Cuba's economic successes of the last ten years. The Powell Commission Report and its recommended policy changes brought the Bush-Cuba policies into clearer focus, but the harder line mandated by the report had been developing incrementally during the first three years of his administration and bore the distinct markings of both his neo-conservative policy advisors, like Donald Rumsfeld and Paul Wolfowitz, and the Miami Cuban thinking of Otto Reich.

One area where the harder line policy began to emerge was in the enforcement of the ban on travel of U.S. citizens to the island. Except for a small number of exceptions, primarily Cuban Americans, it was in reality illegal for U.S. citizens to travel to the island. The policy was carried out under Department of Treasury rules within the Trading with the Enemy Act, forbidding U.S. citizens to spend money on the island unless they were permitted to do so by the Office of Foreign Assets Control (OFAC). These regulations were put in place in 1982 by President Ronald Reagan, reversing a five year period where U.S. travel to the island had been legalized. By 1982, 100,000 U.S. citizens per year were going to Cuba, primarily as tourists. In 1984, the U.S. Supreme Court, in a bitterly contested 5-4 decision, ruled the ban to be constitutional. However, in the first twenty years of the ban, there were virtually no prosecutions under the law and as a result tens of thousands of U.S. citizens traveled to Cuba illegally through third countries every year. In the mid-1990s, activist groups seeking to get a test case that might reverse the 1984 Supreme Court decision openly flaunted the law, but ultimately the Clinton administration foiled that effort by refusing to prosecute the civilly disobedient travelers.

However, once in office, the Bush administration began to step up its enforcement of the ban and that policy has become a centerpiece of its campaign
against Cuba, especially the regulations effective July 1, 2004.

The new rules include the following:

1. Full-hosted travel. The previous authorization for "fully-hosted" travel to
Cuba (for which all costs and fees either are paid for by a third-country national
who is not subject to U.S. jurisdiction or are covered or waived by Cuba) is
eliminated. Moreover, the regulations now include a prohibition on the receipt
of goods or services in Cuba when they are provided free-of-charge or received
as a gift, unless otherwise authorized by an OFAC general or specific license.
OFAC now considers this a prohibited dealing in property in which Cuba has an
interest.

2. Importation of Cuban merchandise. The general license that authorized
licensed Cuba travelers to purchase in Cuba and return to the United States with
up to $100 worth of Cuban merchandise for personal consumption is eliminated.
Thus, no merchandise, other than informational materials, may be purchased or
otherwise acquired in Cuba and then brought back to the United States.

3. Accompanied baggage. The amount of baggage carried by an authorized
traveler to Cuba is now limited to forty-four pounds per traveler, unless a higher
amount is authorized by OFAC.

4. Family visits. Under prior regulations, a general license authorized a person to visit a close relative (defined to include second cousins) once every
twelve months (and more often under a specific license). There was no stated
limit to the duration of the first visit and travelers could spend up to the State
Department per diem (currently $167) for living expenses in Cuba, plus any
additional funds needed for transactions directly related to visiting the relative.
The new rule eliminates the general license and requires a specific license issued
by OFAC that will only authorize travel-related transactions incident to visits to
members of the traveler's "immediate family" once per three-year period, meas-
ured from the last departure from Cuba, for no more than fourteen days. No
additional visits will be authorized by specific licenses, according to OFAC,
apparently even for exigent circumstances. Travelers may obtain an OFAC license to visit an immediate family member who is not a Cuban national (such as
a student in Cuba under a university educational activity license) in exigent
circumstances, provided that the exigency has been reported to the U.S. Interests
Section in Havana and that the issuance of the license would "support the mission of the U.S. Interests Section." The amendments reduce the amount of money travelers who are visiting immediate family members can spend for living
expenses to $50 per day, plus up to an additional $50 per trip to pay for trans-
portation-related expenses.

The restrictions on family visits have divided the Cuban American community and the changes in the Cuban American community that are part of a long
term demographic shift that is underway in the Cuban American community.
The opposition to any engagement with the island remains strongest in the Cu-

bans, primarily from the upper classes, who came to the United States in the early 1960s. Politically this group still dominates the community and their views are pursued with vigor by the three Cuban American representatives and two senators. However, a variety of polls demonstrate that the second generation of the immigrants, largely born in the United States together with those arriving since 1980 are much more likely to support a change in U.S. policy. Another trend underway in Florida politics is that non-Cuban Latinos with no commitment to U.S. policy on Cuba are becoming an increasing factor in Florida politics. The impetus for change in U.S. policy is represented by organizations such as the Cuban American Alliance Education Fund and Puentes Cubanos which advocates immediate engagement with Cuba. These groups and their supporters regularly visit the island and are more likely to send remittances to their families.

5. Educational activities. Specific licenses are limited to undergraduate and graduate institutions (i.e., no secondary schools), and the duration of such licenses is shortened from two years to one year. Only students enrolled in the licensed institution may travel on that license; therefore, students may no longer travel to Cuba under the license of an educational institution other than their own, even if their own institution accepts the licensed institution's program for credit toward the student's degree. Employees who travel under the license must be full-time permanent employees of the licensed institution. Certain educational activities in Cuba may be no shorter than ten weeks; others may be for a period of less than ten weeks. The impact of the new regulations on educational travel to the island has been dramatic. Using the openings provided by the change of regulations in 1995, scores of U.S. universities organized a variety of courses that visited the island. Generally, the courses were short term, two to four weeks, conducted during interior, summer school, or as a short part of a semester-long course. By 2004 more than 30,000 students participated in the courses. The Powell Commission report was very explicit that it intended to close down such programs. The political logic of the report was that students in such programs would have little ability to influence Cubans to think in the democratic or capitalist manner and that such programs generally used the Cuban tourist sector with money going directly to the Cuban government. The new regulations only allowed the continuation of programs of ten weeks or longer (semester) conducted by a single university for its own students. The logic of the Powell Report was that such students could be better ambassadors for capitalist ideas and that given the long term nature of their stay, accommodation would be with families and the money going directly to private individuals not the Cuban state. New regulations also sharply limited the rules under which such programs could be carried out. The result is that today fewer than one hundred U.S. students study in Cuba per year, attending programs conducted by such schools as American University, Sarah Lawrence College, the University of North Carolina, and Harvard University. Under the current regulations, it is highly unlikely that any significant number of new programs will be organized. Political response from

the academic community to the removal of programs and academic exchanges has been strong. In early 2005 a new organization was formed to oppose the new regulations, the Emergency Coalition to Defend Educational Travel (ECDET) was formed under the leadership of Wayne Smith of Johns Hopkins University, former head of the U.S. Interests Section in Havana and long-time critic of U.S. policy toward Cuba. Over 450 professors and educational administrators have joined the organization. On June 13, 2006 ECDET filed suit in U.S. District Court challenging the 2004 regulations on study abroad in Cuba. The suit filed against the U.S. Treasury Department claims that the restrictions violate academic freedom as defined by the Supreme Court. ECDET argues that the First Amendment to the Constitution protects academic freedom, defined as the right of educators to decide, without interference from the federal government what courses will be taught, how they will be taught, who will teach them, and who can take them. The lawsuit enters into some very contentious areas regarding the prerogative of the Executive Branch to determine U.S. foreign policy. Its ultimate fate is uncertain, but it could result in a revisiting of the 1984 U.S. Supreme Court Case that sets the framework for restricting U.S. citizen travel to Cuba.

6. Sporting events, clinics and workshops. The general license for amateur and semi-professional athletic competitions sponsored by an international sports federation is eliminated and OFAC will only authorize such activities under a specific license on a case-by-case basis. The policy of specifically licensing participation in workshops and clinics, whether sports-related or otherwise, is also eliminated.

7. Family remittances. The general license authorizing quarterly $300 remittances sent by any U.S. person eighteen years of age or older to any household or national of Cuba is eliminated. The new general license authorizes such remittances only when they are sent to the remitter's immediate family. They cannot be remitted to certain Cuban government officials and members of the Cuban Communist party. The total amount of family remittances that an authorized traveler may carry to Cuba is reduced from $3,000 to $300.

8. Remittance-related transactions. The general license authorizing depository institutions to act as forwarders for family and emigration remittances is eliminated. A specific authorization as a remittance forwarder is now required. Depository institutions are still authorized under general license to provide services related to other authorized financial institutions, such as transferring funds to Cuba covered by a specific license allowing overflight payments.

The Bush administration also adopted over time a much more stringent policy on the travel of Cubans to the United States. Especially targeted by the new policy were musicians and academics. During the Clinton administration, both groups began to travel more freely to the United States. Cuban music became increasingly popular in the United States following the release of the Ry Cooder film, *Buena Vista Social Club,* in 1998. In the years that followed, artists featured in the film including Ruben Gonzalez and Compay Segundo traveled to the United States for multiple city tours and played in front of sold out audiences. In spite of the embargo, promoters were permitted to pay the Cuban performers who returned to Cuba with thousands of dollars earned in the United States. Cuban artists received music awards in the United States and were able to travel to receive those prizes.

Academic exchanges had begun to be regularized in the late 1980s but during the Clinton period they reached new levels. The most dramatic example of this cooperation occurred with semi-annual meetings of the Latin American Studies Association. From a delegation of just twenty-five Cubans in Miami in 1989, the Cuban delegation had reached over one-hundred by the time that LASA visited Miami again in 2000. Cuban scholars regularly traveled to make scholarly presentations at U.S. universities, and in one case, Esteban Morales received permission to teach for an entire semester at the University of St. Thomas in St. Paul, Minnesota.

Initially, the Bush administration did not change the policy on cultural and academic exchanges. For example, over one-hundred Cuban scholars were approved to attend the LASA meeting in Washington in early September, 2001. However, following September 11, a much harder line developed regarding Cuban academic travel to the United States. Admittedly, part of the process is a security review that has been instituted for virtually all academic visitors to the United States. Under the new procedures, each Cuban applicant must undergo an interview at the U.S. Interests Section in Havana and pay a non-refundable fee of $100 to make the application. The impact of this new procedure was significant. In spite of intense lobbying by numerous academic institutions, including Harvard University, only sixty-five of the 101 Cuban academics who applied to attend the March 2003 LASA meeting in Dallas received their visas. Several prominent Cuban scholars never received any answer to their request. Since the 2003 LASA meeting, the situation has grown even worse. Scholars such as Esteban Morales and Carlos Alzugaray of the Superior Institute of International Relations have been repeatedly denied in their efforts to attend academic conferences in the United States. They have been denied entry under a clause that allows the U.S. government to deny access to high level Communist Party or governmental officials. These denials come in spite of the fact that both men traveled frequently to the United States prior to 2002 and there has been no change in their standing in Cuban society in the meantime. It became clear by 2004 that the Bush administration was reversing the position of two previous administrations in fostering academic contact between the two countries. The extent of the new policy was made fully clear in October, 2004 when the entire delegation of close to one-hundred Cuban scholars scheduled to participate in the LASA meeting in Las Vegas were denied entry to the United States.

The hardline on academic travel continued in 2006 when all Cubans applying to attend the LASA meeting in Puerto Rico were denied visas. In response to the denial of the Cuban visas, LASA moved its 2007 conference from Boston to Montreal and has stated that it will not return to the United States until there is a clear change in the position of the U.S. government on visas. The 2009 meeting of LASA has already been committed to Brazil. It has also been almost impossible for Cuban academics to visit their counterparts in the United States. Since 2003 fewer than ten visas have been granted for Cubans to come to the United States. The effort to limit academic contact for U.S. professors in Cuba has also increased. U.S.-based academics are no longer permitted to attend conferences in Cuba sponsored by the Cuban organizations. Travel to Cuba is limited to those U.S. academics that have a specific research focus on Cuba with a demonstrated ability to publish the results of the research. This provision makes it very difficult for graduate students that might develop a Cuba specialization to visit the island. The U.S. Interests Section in Havana maintained that it was committed to continuing the exchanges, but at the higher levels of the State Department in Washington, it was obvious that reducing the number of Cuban academics coming to the United States was part of a wider policy of placing greater pressure on the Cuban state. Artists also began receiving a harder time in gaining visas to perform in the United States. This shift in policy was epitomized by the refusal in March, 2004 of visas to Cuban artists scheduled to receive awards at the Latin Grammy awards ceremony in Los Angeles. In the ensuing years, few Cuban performers have been able to obtain permission to come to the United States.

Political Motivations in the Bush Policy

The hard-line policies of the Bush administration, in part, represented its political debt to the right-wing Cubans in Miami. The timing of the new measures during the heart of the 2004 presidential election campaign where Florida is again a battleground state was fairly obvious. However, the Bush policies are not primarily driven by the Miami Cubans. The neo-cons who surrounded Bush are especially ideological and consider the continuation of the socialist project in Cuba to be an affront to their plans for U.S. global hegemony. Of course, Cuba is no military threat to the United States, but it is the power of the Cuban example to others in the Third World that must in their view be expunged from the world. Cuba's economy has continued to move forward in the new century, but it still faces key obstacles to long term success, especially given the vulnerability of tourism and remittances. In that context, the neo-cons in the Bush administration believe that Cuba is vulnerable and therefore new pressures are warranted.

Opponents of the ongoing embargo viewed 2005 as a year where possible breakthroughs could occur in changing U.S. policy. Their logic for change was based on the idea that during George Bush's second term, the President and his allies in the most conservative wing on the Republican Party, including the three Cuban-American representatives from Florida (Lincoln and Mario Díaz-Balart, Ileana Ros-Lehtinen) would be in a weakened position to resist the growing majority of Congress—people in both houses that favored an end to the travel ban and a lessening of the embargo. However, in late June, a series of votes in the House of Representatives went definitively against the anti-embargo coalition. Rather than seeking a fundamental reversal of the embargo and travel ban, the coalition (House Working Group on Cuba) decided to continue the challenge to the most controversial Bush policies introduced in 2004. Representative Davis (D-FL) introduced an amendment to the Transportation-Treasury Appropriations bill to roll back the new regulation barring Cuban-Americans from visiting family members in Cuba more than once every three years. The amendment failed by a vote of 211–208. Discouraging to the opponents of the travel ban was that an identical amendment passed last year 225-174 before being removed in conference committee negotiations. More than 20 Representatives who had supported the bill in 2004 in addition to the majority of newly elected members voted with the administration. It is interesting to note that the *Miami Herald*, which normally supports U.S. policies toward Cuba, editorialized against the failure of the Congress to reopen more liberal Cuban-American travel to the island by calling the vote "cruel and un-American."

Representative Barbara Lee (D-CA) introduced an amendment that would have permitted the restoration of the hundreds of educational exchanges that were blocked by the 2004 policy revisions, but that amendment was defeated by a vote of 233-187. Representative Charles Rangel's annual bill to completely end the travel ban and embargo was defeated 250-169. The bill has never passed the House, but for the first time in a number of years it received fewer votes than the previous year. Due to the disappointing set of reversals, Representative Jeff Flake (R-AZ) decided to not offer his annual amendment to lift the travel ban. After winning several years in a row, Flake did not appear to have the votes for passage and did not want to have a losing vote on record. Efforts in the Senate to establish new policy were also unsuccessful. Senator Byron Dorgan (D-ND) gained 60 votes in favor of an amendment to permit humanitarian exceptions for travel to Cuba. The amendment would allow Cuban-Americans to apply for licenses from OFAC to visit immediate family in Cuba during family emergencies. Such travel had been permitted prior to the policies placed in effect in 2004. However, Dorgan's efforts were blocked in a procedural move by supporters of the administration, and the ban on that type of travel continued. Soon after the defeat of these proposals, Cuba suffered significant damage and storm-related deaths at the hands of Hurricane Dennis.

Efforts by opponents of the travel ban attempted to use the difficulty of the moment to allow for the lifting of restrictions on gift parcels and travel to the island, but these efforts were rebuffed by the Bush administration in spite of pleas to the contrary by several leading "dissidents" on the island. Prior to Hurricane Dennis, scattered protests had occurred in Cuba in response to the frustrations caused by daily blackouts. With the power situation only likely to be made worse by the effects of Dennis, the Bush administration maintained its hard line arguing that its policies of undermining support for the Cuban government was beginning to bear fruit. A new element in the Congressional battles in 2005 was the weight of the U.S.-Cuba Democracy Political Action Committee (DPCAC). The DPCAC was founded in August 2003 to counter the efforts of the anti-embargo forces. The PAC has raised about $750,000 since it opened its doors, and according to the Center for Responsive Politics, has given $214,000 to 113 House candidates and $54,000 to twelve Senate candidates with the understanding that they would reject any legislation that would ease sanctions against Cuba. Of these members 33 had consistently voted to lift restrictions on travel to Cuba in previous years. After accepting an out of state campaign donation these members reversed their support for measures easing the travel ban in 2005. It appears that campaign contributions, in the absence of any changes in the Cuba situation, "bought" the support of representatives who had formerly favored restoring at least some important relationship with Cuba. The work of the pact continued in 2006 with large donations to two pro-embargo Senators who won tough reelection battles, Robert Menendez of New Jersey and Joe Lieberman of Connecticut.

2006 Cuba Report

In December 2005, U.S. Secretary of State Condoleezza Rice reconvened the cabinet-level commission for Assistance for a Free Cuba with the stated intention of presenting President Bush with a new report by May, 2006 with the charge of updating the changes that had been made in U.S. Cuba policy in June, 2004, following the issuance of the Powell Commission report discussed earlier in this chapter. The stated goal of the new effort was to provide "updated recommendations to hasten democracy and an interagency strategic plan to assist a Cuban-led transition…and Cuba's reintegration into the inter-American system." The latter point was especially indicative of the non-factual basis of the U.S. position. It is true that Cuba is excluded by the United States from the Summits of the Americas process and from exercising its rights as a member of the OAS, but Cuba regularly participates in a variety of regional forums from the Association of Caribbean States to the Ibero-American Summits.

The new report, eighty-five pages in length, was formerly issued on July 10 after an unexplained two month delay. It was presented under the names of Rice and Carlos Gutierrez, Secretary of Commerce. The report contains seven chapters, including "Hastening the End of the Castro Dictatorship: Transition, not Succession," "Helping Cubans Create Market-based Economic Opportunities," and "The Vital Role of Cubans Abroad." In a break from the 2004 report the 2006 document indicates that there is a "classified" portion of the report that will not be revealed due to "reasons of national security." There may well have been a classified addendum to the 2004 report, but it was not openly revealed as it was in this case. It is widely speculated that the classified part of the report contains specific plans for overthrowing the Cuban government. The new report does attempt to respond to certain criticisms of the earlier report with such statements as "If asked, the United States will . . ." or "Should the Cuban Transition Government request United States assistance, the U.S. government can . . ." The tone of the report is that the U.S. government is simply an interested bystander ready to respond to an invitation from a new, pro-U.S. government in Havana. Such tone seems disingenuous given the long-standing policy of the U.S. government and the fact the report is full of U.S.-inspired plans from reorganizing Cuba's economy along free-market principles to revamping the Cuban educational system to holding multiparty elections within 18 months. For U.S. government assistance to be provided the U.S. president must determine that the successor Cuban government is worthy of aid (i.e. purged of any key figures in the current system). How such a dramatic change is to occur in the absence of significant, organized opposition to the current system, is unclear. It can be assumed that this is where the classified section of the report comes into play.

Three U.S. goals are repeatedly referenced: political freedom, economic opportunity, and free and fair elections. To further these goals, $80 million over two years is recommended by the Commission report in support of what it calls "Cuban civil society" to increase international awareness and to "break the regimes information blockade." An additional $20 million in ongoing annual funding is recommended "until the dictatorship ceases to exist." Such funding is routinely passed by Congress because these are small amounts in the scheme of the overall budget and the policy of opposing the current Cuban government has traditionally had broad, bipartisan support.

A significant policy shift in the 2006 document is the tightening of controls on legal humanitarian aid to the island. The report calls for the prohibition of humanitarian aid to the Cuban people that is delivered through entities that are "regime administered or controlled organizations, such as the Cuban Council of the Churches." The 2004 report had created the framework for distinguishing between legitimate and illegitimate humanitarian aid but the 2006 report gives more clarity to the issue. The U.S. based National Council of Churches of Christ in the USA (NCC) and its sister humanitarian agency, Church World Service, have protested that licenses may be refused for ongoing shipments of humanitarian aid that are handled by the Cuban Council of Churches, their long-time ecumenical partners. Such categorization also places in legal jeopardy the humanitarian aid channeled through Pastors for Peace, a New York-based interfaith organization that openly challenges the U.S. embargo/blockade. Pastors for Peace works closely with the Martin Luther King Center in Havana which like the Cuban Council of Churches maintains cooperative relations with the Cuban government. Not surprisingly, the new report received little support beyond those political forces in the United States long connected with support for U.S. Cuban policy. Ricardo Alarcon called it a continuation of the 2004 report and a "plan for the annexation of Cuba." European sources worried that U.S. policy was placing the United States and Cuba on a collision course. The head of the Organization of American States was more pointed in his criticism when he stated, "There is no transition and it's not your country."

The 2006 report may have been no more than a small item in a long standing U.S. policy toward Cuba but unknown to its sponsors it predated by only three weeks a dramatic announcement from the Cuban side. Cuban President Fidel Castro was entering the hospital for serious surgery and that power was being transferred temporarily to the Cuban Vice President, his brother, Raul Castro. Eighteen months later, Fidel has not appeared in public, remaining somewhat active in Cuban public life, issuing public speakers and meeting visiting dignitaries in his place of recovery. Most significantly, little has changed in Cuban public life over the course of the last year, demonstrating what has always been true, the Cuban revolution is much deeper than the leadership of Fidel Castro, as important as that has been. Also, not surprisingly, the year of Fidel not in power has seen no change in U.S. policy toward the island. After initial official U.S. speculation that Castro's illness would cause chaos on the island, U.S. officials have been forced to recognize that no such unrest is forthcoming. Before the end of 2006, Raul Castro stated as Fidel had before him, that Cuba is always open to dialogue if the U.S. government accepts Cuba's system as a starting point. Not surprisingly, U.S. officials rejected the overture.

Notes

1. For a detailed discussion of the Clinton years see Max Azicri, *Cuba Today and Tomorrow* (University Press of Florida, Gainesville, 2000).

2. For detailed information on the AHTC, see their website, www.ahtc.org.

3. Retrieved from www.ahtc.org.

4. Penni Crabtree, "CancerVax Wins Rare OK from U.S." *Union Tribune*, July 15, 2004.

5. Retrieved from www.cubatrade.org.

6. Retrieved from www.cubatrade.org.

7. Retrieved from the official website of the Sister Cities Association, www.uscsca.org

8. Retrieved from www.cubamer.org.

9. *El Nuevo Herald* (on line), January 24, 2002.

10. Fact Sheet, USAID Cuba Program, Issued January 15, 2004. Accessed at www.usaid.gov.

Chapter Nine

Conclusion

Several years into the twenty-first century and on the eve of the fiftieth anniversary of the triumph of the Cuban revolutionaries we ask the question, what lies ahead for the relationship between the United States and Cuba? The illness of Fidel Castro and his stepping down from a day to day governance role in the Cuban system is obviously a significant moment in Cuban history. Will that important Cuban development have any significant impact of U.S. Cuban relations, especially if Fidel were to die in the immediate future? What is the impact on U.S.-Cuban relations of changing political dynamics in the Western Hemisphere and in the wider world? The last ten years, beginning with the electoral triumph of Hugo Chavez in Venezuela in 1998, have seen a significant leftward shift in Latin American politics in the wake of the failure of the neoliberal economic strategies pursued in the framework of the Washington Consensus in the 1990s. In that era, immediately following the collapse of the Soviet Union, free market ideology was dominant worldwide and in Latin America it meant neoliberal regimes like Menem in Argentina and Cardoso in Brazil, carrying out conservative economic policies that lowered tariff barriers, privatized state companies, and cut government social services. The centerpiece of this neoliberal strategy was the creation of a hemisphere-wide Free Trade Area of the Americas (FTAA) that would have by 2005, deepened the control of the United States over Latin America, politically and economically. Cuba's political stance against this U.S. strategy was clear, but for a certain time period in the 1990s seemed like a voice in the wilderness and the Cuban leadership was forced to focus primarily on their own survival in the midst of this new, neoliberal consensus.

However, the false promise of the neoliberal agenda that it would provide broad economic gains for the Latin American people was very quickly exposed as a lie. The neoliberal policies did succeed in lowering inflation and increasing macro-economic growth rates, but these changes did nothing to attack the long-standing factors that had kept the majority of Latin American people in poverty for centuries. In reality, the economic reforms did create benefits, but those advantages went almost exclusively to Latin America's already wealthy elites and their counterparts in North America. In the short term lower inflation rates, benefiting most Latin Americans, bought some time for the neoliberal regimes. In both Argentina and Brazil the rightwing governments were reelected in the mid-1990s.

In 1998, the first blow to the political consensus around neoliberalism occurred in Venezuela, where populist and former army officer Hugo Chavez won the presidential election on a platform that was decisively anti-neoliberal. His electoral triumph was the culmination of street demonstrations that began in 1992 against the neoliberal policies of social democrat Carlos Andres Perez. Chavez's triumph and his subsequent rise to a position of leadership in the Latin American left has been part of a dramatic political turnaround on the continent. Since the Chavez triumph in 1998, the political landscape of Latin America has undergone significant transformation through a combination of revived social movements and electoral results. The harsh reality of neoliberal reforms sparked the emergence of new social movements, often led by indigenous peoples, that challenged the status quo in their countries. In the forefront of these movements were Argentine demonstrators that brought down four governments in one month in 2001, Ecuadorian protestors who have twice toppled governments since 2001, and the Bolivian strikers who toppled governments in both 2003 and 2005. In each of the above cases, the intervention of powerful social movements also resulted ultimately in the election of progressive leaders: Nestor Kirchner in Argentina in 2003, Evo Morales in Bolivia in 2005, and Rafael Correa in Ecuador in 2006. Equally important in the political transformation of Latin America was the election of Workers Party leader Luiz Inacio da Silva in Brazil in 2002 and his subsequent reelection in 2006. In the same time period came the election of socialist Tabre Vasquez, former guerrilla, to the presidency of Uruguay and two additional electoral triumphs by Hugo Chavez in 2002 and 2006.

What has been the meaning of this changed Latin American political landscape for Cuba? Most importantly, the relative hemispheric isolation of the 1990s came to an end and the newfound allies, especially Venezuela, delivered concrete economic benefits to Cuba and also gave Cuba renewed confidence in a Latin American future not fully dominated by U.S. power and ideology. Over the last decade Cuba and Venezuela have developed a dynamic bilateral relationship that has benefited both countries. Cuba has benefited from the receipt of oil at stable, subsidized prices during a time when volatile world oil prices could have heavily damaged Cuba's economic recovery. This benefit is not unlike the manner in which Cuba was shielded in the 1980s by their oil trading relationship with the former Soviet Union. The availability of Venezuelan oil to supplement Cuba's own inadequate domestic supplies has been crucial to the positive macroeconomic performance of the Cuban economy, especially over the past five years. Cuba has paid for the oil in part by sending to Venezuela thousands of teachers, doctors, and technicians that have been key players in Chavez's Bolivarian revolution, designed to dramatically benefit Venezuela's majority poor through increased access to housing, health care, and education. The Cubans working in Venezuela over the last decade have been crucial to the delivery of the above services to the Venezuelan people. It is too early to gauge the long-term success of the Bolivarian revolution, but in the short term there has been a reduction in Venezuela's infant mortality rate and its illiteracy. The successful bilateral relationship has in the last two years, morphed into a wider project under the leadership of both Cuba and Venezuela. Called the Bolivarian Alternative or ALBA, it is a transnational formation that has as its ultimate goal, the realization of Simon Bolivar's nineteenth century dream of a united Latin America. In 2007 three additional countries, Bolivia, Ecuador, and Nicaragua have joined ALBA and a variety of social and economic projects modeled after the Cuban-Venezuelan relationship are being developed. ALBA is presented as a clear alternative to the now defeated U.S.-led project of the Free Trade Area of the Americas.

From the above, it is clear that Cuba is no longer isolated from Latin America, but it is not the only factor in its twenty-first century international relations. The most interesting developing relationship for Cuba is with the Peoples Republic of China. In the last five years China has become an important trading partner for Cuba. The Chinese see Cuba as an important link in their economic outreach to Latin America. In the coming years thousands of Chinese will be educated in Spanish at schools in Cuba. China is set to begin manufacturing household appliances in Cuba for both the local and Latin American markets. Agreements are being negotiated for joint Chinese-Cuba exploration for oil in the Gulf of Mexico. Cuba has begun to manufacture drugs in China for both the Chinese and international markets. The relationship is in its earlier stages and its ultimate importance to Cuba is not fully clear, but it gives to Cuba options for its economic development that did not exist as recently as a decade ago.

What is the meaning of these regional and international developments for Cuba's relationship with the United States and its own internal development? On the U.S. side there remains virtually no change in the views of the dominant political establishment toward Cuba. The bases of the policy, some of which go back to the nineteenth century, remain largely unchanged. For U.S. leaders, the last fifty years remain an aberration, Cuba is still viewed as "ripe fruit" that will inevitably fall from the tree and be reintegrated into the U.S. sphere of influence as it was from 1898-1959. This long-standing position of U.S. elites fails to recognize the legitimacy of Cuba's project of national independence and assumes Cuba to be an extension of its continental territory. This position is rooted in a fundamental aversion to Cuba's socialist system and the alternative that it presents to the United States' unbridled promotion of the primacy of capitalism. This sense of ideological superiority is most recently manifested in the Powell Commission's total dismissal of the social and economic achievements of Cuba over the last fifty years. The survival of Cuba's revolutionary socialist system into the twenty-first century, even with its inevitable compromises with the world capitalist system, is particularly galling to the U.S. leaders. Today, Cuba is viewed as an even greater threat than before because of its alliance with countries like Venezuela, Bolivia, and Ecuador, whose leaders speak of creating twenty-first century socialism. President Bush has gone so far as to refer to the new relationships led by Venezuela and Cuba as representing a "Latin American axis of evil," a label previously reserved for Iraq under Saddam Hussein, Iran, and North Korea.

The last fifteen years of Cuba's continued independence from the United States have been especially frustrating for U.S. rulers. Most U.S. analysts clearly believed that the demise of the Soviet Union meant that Cuba would soon again be a "ripe fruit." When Cuba successfully engineered a post-Soviet strategy, U.S. hopes for retaking control of the island were dashed. As a result, U.S. leaders turned to a new hope, the Cuban revolution could not outlive its preeminent leader, Fidel Castro. Once Castro was gone from the scene, there would be dramatic political upheaval on the island and Cuban forces friendly to U.S. interests, possibly aided by U.S. intervention, could seize control and return the relationship to pre-1959 status.

In an ironic way, statements by Fidel himself, in the fall of 2005 may have validated that outlook on the part of U.S. officials. Speaking to the Cuban people in worlds he had never used before, Castro declared that the continuation of the Cuban revolution was not inevitable. If they were to fail it would not be the result of external aggression but rather from defects within the system itself that could be capitalized upon by enemies of the revolution, both internal and external. In the speech Fidel attacked those within Cuba that were undermining the system through thievery and corruption. He highlighted problems that were familiar to ordinary Cubans. Some individuals were taking advantage of the framework in which Cuba had opened itself to the capitalist world to enrich themselves personally. He recommitted the focus of the work of the Communist Party and the government to combating these problems within the system. How much of a threat to the continuation of Cuban socialism these problems represent is open to debate, but there is no doubt that their public airing served to bolster the view within the U.S. ruling circles that Cuba's vulnerability to U.S. pressure was very real.

When Fidel Castro fell seriously ill in July 2006 and temporarily ceded power to other officials, including his brother, Raul, under established Cuban constitutional guidelines the world watched with considerable anticipation how the Cuban people would respond. U.S. leaders were clearly hoping for a scenario of unrest that might benefit U.S. interests. More than one year later, the primary story, is that there is no real change. Raul Castro has assumed the presidential duties and the country has gone forward, seemingly oblivious to the changes at the top. The last year and half have confirmed what has always been true, the Cuban revolution is much more than Fidel, however important he may be in Cuban life. Fidel has apparently settled into a new role, staying active as much as his health permits. He has assumed the role of senior leader, meeting foreign dignitaries and writing on a range of issues, including the environment.

Not surprisingly, Raul Castro has continued the same basic policies as his brother. Such continuity comes as no surprise to those who understand the Cuban revolution, given the long-standing collaboration between the brothers and the consistent dynamic of the revolutionary project that they represent.

This latest development in Cuba's political history, the beginnings of a potential full transition to a new generation of Cuban leaders will not likely result in any significant change in U.S.-Cuban relations. From the Cuban side, Raul Castro has made clear that negotiations leading to better relations with the United States are possible, but only if the United States fully accepts the legitimacy of its revolutionary government. At this moment in history Cuba can confidently state that negotiating position because its international standing economically and politically is reasonably strong and would not be advantaged by significant concessions to the United States. There is no doubt that Cuba could benefit from better relations with the Untied States, especially in terms of greater trade and commerce, but those benefits are in no means necessary for Cuba's survival. Today, Cuba has more alternatives to a subservient relationship with the United States than at any point in its history.

From the U.S. side there is also not a significant impetus for change, especially in the wake of Fidel's apparent recovery from his near fatal illness. Because Fidel survives, albeit in a more limited role, the U.S. leaders still hold out hope than when he does die, the moment will then be ripe for unrest in Cuba and possibilities for U.S. intervention. The argument can be made that a real transition to the next generation of revolutionary leaders is well underway in Cuba, but this argument is not likely to win the day in Washington, since it would only underscore the fallacy of U.S. thinking over the last fifty years. It may well be that only after the passing of Fidel could there be a significant change in U.S. policy toward the island. In keeping with our thesis that U.S. policy is ultimately driven by developments on the island, change may come if U.S. rulers, in the wake of Fidel's passing, arrive at the realization that Cuban socialism has survived and is therefore an even longer term reality than they had ever dreamed. A version of that acceptance of reality came with the eventual U.S. recognition of the Communist governments of China and Vietnam. However, the authors recognize the parallels are not exact and that such concessions made in Asia were easier to make for a variety of reasons than it will ever be for the United States to acknowledge the legitimacy of revolutionary Cuba.

As a sovereign nation, Cuba is reaping the fruits of its long struggle, which permits it to play an independent role on the international stage. This objective, however, is only feasible if Cuba continues its economic recovery, preserves its social projects, and guarantees the stability of its political system. It is not possible to know for sure when the present U.S. policy toward Cuba will change, but what appears certain is that if the island cannot continue resisting U.S. pressure, difficult economic conditions and their internal social consequences, and the other problems facing it, while continually moving forward on all fronts, no change in U.S. policy agreeable to Cuba can ever take place. However, if the

Cuban people do continue to persevere under a new generation of leaders, it has the potential to create a dynamic in U.S. policy making circles where the United States, while still hoping for long term domination, chooses a more pragmatic policy of engagement with the Cuban government.

Bibliography

Ambrose, Stephen E. *Towards a Global Power*. New York: Latin American Editing Group, 1991.

Azicri, Max. *Cuba Today and Tomorrow: Reinventing Socialism*. Gainesville: University Press of Florida, 2000.

Blight, James and Philip Brenner. *Sad and Luminous Days: Cuba's Struggle with the Superpowers After the Missile Crisis*. Lanham, MD: Rowman and Littlefield, 2007.

Bonsal, Philip. *Cuba, Castro, and the United States*. Pittsburgh: Pittsburgh University Press, 1971.

Boucher, Lynn Francis, Roger W. Fontaine, David C. Jordan and Gordon Sumner. *The Santa Fe Report: A New Inter-American Policy for the Eighties*. Prepared by the Committee of Santa Fe, New Mexico for the Council for Inter-American Security, Inc. (CIS), Washington, D.C., 1980.

Brenner, Philip. *The Limits and Possibilities of Congress*. New York: Palgrave Macmillan, 1983

Castro Ruz, Fidel. *History Will Absolve Me,* The Moncada Trial defense speech, Santiago de Cuba, October 16, 1953. Jonathan Cape, London: Cape Editions, 1974.

———. *Informe central: Primer Congreso del Partido Comunista de Cuba (Report to the First Congress of Cuba's Communist Party)*. Havana: Editora Politica, 1975.

Chang, Laurence and Peter Kornbluh, eds. *The Cuban Missile Crisis*. New York: The New Press, 1992, 1998.

Cotayo, Nicanor Leon (quoted by). *El bloqueo a Cuba (The Blockade to Cuba)*, Havana: Editorial de Ciencias Sociales, 1983.

Crabtree, Penni. "CancerVax Wins Rare OK from U.S." *Union Tribune*, July 15, 2004.

del Llano, Eduardo. *La exportación de capital de Estados Unidos hacia Cuba (United Status capital export to Cuba)*. Havana: Editora Politica, 1979.

Diez, Tomas. *Chronology on the October Crisis*. Havana, Cuba: History Institute.

Duetschmann, David, et. al. *Guantánamo: A Critical History of the U.S. Base in Cuba*. Melbourne: Ocean Press, 2007.

Duetschmann, David and Deborah Shnookal, eds. *Fidel Castro Reader*. Melbourne: Ocean Press, 2007.

Escalante, Fabian. *JFK: The Cuba Files*. Melbourne: Ocean Press, 2005.

Foner, Phillip S., *A History of Cuba and its Relations with the United States*. New York: International Publishers, 1962.

Franklin, Jane. *Cuba and the United States, A Chronological History*. New York: Ocean Press, 1997.

Gleijeses, Piero. *Conflicting Missions: Havana, Washington, and Africa, 1959-1976*. Chapel Hill, NC: University of North Carolina Press, 2002.

Hamilton Jenks, Leland. *Our Cuban Colony: American Imperialism*. New York: Vanguard Press, 1928.

Instituto de Historia. *Historia de Cuba: Las luchas por la independencia nacional y las transformaciones Estructurales 1868-1898 (History of Cuba: The Struggles for National independence and Structural Transformations)*. Vol.11. Havana: Editora Politica.

Jefferson Papers "The Library of Congress," Monroe-Jefferson, Washington D.C., June 30, 1823.

Krinsky, Michael and David Golove. *United States Economic Measures against Cuba: Proceedings in the United Nations and International Law Issues*. Northampton: Alethea Press, 1993.

"Letter of Thomas Jefferson to John Stuart: Conservative Politician from Virginia," January 25, 1786, in José Fuentes Mares, Poin Sell, *Historia de una intriga (History of an Intrigue)*, Mexico City: Ediciones Oceanos, S.A., 1985.

Lind, Michael. *Made in Texas: George W. Bush and the Southern Takeover of American Politics*. New York: Basic Books, 2003.

Lopez Segrera, Francisco. *De Eisenhower a Reagan (From Eisenhower to Reagan Administrations)*. Havana: Editorial de Ciencias Sociales, 1987.

Matthews, Herbert. *Revolution in Cuba*. New York: Charles Schribner's Son, 1975.

Miranda, Olga. *Las nacionalizaciones cubanas, las cortes norteamericanas y la enmienda Hickenlooper (Cuban Nationalizations, U.S. Courts and the Hickenlooper Amendment)*. Havana: Biblioteca del Ministerio de Relaciones Exteriores, August, 1971.

Morales Dominguez, Esteban, Carlos Batista, and Kanaki Yamaoka, *The United States and Cuba's International Economy Reinsertion*. Joint Research Program Series no. 126. Tokyo: Institute of Developing Economies, 1999.

Olivo, Verde. "Dangers and Principles. The October Crisis from Cuba." Havana: Editorial MINFAR, 1992.

Pinos Santos, Oscar. "The Complot," "Nuestro Tiempo" Mexico FD: Editorial, S.A., 1992.

Portuondo del Prado, Fernando. *Asalto a Cuba por la oligarquta financiera yanqui (Assault on Cuba by Yankee financial oligarchy)*. Havana: Casa de las Américas, 1965.

———. *Historia de Cuba (History of Cuba)*. Havana: Editorial Nacional de Cuba, Vol. I, 1965.

Rendez, Rafael. *El costo de las agresiones de Estados Unidos contra Cuba (The Cost of Aggressions against Cuba)*, Centro de Estudios sobre Estados Unidos, Universidad de La Habana (CESEU-UH,) Working Paper, July, 1987.

"Report of a Special Study Mission to Cuba." *Toward Improved United States-Cuba Relations*, February 1977. Washington, D.C.: U.S. Government Printing Office, 1979.

Robbins, Carla Anne. "Dateline Washington: Cuban American Clout." *Foreign Policy*. Fall 1992.

Rodríguez, José Luis and George Carriazo. *Erradicacion de la pobreza en Cuba (Eradicating Poverty in Cuba)*. Havana: Editorial de Ciencias Sociales, 1987.

Roig de Leuchsenring, Emilio. *Cuba no debe su independencia a Estados Unidos (Cuban independence does not rely on the United States)*. Buenos Aires: Editorial Hemisferio, 1965.

———. *Los Estados Unidos contra Cuba libre (The United States against Free Cuba)*. Santiago de Cuba: Editorial Oriente, 1982, Vol.1.

Sklar, Barry. *Cuba: Normalization of Relations*. Washington, D.C.: Congressional Research Service, 1978.

Smith, Wayne. *The Closest of Enemies*. New York: W.W. Norton , 1987.

Index